The Syriza Wave

The Syriza Wave

Surging and Crashing with the Greek Left

by HELENA SHEEHAN

MONTHLY REVIEW PRESS
New York

Library of Congress Cataloging-in-Publication Data:
available from the publisher—

ISBN (paper): 978-158367-625-7
ISBN (cloth): 978-158367-626-4

Typeset in Minion Pro

Monthly Review Press, New York
monthlyreview.org

5 4 3 2 1

Contents

To the Greek left,
who struggled so bravely for so long,
who brought forth Syriza,
who will transcend Syriza

Preface

Greece lived in my imagination long before I ever set foot in it. From a young age, I reached out to the whole. I sought a wider and deeper understanding of the world than what I saw around me. As a teenager, outside the school curriculum, I read the Socratic dialogues and imagined ancient Athens. I studied philosophy in university to the doctoral level. I became a philosopher. I also became a Marxist, which led me to reconceptualize the history of philosophy and reimagine ancient Athens, as I learned how to see ideas in sociohistorical context. As a university teacher, I incited my students to imagine the ancient world in the interactions of intellectual, political, and economic forces that unfolded there and came rippling into our own time. As I walked among ruins during my times in Greece, this history flowed through me again. I channeled that energy back into my teaching of the history of ideas, and my writing focused on class, race, and gender in the history of knowledge.

From 1980, I felt the allure of the Balkans. I accepted an invitation from the Praxis philosophers to come to Yugoslavia. Later I was invited by the ruling party. These were conferences—not the detached academic kind but the intellectual activist kind. There was intense interaction with others who wanted to understand and to change the world. Not only that, but it was warm and near the sea. These were meaningful and memorable experiences. It was in Cavtat where I first met Paul Sweezy and Harry Magdoff and I began my association with *Monthly Review*. There were also holidays, mostly in Yugoslavia but sometimes in Bulgaria. My partner, Sam Nolan, and I called these our 4-S holidays: sun, sea, sex, and socialism.

As an organic intellectual, that is, a precariously employed PhD, I combined financing my holidays with making arguments about socialism by writing about my trips for the *Irish Times*. This pushed me to reach out to penetrate places and engage in conversations I might not have had otherwise. As the tide turned in Eastern Europe, from the German Democratic Republic to Yugoslavia, I wrote about this world-historical change in terms of the big events and arguments as well as the everyday lives of those whose world was being turned upside down. I was interested in history from the point of view of the vanquished. I experimented in synthesizing travelogue and theory.

I turned to Greece when Yugoslavia died. In 1992, Sam and I traveled to Greece, regretting the loss of a crucial S: if we couldn't have socialism, we could still have socialists. I investigated the Greek political spectrum and decided that the position I supported was that of Synaspismos, because it came from the critical communist movement, which corresponded to my own ideological position. Many of its members had belonged to the KKE, the Communist Party of Greece, one of the most formidable communist parties never to take state power. They had left the KKE because of different positions on Eastern Europe and Eurocommunism and also because the KKE, which had been part of Synaspismos as a coalition, had left it.

After 1994, when I finally became a tenured academic, I wasn't as pushed about writing up my holidays for newspapers, but I got most out of the trips when I did that. My last journalism-funded holiday was in 1993, when I wrote "Rhodes Diary" for the *Irish Times*, which was also published in *Neues Deutschland*. I contacted the head office of Synaspismos in Athens to say that I was writing an article about Greece. They put me in touch with Thanasis Anapolitanos, the president of Synaspismos in Rhodes and a civil engineer for the Ministry of Culture who was my primary guide to Rhodes on this and subsequent occasions. When I dug this article out of my files and read it again, it seemed so long ago. Yet I was struck by the echoes from the past in the present. There was a general strike about privatization of public utilities. The hotel lobby was in darkness, the computers were down, the refrigerators were defrosting, and the elevators were disabled. At the post office and other public buildings there were handmade signs saying "We are on strike."

There was an election coming and Thanasis was a Synaspismos candidate. Andreas Papandreou headed the Pasok list in Rhodes. He was the leader of the Panhellenic Socialist Movement—which was ahead in the polls. Most treated this with a shrug of the shoulders, devoid of the hope and enthusiasm that greeted the victory of Pasok in 1981. Pasok had raised wages, created a national health service, repealed anticommunist laws, initiated many progressive reforms, and pursued an independent foreign policy, but it became mired in corruption and financial scandals, imposed austerity measures, and retreated on foreign policy. Thanasis regretted that Pasok "took the best traditions of the left and soiled them. Their scandals discredited socialism." I spoke to Vangelis Pavlidis, a cartoonist for the newspaper *To Vima*, who had been on the central committee of Pasok but now said he wouldn't even vote for them again. "Pasok encompassed so much talent, creativity, and energy, which is now dissipated." I asked where all these people had gone. "They went home," he replied. Even the people who stayed in Pasok agreed with much of the critique but said, "So what?" because they still had enough support to win. Those who were voting for them were doing so as a vote against the conservative New Democracy (ND) party and not because they hoped for much from Pasok anymore. For Pasok, it took several years of real achievements and then reversals for it to come to this. For Syriza, it all unfolded in months.

One thing that was different was that the KKE had seen some promise in Pasok at that time that it subsequently never saw in Syriza.

Panos Michailidis, who had spent seventeen years in prison for being a communist, felt disappointed in Pasok. "They came to power with a good left program. Some of their policies were to the left of the KKE." In 2004, Synaspismos coalesced with other forces to form Syriza. On our trips to Crete, Rhodes, Kos, and Corfu we had many discussions of Greek politics across a wide political spectrum, but we felt the greatest affinity with Synaspismos, and then Syriza.

I was interested, then as now, in how Ireland looked from Greece and vice versa. The major story involving Ireland when I was in Greece in 1993 was the perceived inequity in the distribution of European Community (precursor of the EU) structural funds. It was noted that Ireland received 1,049 European currency units (precursor of the euro) per citizen, whereas the figure for Greece was only 667 ECUs in the period from 1989 to 1993.

The comparisons and contrasts between Greece and Ireland came to my attention again under the impact of the global economic crisis that began in 2008 and intensified in Europe in 2010. Private debts were transmuted into public debts, leading to drastic expropriating measures and the plundering of public services to pay private investors. To "bail out" the states doing so and enforce "austerity," the troika—the International Monetary Fund, the European Union, and the European Central Bank—came first to Greece and then to Ireland. These years demanded intensified political activity in Ireland and renewed focus on Greece.

Only in 2012 did I start writing up my trips to Greece again. In May 2012, when my Facebook newsfeed and Twitter stream were preoccupied with the French presidential election, rooting either for Hollande or Mélenchon, I tweeted "SYRIZA!" Others too took notice. From then on, the international left looked on them in a new way, and I paid a lot more attention too.

I was riding the Syriza wave, as were many on the international left, some of whom had never heard of the party before this. I wrote my way through my trips to Greece in 2012 and 2013 for the *Irish Left Review*. These articles received a lot of attention and were republished in *Links, Counterpunch,* and other places, as well as being translated into a few other languages. Most of chapter 1 and part of chapter 2 of this book are based on these articles.

Whatever plans I had for 2015 (writing a different book from this one) were suspended when the general election in Greece was called for January 25. It was nearly a full-time job to keep up with all that was happening, to read all that was being written, to respond to requests to give speeches or engage in solidarity activities. In the midst of this, Monthly Review Press asked me if I would write a book about Greece. I resisted at first, arguing that there was a lot of good writing about Greece from those more qualified than I. I'm not Greek. I don't speak Greek. I don't live in Greece. I'm not a professor of economics. All I had to offer was the sort of thing I had written already, a narrative of my experiences and reflections, stemming from my interactions with Greece in the hope that this would contribute to a big-picture understanding of the crisis in both Ireland and Greece. Why not do that? they said. In due course, we all agreed and this is the result.

The weight of this book is on the post–July 2015 period, because least has been written about this time. It is not only the least known part of the story, but it is the saddest part of a sad story. It is true tragedy on a scale with the ancient tragedies in the land where the word tragedy originated. This has been a difficult book to write, but such difficulty pales beside the burden borne by those who live with the crushing consequences of the events elaborated here. I hope that this book can play some role in mediating between their lives and those of my readers.

—HELENA SHEEHAN
Dublin, 2016

Acknowledgments

Because of the nature of this book, my debts to others are transparent in the text itself.

I thank all those who shared their thoughts, hopes, fears, grief, time, food and wine with me. The surging and crashing was in the best of company.

I also thank Monthly Review Press for the push to write this book and the care they have taken with it.

Timeline

The international financial crisis of 2007–2008 began in the United States and spread to Europe, where it had ever more severe consequences, bringing extreme economic and political instability to both Greece and Ireland. Ireland became the first country in the Eurozone to enter into recession in 2008 followed by Greece in late 2009.

2008

September 29: Irish government gives blanket guarantee to banks, which eventually left the public sector liable for billions of private debt.

2009

February 21: 100,000 protest on the streets of Dublin against financial scandals, public sector wage cuts, and rise in unemployment organized by Irish Congress of Trade Unions.

Oct 4: General election in Greece. Pasok receives 43.9 percent of popular vote and takes 160 of 300 seats in parliament. George Papandreou becomes prime minister.

Oct 20: Greek budget deficit set to reach 12.5 percent, exceeding 3 percent of GDP threshold allowed in Eurozone. A series of downgrades by rating agencies ensues.

December 21: Ireland sets up the National Asset Management Agency (NAMA) as a "bad bank" using government bonds to acquire distressed loans arising from property bubble.

2010

February 9: Austerity measures passed in Greek parliament. Through the year this continues with increases in taxes and cuts in wages, pensions, and public services.

April 23: Greece requests loan from EU, ECB, and IMF (troika).

May 2: First memorandum agreed between Greek government and the troika.

May 5: Forty-eight-hour general strike is accompanied by violent protests throughout Greece.

November 21: Ireland requests loan from troika.

November 27: Over 100,000 march in Dublin. Although organized by the trade unions, trade union leaders are booed in the streets for lack of militancy in standing up to the government.

November 28: Memorandum agreed between Irish government and troika.

2011

Throughout the year, both austerity measures and protests escalate in Greece and Ireland.

February 25: General election in Ireland results in massive defeat for Fianna Fáil-
Green government. Most cabinet ministers lose their seats. Fine Gael and
Labour form a new government. Despite being elected on a scathing critique of the previous government, the new government continues on the
same course of raising taxes and charges, cutting public services, privatizing public assets, and complying with troika demands.

May 25: Movement of the Squares occupies public spaces in protests in Greece
following the eruption of the *indignados* movement in Spain.

October 8: Occupy movement comes to Ireland with Occupy Dame Street in
Dublin followed by occupations in all Irish cities and many towns. Starting
with Occupy Wall Street from September 17 in New York, this movement
of the 99 percent against the 1 percent spreads like wildfire through every
continent except Antarctica with marches, assemblies, and tents occupying
public spaces for months.

October 27: Michael D Higgins, the most left-wing of the seven candidates running for president of Ireland, is elected.

October 31: Papandreou calls for referendum on EU summit deal on Greece.
Opposition to the referendum forces Papandreou from office. Referendum
is never held.

November 4: Papandreou resigns.

November 6: Lucas Papademos becomes prime minister of Greece with a new
government coalition of Pasok, New Democracy, and LAOS.

2012

February 21: Second memorandum is agreed for Greece.

May 6: General election in Greece. Syriza comes second with 16.7 percent. Pasok
plummets to 13 percent. Golden Dawn candidates are elected to parliament for the first time. No government can be formed.

June 17: Another general election in Greece. Syriza again comes second with
26.8 percent. ND, Pasok, and Dimar form government. Antonis Samaras
becomes prime minister and Alexis Tsipras becomes leader of the opposition.
Although Samaras in opposition was critical of the previous government's
compliance with trioika policies, he implements them in government.

2013

*Further austerity measures, general strikes, and protests all through the year in
Greece. No general strikes in Ireland, but many other protests.*

June 11: Greek government announces that it will close ERT, the public broadcaster, at midnight. ERT continues broadcasting for two years.

December: Ireland officially exits the troika program.

2014

May 25: Elections to the European Parliament. Syriza wins most seats (6) in Greece.
Sinn Fein wins 4 seats in Ireland. Podemos enters EP for the first time.

December 29: Greek government fails to elect its candidate for president, triggering a general election.

2015

January 25: Syriza wins general election with 36.3 percent of the vote and forms government with Anel. Alexis Tsipras becomes prime minister.

February to July: Dramatic and unproductive negotiations with troika over debt and austerity.

February 20: Interim agreement with Eurogroup.

June 4: Greece fails to make payment due to IMF.

June 11: ERT is reinstated.

June 18: Negotiations break down.

June 27: Tsipras announces referendum on troika proposals. Massive mobilization of the population for and against proposals.

June 28: Greek banks and stock market close and capital controls are introduced.

June 30: Greece defaults on IMF payment. Second memorandum expires.

July 5: Referendum produces 61.3 percent vote for Oxi (no).

July 13: Tsipras signs an agreement that is even more unfavorable than the one rejected in the referendum.

August 14: Third memorandum passes in parliament.

August 20: Tsipras calls general election to purge his own party.

August 21: Laïkí Enótita (Popular Unity) (LAE) is formed by Syriza MPs voting no to the memorandum.

September 20: Syriza wins general election with 35.4 percent and forms another government with Anel.

From summer 2015, a refugee crisis intensifies, due to war in Syria. After other European countries close their borders, massive numbers of refugees become trapped in Greece.

2016

Through the year, the Greek government struggles to implement the third memorandum, hampered by strikes, occupations, and many forms of protest, many of them involving those who previously supported Syriza.

February 26: General election in Ireland results in defeat for the outgoing government, with a significant increase in votes for smaller parties and independents, but with no obvious winner. The Labour Party plummets from 37 to 7 seats (of 158). It takes more than two months to form a government.

March 20: EU-Turkey agreement comes into effect, requiring Greece to return refugees to Turkey unless they apply for asylum in Greece.

April 29: Fine Gael and independents form a minority government with cooperation from Fianna Fáil.

June 23: Britain's referendum on EU membership results in vote for Brexit, destabilizing EU.

CHAPTER 1

2012: Almost Winning

Traversing the Crisis

The crisis demanded intensified scrutiny of the global system as well as heightened political activity in relation to it. The crisis brought the troika first to Greece and then to Ireland. In Ireland we watched Greece very closely. We did so with different degrees of trepidation, terror, hope, and inspiration. Our successive governments, and indeed many of our fellow citizens, were keen to make the point that we were not Greece. Although all measures enforced on us pointed in the same direction, the idea was that we would be compliant and it would go better for us. The narrative of Irish exceptionalism prevailed. It was put to me on a radio program: "We don't want to be like Greece, do we?" I couldn't agree. Naturally I did not want wages and pensions and social services to plunge so low and for poverty and suicide to blight even more lives, but I did want us to resist in such massive numbers. Moreover, I wanted us to have an alternative on offer such as what I saw shaping up in Greece.

In international television coverage of demonstrations in Greece, we saw a banner declaring "We are not Ireland" and we heard of protesters chanting "We are not Ireland. We will resist." It stung. Those of us who were resisting felt acutely our failure to mobilize sufficient numbers to put up the resistance the situation required. Nevertheless, the Irish left looked with respect and solidarity at the Greek resistance and continued in our efforts to up our game here.

The forces swirling around Greece were swirling around us all. What I saw when I looked at Greece demanded the attention of Ireland and the rest of the world.

A Greek Tragedy

A monumental drama was playing out before our eyes. It was a true Greek tragedy. The plot: a society was being pushed to its limits. The denouement was not yet determined, but survival was at stake and prospects were precarious. Greece was at the sharp end of a radical and risky experiment in how far accumulation by dispossession could go, how much expropriation could be endured, how far the state could be subordinated to the market. The process, long underway in the third world and then the second world, was coming to the first world now. It was a global narrative, but the story was a few episodes ahead here.

Greece was the crucible. It was a cauldron where concentrated forces were colliding in a process that would bring forth either a reconfiguration of capitalism or the dawn of its demise.[1]

Salaries, pensions, and public services were falling. Prices and taxes were rising. Massive asset stripping was underway. Water, power, ports, islands, and public buildings were up for sale. Unemployment, emigration, and evictions brought a sense of a society unraveling. Homeless people wandered the streets and scavenged for food in bins or begged it from the plates of those eating in tavernas. If they were immigrants, they were terrorized. Those looking into a horizon without hope either drifted into desolation or performed the ultimate decisive act of suicide. Some did so in private spaces, while others chose public places to underline the political nature of their fate, as they jumped from heights, set themselves on fire, or shot themselves. In April 2012, Dimitris Christoulas, a retired pharmacist who felt he could no longer live a dignified life after his pension had been slashed, shot himself in front of parliament. His last words were: "I am not committing suicide. They are killing me." He urged younger people to fight.

Speaking to Greeks, it was hard to find any without a far-reaching systemic critique. They told you so many details of the deceits of the troika, the corruption of government, the decline in their own standards of living, the pervasive sense of social disintegration. When asked if they saw any hope, few answered in the affirmative. Nevertheless, some did. It was a precarious hope. For some, it was hesitant and weak, full of doubt, but a faint sense of a possible way out of the morass. They protested, they marched, they went on strike, even if they sometimes felt as if they were just going through the motions because they did it so often. They were not sure what it would take to break this cycle and move it to another level, but they knew it could not go on as it was. For others, hope was clearer and stronger, although not without doubt and not without a sense of nearly overwhelming forces that could swamp all their best efforts. These were the ones who were not only critiquing and resisting, but also strategizing and organizing for a social transformation that would chart a path out of the crisis, ultimately a new path out of capitalism and to socialism. Conscious of all previous attempts that had crashed and burned or betrayed the hopes they engendered, they were sober about their chances but determined in their work.

The Whole World Was Watching

International focus on Greece had soared when Syriza came second in the May 2012 election, leaping from 4.6 percent to 16.8 percent, with polls indicating that it could come first in another election to be held in June. Massive media attention ensured that all eyes were on Greece during this interval. The global elite warned of the dangers. Indeed it could be construed as international intimidation. RTÉ, Ireland's public service broadcaster, adopted the tone of the masters of the universe as it reported the situation in Greece. Most international commentators were warning the Greek people not to vote for Syriza.

The United Left Alliance (ULA), which had won five seats in Dáil Éireann in the 2011 election, organized a meeting where Syriza MP Despina Charalampidou spoke. Few remarked upon it, but I was aware of how impossible it would have been in previous decades to have Trotskyists sharing a platform so harmoniously with a left Eurocommunist. In fact, Joe Higgins of the Trotskyist Socialist Party was of the opinion that it was essential to get the KKE on board to form a left government. On the day before the June election, we held a demonstration of solidarity with Greece on O'Connell Street in Dublin. It was initiated by people associated with the Occupy movement and inclined to be skeptical of electoral politics, which I also thought was a remarkable feature of the new atmosphere. Although the demonstration was to support the Greek resistance and not Syriza specifically, there was strong support for Syriza in evidence. I spoke at it myself in this vein. It was also Bloomsday, with the two themes held together by James Joyce's *Ulysses*, which was a theme of certain speakers, some of them in period costume from other events. An unsympathetic passerby told me she had been to Greece many times and found that Greeks just don't work. I told her that I had been there as many times and thought otherwise. Apparently this pampered person was not served to her satisfaction a few times when on holidays, so Greeks deserved what was happening to them. Meanwhile, Paul Murphy, a Member of the European Parliament (MEP), had traveled to Athens to be there for the final Syriza rally and election results. I wished that I was there too.

As it turned out, although Syriza leapt to 26.9 percent, it came second again to New Democracy, which formed a coalition government with Pasok and Dimar, two supposedly left parties. The international media, which was giving Greece saturation coverage between the two elections, then turned their attention elsewhere. The left kept its eyes on Greece, however, and watched as Syriza rose in the polls, consistently coming out the highest party and raising the prospect that Syriza would win the next election. There was a strong sense that this was what was needed to break the logjam.

Despite this, much of the international media attention saw Syriza reduced to a footnote, focusing on the rise of Golden Dawn (XA), which was now the third party in most polls. This did deserve attention and analysis, but it was almost never proportionate. This xenophobic party demanded deportation of immigrants, attacked them on the streets, overturned their market stalls, threatened dire consequences if they remained in Greece. Their theatrics created media spectacle: Nazi salutes in parliament, distribution of food and collection of blood for Greeks only, denouncing a theatrical production as blasphemous and driving it out of town. Many of their antics and claims were comical, particularly the conceptualization of themselves as in a direct line in the story stemming from the glories of ancient Greece. What was most worrying was the vigilante role they were playing, with support from the police. Using demagogic techniques, they won significant support in destitute city neighborhoods with large immigrant populations by stirring up desperate Greeks against them. This toxic syndrome even penetrated schools, with students threatening each other or their teachers with a call to XA.

Syriza as Synthesis

The more sober and serious story line at play was the transition of Syriza from a coalition of 4.5 percent to a party of 26.9 percent to a potential left government in a scenario of epochal crisis. When the international media turned elsewhere, this was the story that I was following most intently after the June election, as were others on the international left, who were galvanized by the success of Syriza in a way that raised our sights and held hope of becoming a force up to the demands of our times.

What was it about Syriza that so stirred the international left? Was it because a left party suddenly surged from being one of many parties confronting those who ruled the world to one that could come to power in a way that could chart a new path for the left? Was it because we wanted not just to struggle but to win somewhere? Yes, this was surely part of it, but I thought that it was more than that.

For me, Syriza was synthesis. It was a convergence of the old and new left. Within that, it was a convergence of old left traditions that were once so divergent, as well as various new left forces. Gathered up into Syriza were ex-CP communists, Trotskyists, Maoists, and left social democrats as well as independent leftists, feminists, ecologists, alter-globalization activists, and *indignados*.

This was particularly meaningful to me, because I have been part of both the old and the new left. I have participated in and sometimes polemicized against all of these forces. I was an activist in the 1960s New Left as well as the more recent Occupy movement. I have been a member of social democratic and communist parties. I have reflected over the years on the best and worst of all these strands. I have had a particularly intense relationship with the communist movement, which set the last century on fire, attracted the commitment of brave and brilliant comrades, and ultimately, often tragically, disappointed so many of the hopes it engendered. My engagement with it, both as an author and an activist, was much of what drew me over the years first to Synaspismos and then to Syriza. It represented a critical continuity with that history along with a radical openness to a different future.

I believe in a politics that makes the long march through all the institutions of society. This includes electoral politics, but not in a myopic fixation on parliaments. It struggles for power and creates alternative structures in the streets, workplaces, schools, universities, media, arts. I saw Syriza as oriented to this kind of politics, seeing its presence in parliament as part of a wider social movement. It was even bringing in those in new movements who were skeptical about state power, who saw the state as so limited, so subordinate to capital, so controlled by oligarchy, and persuading them that states still have some power and that the state must be a site of struggle. Syriza envisioned governing in such a way as to combine horizontal and vertical power, both representative and direct democracy. It was attuned to the demands of the historical moment, requiring the left to surpass itself.

A Mini-Odyssey

This brought me back to Greece in August and September and again in October of 2012. I had been there many times over the past two decades, swimming in the sea, drinking in tavernas, discussing politics, reading novels and histories that shed light on Greek society and especially the Greek left. Now I came because I wanted to test my sense of Syriza and its importance for the international left, to extend my interaction with it, to explore the dynamics of the older and newer forces within it, to discover what discussions and debates were underway and to probe how they were preparing for power. I knew that power was much more than winning elections and forming a government. I wanted to know more about what sort of social transformation they envisaged.

There were a number of visits after the election from leftists from abroad asking: What next? Several of these were in July during an interval of post-strike, post-election exhaustion and sweltering heat, which brought the level of activity down a few notches. Laurie Penny wrote a book called *Discordia*, based on one week in Athens. She had come expecting to see riots and instead saw "what happens when riots die away and horrified inertia sets in."[2] Hilary Wainwright in *Red Pepper* reported on the quieter political activity going on under the surface, describing Syriza as "Like a swan moving forward with relaxed confidence while paddling furiously beneath the surface."[3] I wanted to follow up on this a few months down the line, especially in the autumn when the tempo was rising again.

Sojourning in Zakynthos

I started in Zakynthos, combining a holiday in late August and early September with seeking and finding Syriza there. I contacted the local secretary of Synaspismos with a referral from Athens. Along with my partner, Sam Nolan, secretary of the Dublin Council of Trade Unions and a longtime left activist, I met Nikos Potamitis, an orthopedic surgeon and an astute and articulate activist. For hours we talked politics in a café in Bohali as the sun set over a panoramic view of the town. We started with his own political trajectory, from KKE through Synaspismos and Syriza, and covered a wide range of topics, from the end of the USSR to the next phase of Syriza. We met again at the Syriza office in Zakynthos, where he showed us election literature and posters and described the range of the party's activities on the island. Syriza won the June election on the island and sent a left MP to the national parliament for the first time in many years. Support for Syriza leapt from 4 percent to 35 percent and activist numbers swelled from fifty to five hundred between May and September. We then experienced the generous hospitality of his home in Akrotiri over a dinner of many courses with his wife Efi, a drama teacher, and his three children, as well as Syriza candidate Athina Mylona. Again we talked politics for many hours. We left laden with gifts of cake, chocolate, wine, brandy, a CD of local music, and a Syriza poster and flag. The following week, we were invited back to the office, where we met the central committee of Syriza in Zakynthos, who welcomed us warmly. I inquired about their occupations. There were two doctors, an actor-director, a financial consultant, a tourist shop owner, a teacher, an architectural detailer, and several people who worked in the agricultural sector. They commented that Sam and I embodied the ideal combination for the left: a carpenter and a professor. We took our leave with a flurry of warm good-byes and *kalinichtas* and *venceremoses* and *efharistos*. We walked along the harbor in the evening, feeling more hopeful than we felt at home. My daily swim in the sea at sunrise made for a great sense of well-being too.

Our discussions, particularly with Nikos, raised themes that would recur in most of my conversations with Syriza activists: the concrete manifestations of the crisis in Greek society; the need for a radical alternative; the transformation of Syriza to a bigger, more diverse, yet more unified party; the debate about whether or not to exit the Eurozone. Nikos was on the left of Synaspismos and Syriza and wary of Syriza becoming the new Pasok. He was strongly in favor of nationalizing the banks and exiting the Eurozone, so as to take control of the economy. He gave many details of the manifestations of crisis in Greek society: impoverishment, emigration, suicide. He described the collapse of the middle strata and the proletarianization of professionals. Well aware of what doctors abroad earned, he was determined to stay, although the economics of a basic salary of €1,500 a month and falling were not so easy. Before the crisis, his basic salary was €2,800. He was also conscious of the struggle of those who worked for €500 a month and those who had no work and no pay at all. He was acutely concerned about the deterioration of the health service, which could not meet people's needs.

Some of those on low wages in Greece were highly educated. The woman who was cleaning our room had been a mathematics teacher in Albania who was delighted to discuss the novels of Ismail Kadare with me. Many Albanians had returned, but she had lived in Greece for fifteen years and didn't want to go back to a country run by mafia. A waiter serving us was from Bulgaria and aspiring to be a professor of philology. He liked the idea that I was a philosopher until it came out that I was a Marxist. He said that socialism wiped out traditions that took thousands of years to build. He was an orthodox Christian and a constitutional monarchist. The fluency in multiple languages among those working in the service sector was striking.

We stayed in touch with Nikos after we left and were delighted to receive a link to a video of a creative protest where the people burned in the public square a representation of Cerberus, the mythical three-headed dog guarding the entrance to the underworld, from which it was impossible to return. This dog was made in the theatrical laboratory in the Potamitis home. The three heads of the dog were named for the troika and the hind flanks were Pasok and New Democracy However, young Katerina was upset to see the creature they had so carefully created being burned.

The crisis was not so evident on the islands as in the cities. Tourists came for their holidays and most went away having seen little sign of it. I walked around Tsilivi past a Molly Malone pub and another bar with a jukebox belting out "Jolene" and wondered yet again why people would come to Greece only to wrap themselves in the culture of home and insulate themselves from the culture of Greece. Tourism was bringing income and employment to these islands and spared them many of the indignities of the cities, where people were begging and scavenging in the streets. However, when you asked people about their lives—the working people who staffed the hotels, shops, hospitals, and schools—they would tell you how their incomes had dropped, how their conditions of work had deteriorated, how many were leaving, how their society was unraveling. If they were immigrants, they would tell you that their children feared XA coming for them in their schools and kindergartens. Even though the neo-Nazi presence was not so strong on this island, they saw them on television and a sense of menace had skewed their forward gaze.

Arriving in Athens

When I arrived home from Zakynthos in September, I began planning my October trip to Athens. I started building my network of contacts, beginning with my existing professional and political counterparts—professors of philosophy and former members of the KKE now in Synaspismos and Syriza. From there, I branched out, especially after I arrived in Athens. I spoke to university professors, members of parliament, party workers, trade union officials, journalists, teachers, doctors, lawyers, hotel staff, taxi drivers, shop assistants, waiters, the unemployed. I heard the stories of people from all stages of the life cycle, articulating political views ranging from communist to neo-Nazi, from KKE to XA. I walked miles on the streets of Athens every day, mostly alone, but sometimes with academics, activists, and journalists. I looked and listened with the heightened awareness of the curious visitor.

I arrived on October 9, an hour after Angela Merkel also arrived. My flight had already been booked when her visit was announced. The timing was unfortunate in that it meant a lot of logistical stress about whether and how I would get there with all the police restrictions and work stoppages and, even worse, arriving too late to join in the protests. Because of the road blocks and the cancellation of public transport options, I had to get a taxi. The taxi driver drove while talking on his mobile, spreading a huge map over the steering wheel and writing on it, which was really nerve-wracking. When I arrived at my hotel, it was so shuttered down that it was hard to find a way into it. My Twitter feed showed that tens of thousands of people were gone from Syntagma Square and only small numbers scuffling with riot police remained. I strolled around the area surrounding Omonia Square and struck up conversations about the events of the day. No one welcomed Angela Merkel. Many referred back to the German occupation of Athens during the war and claimed that they still owed war reparations. In the hotel, visitors wanted to know where not to go to avoid danger. The receptionist on duty told me that he had been in Syntagma Square for the mass protests. Eventually the shutters went up and the road blocks came down. On the television I saw Merkel leaving. Footage of the visit was on a loop, the weirdest part being Samaras and Merkel walking down a leafy deserted street, talking sedately. It was so surreal, considering the real atmosphere on the streets. Only riot police could create that bubble for her. It reminded me of watching Gaddafi on the last days of Jamahiriya television, when I was trapped in Tripoli during the 2011 uprising. Over and over he paraded in ceremonial loops, in gowns of many colors, while sights of burning buildings and sounds of gunfire filled the air outside my window. I watched hours of news and current affairs on Greek television in the evening, as I was to do every other evening, getting the gist but missing the nuance, but finding it riveting notwithstanding. That wasn't like Libya.

My first port of call the next day was the office of Synaspismos-Syriza in Eleftherias Square. It was a multistory building. Seventy people worked there. Another hundred or so worked for Syriza in the parliament. I was greeted warmly by Dimitra Tsami, with whom I had been in email contact for some months. I met a number of other comrades and settled into a meeting with Costas Isychos, who was in charge of international affairs. He knew more about Ireland than most people I met in Greece and asked me for my assessment of various forces, especially ULA and Sinn Féin. Mostly we spoke of Greece and Syriza. Again the main themes were those characterizing all my conversations with Syriza activists: the manifestations of crisis, the transformations of Syriza, the preparations for power. Costas covered much ground with great clarity. There was extreme alienation from the political system. The class structure was changing. The middle strata were becoming proletarianized. The wealthy bourgeoisie had a new layer: in addition to the old oligarchs, typified by the ship owners, it now included the casino capitalists, who had XA as their reserve force. As the crisis deepened, people were moving from the center to the right or left. The influx into Syriza, while a source of optimism, was a source of danger too, as some of the newer elements had been infected with neoliberalism and clientelism. Although the political system was corrupt, it was necessary to engage with it in order to transform it.

It was necessary, they believed and I believed, to show that the left could govern. If Syriza was to take state power, it would do so in an extremely unfavorable geopolitical situation. As Costas spoke, I got some sense of the sober strategic thinking going on about how to deal with various scenarios that might come into play: for example, how to survive if Greece was cut off from international funding and existing trade relations. Syriza had a team of economists working on all possible problems, such as exiting the Eurozone, finding alternative sources of energy, etc. Costas belonged to the Left Platform, which agreed with the economist Costas Lapavitsas about exiting the Eurozone. He stressed the need to build international solidarity. He put a proposition to me, asking me to be part of an international network of political thinkers that they were forming. I said that I would be honored. Syriza was the last hope for Greece, he stressed. After that, it was the fascists. This made people very serious, realizing what a heavy weight of responsibility they bore. Among the disparate elements that had combined to become Syriza, there was at that time a relatively good climate for dealing with differences and converging to put their efforts into the tasks before them.

Professors, Parliamentarians, and Policy Process

The seriousness of the situation and the weight of responsibility that the party bore was a theme echoed over and over in my talks with Syriza, especially by those in leading positions. Aristides Baltas, a philosophy of science professor and an influential thinker in Syriza, told me that he had used my book *Marxism and the Philosophy of Science* on many occasions. We met in Syntagma Square and walked to the University of Athens. It is a very urban university. The main building is a striking classical edifice standing between the National Library and the Academy of Athens on the wide boulevard of Panepistimiou. The rest of its buildings are scattered through city streets in between shops, cafés, and offices. We settled into one of these cafés. So many of my meetings were right out on the city streets, with all the noise of the traffic and bustle of city life. Those months of Occupy University sessions out there on Dame Street in Dublin made me accustomed to this, so I not only managed it but found it bracing and appropriate. I thought of our discussions as in continuity with those of the agora of ancient Athens. In the past few years there had been a collective effort to pull together the best ideas for exiting the crisis and transforming the society into a coherent program. Aristides Baltas had been coordinating an elaborately participative process to develop this program, which was now published in a book of several hundred pages, though largely ignored by the Greek media, who nevertheless kept saying that Syriza had no program. Since the election, a more intensified and encompassing process had been underway. The leadership was thinking very concretely about what to do the day after being elected: what legislation to pass to revoke the memorandum (the agreement to implement economic adjustment, privatization and austerity measures between the troika and the Greek government, first under Pasok in 2010 and then under New Democracy in 2012); how to restore wages, pensions, and public services; how to clear out corruption and clientelism. Moreover, they were strategizing about how to transform the structures of the state itself and how to formulate policy within this transformation. They rejected an approach that concentrated on shadow cabinets and special advisers. When elected, they would call together those who worked in various ministries to ask them how they could best do their jobs and to discuss how the ministry should be run. Indeed, they were already doing this. They were assembling people who worked and had expertise in various areas to come together to form committees and formulate policies now. There were

groups working in economics, energy, culture, education, local government, foreign policy, and other areas.

Indeed I attended one of these meetings. It was set up to coordi-
nate foreign policy and defense. Nearly a hundred people gathered
in the Art Garage in Exarchia. They included professors of international relations, members of parliament, diplomats, public servants
in the ministries of foreign affairs and defense, members of the armed
forces, and others who felt they had a contribution to make to policy
in these areas. They also included people from all the constituent elements of Syriza. At the beginning of the meeting I was introduced by
Sotiris Roussos, a professor of international relations, who had been
given a surprisingly elaborate Internet-researched bio of me, doubt-
lessly prepared by Dimitra. He then translated for me as I spoke of
how I saw Syriza and its importance for the international left. I then
listened to the five-hour deliberation that followed, which was serious
and harmonious. It was not that everyone agreed about everything;
quite the contrary, but there was a constructive atmosphere in discussing disagreements.

Although the room was bursting with expertise, the point was
made that policy was not just about expertise but about politics, about
what class interests were being served. The foreign policy of all previous Greek governments had served certain class interests, and they
would have to go down a different road and serve different class interests. There were proposals to widen policy participation even further
through the creation of interactive Internet portals, not only in Greek
but in other languages. Parliamentarians warned against domination
of the party by the parliamentary group. Rena Dourou, seen at the
time as a possible foreign minister, argued that the center of grav-
ity should not be the parliamentary group, because there was a need
to maintain multilevel relations with wide social forces. (Dourou
became famous abroad when Golden Dawn MP Ilias Kasidiaris threw
a glass of water at her during a television debate.)

There were many speakers who focused on particular countries
or regions. It was striking how little emphasis was put on the EU,
especially the northern part, as opposed to Greece's neighbors in the

Balkans, the Middle East, and North Africa. One of the comrades who did a stint translating for me was Yiannis Bournous, who represented Syriza at the Party of the European Left. Bournous was one of the few Greeks I met with knowledge of Ireland and the Irish left. He made the point that Ireland had no party affiliated with the PEL, which was not good; I agreed.

My discussions with Aristides before and after this Syriza meeting put the process I was witnessing in broader context. There were open Syriza assemblies everywhere, especially in workplaces, universities, and neighborhoods (often outdoors), where people were putting forward their ideas for the future. Not only that, but there were solidarity networks struggling to meet people's needs in the present by providing food and medical care. There were alternative economies for the exchange of goods and services at the grass-roots level. Syriza participated in these. These networks could not solve all these problems, but they could socialize them. These activities had a strong prefigurative thrust to them, enabling a more collectivist experience and an alternative to individual isolation, as impoverishment intensified on the way to a more collectivist future society. It reminded me of our 1960s liberated zones.

The old reform-versus-revolution debate was irrelevant now, Aristides claimed. The space for a social democratic solution was closed now. It was capitalism versus the people. While it would not be possible to do everything they wanted as soon as they wanted, the socialist perspective remained firm, he underlined. It was only Syriza, Aristides insisted, who were doing the transitional thinking. Both the KKE and Antarsya spoke as if it would be possible to move immediately and totally from capitalism to socialism. Indeed, I had read KKE statements and the attitude seemed to be that it was the October Revolution or nothing. It was necessary to learn everything that could be learned from the left of the past and to redefine socialism for the twenty-first century, we agreed.

Preparations were underway for a conference to be held at the end of November, leading to a bigger congress in the spring to reorganize Syriza into a unified party. It was going well, Aristides reported.

When they were smaller, it was more difficult getting the coalition to cohere and stabilize, but now that they were so much bigger and had so much more responsibility to provide an alternative for Greek society, it concentrated minds and a good atmosphere prevailed. The purpose of the conference was to define further their political and ideological identity, to concretize their program for government, and to decide on new organizational structures. They were still trying to find the right balance between their existing traditions and formations and new political forms. The structures of Syriza were radically open, very much in contrast with those of the KKE. It was possible to participate without being a member. Indeed it was only under new structures that some of those who had been participating until then, without being a member of any of the component organizations of Syriza, would actually become members of Syriza.

Aristides was responsible for drafting the declaration for the conference. At the end of our second meeting, he walked with me to the university office of Michalis Spourdalakis, professor of political science, who was also working on this. They discussed various amendments, doing so in English so as to include me in their deliberations. We spoke of the traditions of political education in left parties, something that was stronger in the past than now, which we all agreed needed to be revived. There were no permanent structures for this in Syriza, and they thought that there needed to be. A great thirst for knowledge was in evidence. Lectures at the universities on the history of the left, Marxist theory, and the fate of the USSR had attracted large attendances, they said. Many of the younger generation involved in left politics were highly educated in a formal sense, but not in the traditions and ideas of the left. This was underlined for me a few days later when I asked an educated young woman active in Syriza what she thought about Marxism. She said that she was well disposed toward it but didn't really know much about it.

Both Aristides and Michalis stressed that Syriza was an experiment. It was following the shape of history and the rhythms of the social movements. Both at different stages quoted a line from a poem of Antonio Machado: "We make the road by walking."[4] Both of them had a long history of political activity and had been in Synaspismos from its earliest days. Both were Marxists, but committed to an undogmatic form of Marxism. Syriza as such was not Marxist, they said, but Marxism was a strong force within it, with no one position within Marxism having the status of orthodoxy. There was support for a whole spectrum, from *A* to *Z*, Althusser to Žižek, Aristides said. I winced, since I was not keen on either Althusser or Žižek. Or going further back, he added, from Bukharin to Trotsky to Mao.

Aristides then left and I had a long talk with Michalis. He continued on the theme of transformation of Syriza, the convergence of the traditions of the left with those of the newer social movements. He was involved in the Greek Social Forum as well as the European and World Social Forums. He emphasized, as did others on this question, that Synaspismos and Syriza participated in wider social movements without trying to control them. For example, during the more recent Movement of the Squares, the Greek version of the Occupy movement, Syriza people played their part but respected the movement's autonomy. While the KKE stood aloof and condemned the movement as anti-communist and anti-labor, Syriza argued from within in the face of these tendencies, which beset the Occupy movement almost everywhere. He described the many activities in which Syriza was involved and discussed their prefigurative dimension. Their local bases were more like community centers than party offices.

Syriza was forging a way of strategizing about socialism that critically evaluated all previous attempts at socialism, while overcoming the long disputations and divisions of the left on this question. Michalis believed that capitalism was testing its limits in Greece, which put an extraordinary challenge to the Greek left. This was why it was time for the left to recompose, to transcend both the bankrupt reformism of social democracy and the deluded vanguardism of those still dreaming of storming the Winter Palace. Syriza wanted neither to settle for whatever might be on offer by capital nor to reject whatever reform might lift people's lives now in a paralysis that puts everything off until the ultimate revolution. Syriza was determined neither to settle for governmentalism nor to succumb to governmentophobia.

I also had discussions with another professor at the University of Athens, Kostas Gavroglu. We knew each other from a symposium at the University of Paris on Marxist historiography of science, where we had both spoken. We met at the University of Athens historical archive, of which he was the director, and went to a café across the street for lunch. He spoke of Syriza's long development from KKE Interior, opting for "socialism with a human face" over Moscow domination, basically from the Eurocommunist tradition. He was on the central committee of the KKE Interior and had been part of the various transformations of the Greek left during those decades from the 1960s on. He was hopeful about Syriza's prospects and put a lot of emphasis on its participation in wider social movements, unlike the KKE, which undermined them. This was a constant theme in the conversations I had in Greece.

Generations

It was great talking to my contemporaries about those decades and how we had experienced the same movements, but particularly the communist movement, from different places. There was not only an ideological harmony but a generational sensibility in our interactions. But I needed to speak to the younger generation as well, and Aristides and Kostas both encouraged me to do so and put me in touch with younger activists. On the whole, I found the intergenerational dynamic to be healthy. My contemporaries, the sixty-somethings, referred to it the most, making the point that they should be on the second line these days, with younger faces out front. They were proud to have someone of the caliber of Alexis Tsipras, who was thirty-eight, as the forward face of their party. They were also proud to have Manolis Glezos, who was ninety, out there beside him. Glezos was a Syriza MP, who took down the swastika from the Acropolis during the Nazi occupation, had served time in prison and parliament over the years, as well as working as a writer and editor. He was still a strong voice, still facing the riot police in the streets.

Seeking younger perspectives, I met Dimosthenes Papadatos in Syntagma Square and we proceeded to yet another café in the university area. He was editor of *Red Notebook*, a colorful, energetic, and intelligent online Greek journal that I was able to follow with the help of computerized translations.[5] It dealt with the latest political news; reviewed films, books, and lectures; notified its followers about events; and engaged in critical analysis of everything from the memorandum to the relation of the left to the Enlightenment. Dimosthenes was keen on the left using its voice in social media. He was also working in the parliament on immigration and writing his PhD. He came from a Pasok background and became involved in anti-imperialist and alter-globalization movements while still in high school. He participated in the World Social Forum. He first joined the Greek Socialist Workers Party (SEK) in university but moved to Synaspismos, and then to Syriza, because he believed in left unity.

Syriza had gained much ground among youth through its participation in social movements, working within them, rather than coming into them with an agenda formulated elsewhere. When the Movement of the Squares began, he recounted, left activists were not welcome. There were even banners saying, "Left, go away." However, as a result of the constructive participation of Syriza people, the climate changed. By the end of June 2011, there was a rapprochement between the *indignados*, the left, and the unions, culminating in a two-day general strike. *Red Notebook* published in Greek translation a lot of material from the Occupy movement. Like others in Syriza, Papadatos put huge stress on international solidarity. He saw *Red Notebook* as playing a role in bringing the international conversation into Greece, especially on the crisis. He felt that Greece would need all the support it could get in the coming period. Like others, he was thinking seriously about the next phases of Syriza as a party and as a government. The two hours went quickly and I had to rush away to another appointment, but there were many threads left for another day.

Another activist of a younger generation I met was Ioanna Meitani, who was on the editorial board of *Enthemata*, a supplement on theory and opinion of the daily left paper *I Avgi*. She had a distinctive generational perspective that was a challenge for me to consider. She saw the 1960s generation of the left, my generation, as being young when everything seemed open, whereas her generation came on the scene when everything seemed closed. It was the loss of dreams that led them to revolt, whereas my generation had dreams, but also a habit of defeat—although some of them, she admitted, were still working incredibly hard to realize such dreams in the new circumstances. When I asked about socialism, she said that it was a dream, but she wasn't sure if it was possible. Even in revolt, they had scaled-down dreams, it seemed to me. She knew that there were lots of Marxists in Syriza, but she hadn't engaged with Marxism enough to have formed a position on it. She had been very active in the open structures of Syriza but was not actually a member of it, because she was not a member of any of its constituent organizations. When the new party was formed with direct individual membership, she would be a member. She was in favor of this new direction. There would still be platforms, but these constituent groups would fuse. I asked about gains and losses in this scenario. She saw only gains and no losses. I had to admit that, although I knew that it was the right way to go, I worried about losses, about postmodernist or social democratic sensibilities swamping communist analyses.

Ioanna worked for the Rosa Luxemburg Stiftung, an educational and research network set up by Die Linke with funding from the Bundestag, which had set up an office in Athens. This was where we met. It was a bright attractive space, dominated by red-and-white walls with big black-and-white photos from the history of the left in Germany and Greece. Syriza also had such a foundation, called the Nicos Poulantzas Institute. Both were part of an international network called Transform!, "a European network for alternative thinking and political dialogue."[6]

Aristides said that I must speak to Haris Golemis, the director of the Nicos Poulantzas Institute. This institute was initiated by Synaspismos in 1997 and "aims at fostering the values of the left, systematically developing an awareness of contemporary social, ecological, political and cultural issues and exploring the emerging changes within society" with a "commitment to the ideals of socialism with democracy."[7] We agreed to meet as a march was assembling in the grounds of the National Archaeological Museum. We coordinated our positions by mobile phone. There were many people gathering, so I wondered how I would recognize him. "He looks like Einstein," a comrade told me, and sure enough he did. Haris explained that the NPI came from the renovative communist tradition, but its political space now could be defined as broad left. Although it came from Synaspismos and then Syriza, it was autonomous. It would be expanding further in the future. One of its projects was to study the new political forces in the European left. In describing the composition and activities of Transform!, he noted that one of the few countries without a body affiliated with it was Ireland. We would have to think about what we might do about that, I said.

The Other Left

I thought that I should also speak to those of other political perspectives on the left, both about how they saw the crisis in Greek society and how they saw Syriza. I was especially interested in finding out what was going on in the KKE. I had been reading their statements during and since the elections, where they prioritized attacking Syriza over the troika and the right. "Don't trust Syriza" was their message. Obviously many of their own supporters thought otherwise, as they deserted the KKE and voted for Syriza in significant numbers. The KKE won twenty-six seats in May but only twelve in June. Their leader, Aleka Papariga, was a small combative woman, who lashed out at Syriza even when it was not relevant to the question asked. In Ireland, two parties, the Communist Party of Ireland and the Workers Party of Ireland, both supported the KKE and echoed their attacks on Syriza. The KKE was a formidable party with deep roots in Greek history and considerable support in the Greek working class. Many members of Syriza were once members of the KKE and felt part of a common history. When Syriza reached out to them in the name of left unity, a unity that might have made a crucial difference in being able to form a left government in June, they were spurned and attacked. Syriza expressed regret rather than attacking back, although at a Syriza event in the interval between elections, the Slovenian philosopher Slavoj Žižek referred to the KKE as "the party of the people who are still alive because they forgot to die," which was offensive as well as irresponsible.

Although they drove away people who wanted to relate to the communist tradition in a critical manner, I thought that there still must be people left in it who were reflective and disturbed by the current line. I wanted to meet someone who would speak to me honestly about this. I found a person who was willing to do so, through a trusted intermediary, but it was indicative of the atmosphere in the party that he did not want me to use his name in my writing. We spoke openly for three hours in an outdoor café. He was a young, serious, and highly educated person, who was strongly committed to the party, proud of its past, but worried about its future, because of its present line. He defended the party program, which was committed to appropriate alliances, and he believed that the party's current practice was at odds with its program. The KKE, as he saw it, was the historical party of Marxism in Greece. It was at the forefront of all progressive struggles in Greek society for decades. It resisted occupation, fought a civil war, endured torture and exile, and led the anti-imperialist opposition to wars in Yugoslavia and Iraq.

The attacks on Syriza went back to splits from the party, which were bitter and passionate. He saw those who split as abandoning that history, although I argued that it was still their history too. They saw themselves as carrying it forward in the most appropriate way for these times. He did not see it that way. He thought that they moved to the right. The KKE were organizing for socialism, he argued, whereas Syriza wanted to manage capitalism. He also took issue with their position on both the EU and the euro. I pointed out that many in Syriza agreed with him about the Eurozone. He replied that Syriza was fluid. It was many things. He respected people in it. He was open to an alliance with it, but with many reservations and conditions. Was there much discussion of this in the party? I asked. No, the subject was taboo, he admitted. There was a more general debate about alliances and coalitions, but no open discussion of the attacks on Syriza. The party was losing not only voters but members, he revealed regretfully. There were stricter criteria for membership now. Members were being expelled. This strategy, this atmosphere, would drive the party to extinction, he concluded, as we ended on this sad note.

Another force on the left standing apart from Syriza and making some of the same criticisms was Antarsya, a coalition of the anticapitalist left. I had thought of it as primarily Trotskyist, but Kostas Skordoulis explained to me that it more or less mirrored the composition of Syriza in encompassing Trotskyists, Maoists, Eurocommunists, etc. Kostas was a professor of epistemology of science at the University of Athens. We had only met face-to-face on this day, despite several years of email contact regarding work of mine translated in *Kritiki*, a journal he edited, and an Engels symposium he was organizing for an upcoming international history of science congress. We went walking around Exarchia together, as he showed me the spot, now a shrine, where Alexandros Grigoropoulos, a fifteen-year-old student was killed by police, setting off widespread rioting, especially of youth, in December 2008. We moved on to the famous polytechnic, the scene of resistance, marking the beginning of the end of the junta. We then went to Exarchia Square and eventually settled down in a café across from his party's headquarters. He mapped the current state of Trotskyism globally. I have always found the proliferation of Trotskyist parties and their internationals a bit bewildering. The atmosphere on the left had shifted and those of us from the different streams of the left were interacting more constructively with each other now. With Kostas, it was particularly easy, and we had no problem in establishing a warm, respectful, and honest rapport.

Antarsya, he told me, had four thousand members, organized in all cities and many islands. They had councilors elected in every prefecture. In the May elections, they got 1.2 percent, whereas in June they only got 0.33 percent, as voters moved toward Syriza. There were voices in Antarsya advocating joining Syriza, he admitted, although he was not one of them. Indeed, the international body to which his group was affiliated, the USFI, supported Syriza, against the will of their Greek members. Kostas believed that it was necessary to have a left alternative to Syriza, a mass revolutionary party that could overthrow the system, because Syriza was too adaptationist, too willing to work within the system, too anxious to win the electoral base alienated from Pasok. All the same, unlike the KKE, Antarsya did not adopt a sectarian stance toward Syriza. They worked together in communities, unions, and universities. Indeed, earlier in the day, he was walking past the café where I was with Aristides and a pleasantly collegial conversation ensued. We met again the following week on the day of a march when Kostas was marching with Antarsya and I was marching with Syriza, but nevertheless we were colleagues and comrades.

The Unaffiliated Left

Another person with whom I had been in ongoing contact for a number of years was Christos Kefalis, who translated a number of my publications into Greek. He was editor of the journal *Marxist Thought* and a book called *October and Our Age*, in both of which my work appeared. He was committed to work that united all serious Marxists across the various traditions. He was a freelance writer, editor, and translator, as well as a committed left activist. He had been in the KKE twenty-five years ago but was now part of the independent left. He voted for Antarsya in May and Syriza in June. He had a thorough knowledge of the history of the Greek left. I asked him many questions, which he ably answered, as we walked through Exarchia, settled into a café and then on to a taverna, where the food and wine added to the pleasure of conversation but got in the way of taking notes. Looking to the present, he thought that the current government was the final government that the ruling class could form. He expressed regret that Antarsya and KKE would not unite with Syriza. The KKE had hardened with time, he observed, and it was expelling members. "They are collecting everything obsolete," he said sadly. They were defending Stalinism, and even the Moscow trials of the 1930s that sent honest communists to their deaths.

More recently I had formed contacts in Greece through social media, and I managed to meet face-to-face with at least some of the people who tweeted from Greece and kept me so well informed about what is happening when I was not there. My tweets from Greece brought a message from Damian Mac Con Uladh about meeting, which I was delighted to receive. We met in Syntagma Square and proceeded to a Monastiraki restaurant for lunch. On the way I had my first look at the metro, which was impressive, especially with the display of archeological artifacts unearthed in the building of it. It was one of the best things to come out of all the money spent on the Olympics, he commented, unlike the many rotting stadiums. Damian was working as a journalist at *Athens News*, although he hadn't been paid in months. He also wrote a blog called *A Gael in Greece* and articles on Greece for the *Irish Times*. How did he come to be in Greece? I wondered. He had been working on his PhD in history and met his Greek wife in a German archive. Although I was keen to draw him out about living and working in Greece, we spent a fair bit of time talking about Ireland and the GDR as well. His knowledge of all three countries was impressive, as were his insights into the many ironies of life in them, especially life on the left.

Another person with a connection to Ireland I met in Athens was Eugenia Siapera, a lecturer in Thessaloniki who would soon be taking up a job at Dublin City University as a lecturer in social media. She was sorry to be leaving, but she saw no future for her children in Greece. She spoke not only of the many general symptoms of crisis but of the decline in the schools. She came from a communist background and joined the communist youth organization when she was younger, under the influence of her father, who was arrested and exiled for his activism. She was left but did not belong to any party. She voted for the Pirate Party in May but switched to Syriza in June. She was incensed by the rise of XA. A few years ago people laughed at them, she said, but now the situation was worrying. Lots of threads to be taken up again when she came to Dublin, I thought.

The Once Left: Dimar and Pasok

Dimar—Democratic Left—was a breakaway from Syriza in 2010, in the direction of Pasok. Some of their MPs were ex-Pasok. They had won 6.3 percent in the last elections and were the third party in the government that was implementing the memorandum. Although they abstained in the vote on the memorandum, they voted for the austerity budget based on it. They lost three of their seventeen MPs in the process. It was hard to see them occupying a position on the political spectrum with much of a future, although they were holding steady in the polls.

As to Pasok, it was impossible to consider them part of the left in any sense anymore. The name, Panhellenic Socialist Movement, did not fit it at all. It was the party of the memorandum. The people who had been betrayed had taken their revenge and the party had collapsed, even though it went sputtering on, particularly in the person of its unattractive and unpopular party leader, Evangelos Venizelos. His television appearances and parliamentary speeches brought forth waves of revulsion on the social media, especially during his venomous attacks on the left. Pasok was still in government, despite going down to 12.3 percent in the elections and plunging further in subsequent polls. Many were moving from Pasok to Syriza, which was problematic for Syriza. They needed to grow, but not in a compromising social democratic direction. Not that all ex-Pasok people were pulling to the right. MP Sofia Sakorafa, for example, a former champion javelin thrower, was a radical and prominent face of Syriza.

Past and Present on the Streets of Athens

In between all these encounters, I walked and watched and wondered. Why was this country, with its rich history and culture, at the cutting edge of this current phase in the restructuring of capitalism? How far would it go? I was focused on the current crisis, but I tried to conceive it in terms of a longer story. I was thinking a lot about ancient Athens, which had lived in my imagination from the time I was a teenager and began studying the history of philosophy. It had the frisson of forbidden fruit, because it was venturing outside catholic orthodoxy. I was awed by the Socratic (Platonic) dialogues. Later I was convinced by the Marxist critique of ancient Greek philosophy, especially by the work of British Marxists Christopher Caudwell, George Thomson, and Benjamin Farrington. Thomson's books *The First Philosophers* and *Aeschylus and Athens* had an honored place on my bookshelves. These analyses showed the relation of abstract concepts to the shifting class structures of the ancient world. Ellen Meiksins Wood later wrote about this too. This critique did not dim the attraction of ancient Athens for me, but added a complexity that made it all the more intriguing. I taught the history of philosophy for many years and always did so with a strong emphasis on sociohistorical context. I tried to make ancient Athens live in the imagination of students as it did in mine.

Adding further to the complexity was the question of the relation of the Greek left to Greek antiquity. It had been the Greek right who had always staked a claim to continuity with the glories of ancient Greece, to the point where the left sometimes rebuffed it. In the schools, the teaching of history has been dominated by a sense that Greeks created an advanced civilization, while the rest of the people of the world were still swinging from the trees. Now XA were taking it up in an even more aggressive way, encouraging students to turn on their foreign classmates as compromising this idealized Hellenism.

I discussed the legacy of the ancient world with various people I met, especially historians and philosophers. Kostas Gavroglu pointed out the problematic nature of the continuity asserted by the right. Modern Greeks lived in the same place and spoke a form of the same language, but there had been so much mixing of populations in the Balkans over the centuries that modern Greeks were not the direct ancestors of the ancients. The Greek left, he commented, had veered between ignoring ancient traditions and adopting a milder form of the right's view. Aristides Baltas said that it had been wrong for the Greek left to be so negative about classical Greece and to leave it to the right. He thought that a more complex view of it was being taken now.

I walked to the top of the Acropolis. I didn't focus on the exact dates and details and dimensions of it, but tried to imagine how life had flowed through this part of the world over the ages. I thought of those who erected these structures, those who lived and thought through the centuries here. I then visited the new Acropolis Museum. It was impressive, but needed more in the way of a history-from-below dimension. I kept reciting to myself the great poem of Bertolt Brecht called "Questions from a Worker Who Reads," which begins "Who built Thebes of the seven gates? In the books, you will read the names of kings. Did the kings haul up the lumps of rock?" I reached for the lines of connection between the populations of these streets, ancient and modern. I also affirmed a continuity between the discourses of the ancient agora and my conversations with my contemporaries here. I didn't locate the brilliance of Athens only in its past.

In my times alone I read novels that I hoped would thicken my sense of Greek history, as I had done during all my previous trips to Greece. Some were disappointing, but *The Thread* by Victoria Hislop and *The House on Paradise Street* by Sofka Zinovieff definitely added time and texture to my vista.

I also walked the streets and squares of the contemporary city, seeing the homeless carrying all their possessions everywhere they went, people scavenging in bins for food, immigrants scrambling to sell things to passersby, junkies shooting up, rats scurrying across my path. Sometimes I averted my eyes and walked on quickly, because I didn't really know what to do. There were so many problems I couldn't solve or even engage with at a close level. Like most leftists, I think that my job is to address the nature of the system and to struggle to change it, but sometimes I feel at a loss as to how to help the suffering humanity, who cross our path one by one. Once I was sitting alone in a taverna on the street and a man came up and said he was hungry in a shy and shamed way. I gave him a skewer of souvlaki from my plate and offered him bread from the basket on the table. He seemed so grateful for so little. Mostly when approached in cafés I was in company and engaged in conversation and didn't welcome being asked to buy tissues or flowers or whatever, and all involved had a brief, awkward, and unsatisfactory encounter.

Every day, sometimes several times a day, I came across demonstrations. If I was free, I joined them and asked them about their grievances and goals. I spoke to occupying factory workers, protesting students, journalists, doctors, pharmacists, lawyers, etc. The protest culture was evident, not only in bodies on the streets but in writing on the walls. Athens must be the graffiti capital of the world. In Exarchia, there was scarcely a space without it. It was in various languages, although mostly in Greek. When I asked a Greek what was being said on a particular wall, he responded: "Many angry things about troika, government, police." Perhaps the most striking of what I saw was in English in gigantic red letters on the wall of the Academy of Athens, near the presiding statues of Socrates and Plato. It read: "Capitalism is killing you. Fascism won't save you." At the taverna in Exarchia that I adopted as my local, one wall of it proclaimed "Our Streets."

There was a strong anarchist presence in Athens. You see their "A" symbol everywhere. Aristides told me that anarchists were voting now. The communist tradition was ever present too and the hammer and sickle was also everywhere. One day, while walking in Exarchia, I heard strains of "Avanti Popolo" wafting through the air, although I couldn't locate its source.

One in three shops in Athens was boarded up or burnt out. Of those open, there didn't seem to be much happening in many of them. I entered the posh department store Attica, although not for shopping. I went up and down the escalator to reach the facility I required and saw little evidence of shopping on any of its floors. I wondered how many of the workers standing idle would keep their jobs.

The atmosphere in Athens was being compared to that of Berlin during the Weimar Republic.[8] The high unemployment, fascist threat, street fighting, political paralysis, personal anomie, and so many features of these streets did echo in me what I imagined those other streets were like at that time.

So many sectors were in disarray and decline. Hospitals were running out of crucial medicines and supplies. Universities were in turmoil over new structures of governance, cuts in funding, loss of staff. The neoliberalization of universities, underway everywhere, was more coercive and more resisted here. That restructuring of Greek debt the previous spring, which sounded good from afar, meant that Greek public-sector institutions, which were required to deposit a portion of their funding with the Bank of Greece in government bonds, had their deposits reduced by 60 percent. The disarray in the universities was one more impetus to the brain drain, as the country was hemorrhaging intellectuals and other skilled workers. The mainstream media were controlled by oligarchs and hostile to the left. There was much in the way of alternative media, but the circulation of Syriza newspaper *I Avgi* (The Dawn) was only three thousand a day and the audience of the Syriza FM station Sto Kokkino was limited. Journalists who tried to break stories of scandals and corruption were fired and even arrested. The Lagarde list of Greeks with accounts in one Swiss bank was suppressed by previous governments and then Kostas Vaxevanis was arrested for publishing it in *Hot Doc*. Everyone told me so many stories, with vivid examples from their own sectors, while seeing that parallel processes proceeded everywhere, except in the enclaves of the oligarchs. Every day was filled with tales of woe and symptoms of sociocide.

Life had become menacing on so many levels. Even insect bites were no longer just irritating, but now threatening, as malaria had returned to Greece. Although the solidarity networks and protests brought an enhanced sense of community, there were countervailing patterns in evidence too, as people pushed and even trampled each other for free food supplies. Desperation surrounded food. People were asked to put stale bread and other still edible food in bags hanging on the outside of bins to save scavenging and contamination. The bags disappeared quickly. I was surprised at how many men I saw fingering worry beads. I had associated these with very old men in *kafenios* on islands, but saw young men walking the city streets with them, including a riot cop on duty.

So many were so visibly suffering. Yet the Plaka, built on the slopes of the Acropolis among the ruins of the anceint city, was full of tourists, especially Americans on cruises, who didn't see it. They spent a few days each in various countries without touching anything real in any of them. The chatter I overheard was about food and shopping. Some remarked that it didn't really seem so bad. I suppose that it didn't in their five-star hotels. Even I had moments, I have to admit, when the crisis seemed at bay. I wore my summer dresses and sandals the whole time I was there, in perfect weather most days. On a Sunday I walked around the National Garden and sat on the grass with hundreds of others listening to a symphony orchestra in gorgeous autumn sun. It seemed idyllic. As I looked around, even the homeless seemed briefly released from their burdens.

There was humor amidst all the anxiety too. My Twitter feed from Greece was full of ironic observation. One noted that the recent prime minister, George Papandreou, was now lecturing on crisis management at Harvard because the captain of the *Titanic* was dead. Another advised undercover cops that their Ray-Ban Aviators clashed with their hoodies and black bloc riot couture.

Although I normally walked, I did take taxis on a few occasions. One day, I found myself in conversation with a taxi driver who supported XA. He listed crimes committed by immigrants. He admitted that they were not all criminals and insisted that he was not racist. He realized, he said, that they came to Greece for a better life, but they couldn't have it at the expense of Greeks. There were no longer the resources. Scarcity changed the situation. People were living in fear. When people had problems, the police didn't come, but XA did come and cleaned up the mess.

Another taxi driver told me that he worked seven days a week on twelve-hour shifts for twenty-eight days a month for €900 a month. He had a job as a salesman for a company that went out of business a few years ago. His wife worked too, but they still found it hard to manage. Still, he thought they were lucky, because he saw so much desperation as he drove around the streets of Athens all day and night. He voted Syriza. It offered some hope, he thought. He supported the general strike the previous day.

A General Strike

There had been approximately twenty-seven general strikes in Greece since the start of the crisis. There had been many sectoral and local strikes. It was hard to think of any sector of the workforce that hadn't been on strike during the previous four years. People in Ireland asked what had all these strikes accomplished. It could be argued that they brought down two governments. It was true that they had not mitigated any measures decreed by the troika, but the cumulative impact might be more evident eventually. The politics of the street had increasingly converged with the politics of the ballot box, as people saw that it would take a new government to set the process along a new trajectory.

There was a general strike on October 18 when I was there. In the days preceding it, trade union posters went up all over central Athens. *Oxi*—No to austerity—was the dominant message. That morning the hotel was shuttered down, with minimal staff. Shops and factories were closed. Public services were suspended. Schools were not in session. Flights were grounded. Little traffic was on the road. Riot buses were outside the hotel, as were a contingent of PAME, the All-Workers Militant Front, gathered to march to Omonia Square, where they would converge with other PAME contingents for an assembly before marching to Syntagma Square. PAME and the KKE always marched alone and did not mix with other union and political groupings. I walked to Omonia to take in the atmosphere. It was early yet, so there weren't many there, but there was a platform erected, with red flags flying and militant communist music playing. It was the sort of music that always stirred up my feelings about the communist movement, a mixture of pride and loss. I ran into Damian Mac Con Uladh there. He briefed me on the canon of KKE music, which rejected much contemporary music as decadent, even the GDR version of pop music.

We walked together to the other gathering point at Pedion Areos, where the Civil Servants Confederation (ADEDY) and the General Confederation of Greek Workers (GSEE), the main trade unions for public- and private-sector workers, were gathering with left formations such as Syriza and Antarsya. The ADEDY and GSEE, caught up for decades in habits of class collaboration, had become more militant with the severity of the crisis. The atmosphere here was more diverse, more relaxed, less regimented, more new left than old left. I met Syriza comrades, as arranged, in a café in front of the National Archaeological Museum. I chatted to Antarsya comrades as well and met many new people, although briefly. Eventually we marched. Two comrades, Aliki Papadomichelaki and Lila Mambregianni, were solicitous in looking after me. Aliki had been politically active since the 1950s, spoke multiple languages, and seemed to know everything about the left everywhere. Lila was unemployed after the company for which she worked for twenty-eight years closed and left her with no pension except what she received from the state. She put her energy to good use now in political activism.To mitigate the effects of tear gas, they told me when to smear Riopan on my face and when to put on the gas mask they gave me as we approached Syntagma Square. They translated the slogans for me. Some of these were: "We won't let capitalism kill us"; "History is made by people who don't obey"; "The time of the left has come"; "Athens, Madrid, Lisbon, Rome, all Europe." No mention of Dublin!

In Syntagma Square, the atmosphere was menacing. Riot police were out in force. The air was full of chemicals. I felt some itching in my eyes, nose, and throat, but I didn't get the worst of it. A bloc of professors had got the worst of it. Enterprising immigrants were selling water, tissues, and gas masks. Protesters were being forced to march around the perimeter rather than assembling inside the square. "What now?" I asked. "Nothing," said Lila. "Two years ago we had mothers and babies and we sang songs. We had concerts when we got to Syntagma Square. Now we just fight." People with children, home from school, because schools were closed, could not bring them into the chemical warfare and physical aggression of Syntagma Square. There were scuffles, chemical weapons, Molotov cocktails, stun grenades, injuries, arrests. One man, a member of KKE, an unemployed seaman, who was marching with PAME, died, apparently of a heart attack. I marched on with Syriza around the square and then toward Omonia.

As it was coming up to 3:00 p.m. and I had an appointment at the Plaza Hotel, I left them when we got to the university and headed back to Syntagma Square. I was to meet Georgios Ayfantis, diplomatic adviser to Alexis Tsipras, who had given me his card after I spoke at the international meeting and asked if we could meet. The road into the square was blocked by riot police. I always make a point of arriving at appointments on time, so with steely determination and surprising calm, I walked right through the line of riot police. I got away with it, presumably because I didn't look very combative. When I got to the hotel, it was shuttered down and a concierge said that I had better come inside because there was trouble brewing just outside it. Then they shut down completely, meaning that I was locked in and he was locked out. We ascertained each other's position by mobile phone and he found his way in through the back. He was a career diplomat. He was born into the Greek elite. His father was a judge. He attended an American school in Greece. When he was younger, he joined the KKE, but was expelled from it. He listed his postings in the diplomatic service and then moved on to the future. There would be much tension between the EU and a left government in Greece, he predicted. Summits with Alexis Tsipras there as prime minister would be a nightmare for Angela Merkel. There would be problems at home too. "There will be no velvet revolution in Greece," he said, referring to the transition in Czechoslovakia in 1989, repeating a sentence that I heard many times in Athens. The Greek oligarchy would not give up lightly. However, the oligarchs no longer controlled the military. The police would be more of a problem. He spoke of submarines and prisons and trade relations and natural resources and many other matters. I had the impression that there was much concrete strategic thinking at play in Syriza. He advocated a pragmatic foreign policy, including such relations with Israel as were in the national interests of Greece, a highly contested position in Syriza.

The Party Leader

Speaking of Alexis Tsipras, I was struck by how proud Syriza people were of him without any trace of personality cult. He was young, attractive, canny, even charismatic. He became a global superstar in the international media between the May and June elections. There were attempts in mainstream media to undermine him, concentrating on his youth and inexperience. Reuters revealed to the world that he was "no working-class hero." Why? Because he had a postgraduate degree in engineering. In August, *Der Spiegel* listed him as among "Europe's 10 most dangerous politicians." In Greece, the right cast him as irresponsible and inexperienced, while the left (outside of Syriza) accused him of being too compromising. Some compared him to the young Andreas Papandreou and implied that he would disappoint accordingly. He would almost certainly be the next prime minister. It was true that he was inexperienced in governance, but many Greeks wanted someone not tied into the experience of what governance had been in Greece until now. Syriza people pointed out that he was intelligent and he listened. They said that he was modest and he learned quickly. One person criticized a speech he had given recently as too technocratic but amended this with an account of a press conference he gave the next day where he dealt with political economy in a more astute way. Even those who held positions to the left of him within Syriza thought that he was the appropriate leader.

Left Criticism of Syriza

A number of the criticisms of Tsipras were made against Syriza itself. People said that they were moving to the right with the prospect of electoral success. "They water their wine," several people said to me. "They want to manage capitalism, not create socialism," others added. When I put these criticisms to Syriza people, they rejected them firmly. They insisted that they had not moved to the right, that they were not watering their wine, that they did want to create socialism. Yes, they wanted to manage capitalism in the interests of working people in the immediate aftermath of forming a government, but they wanted to do so in the direction of moving toward socialism. It was not possible to do everything at once, but they would institute a radical democratic transformation from the very beginning, combining forms of direct democracy with representative structures. They would reverse the austerity cuts, restore wages and pensions, and redistribute wealth and power in a way that was not yet socialism, but was intended to open a new path to socialism for the twenty-first century.

The EU and the euro were problematic areas between Syriza and others on the left. Even within Syriza, there were those who were for exiting the Eurozone. The KKE opposed the EU itself as imperialist. Syriza saw the EU, as it did the state itself, as a site of struggle in relation to the euro, debt, and much else. They were aware, however, that they would face serious opposition from the EU and might be forced out of both the EU and Eurozone. There was much plan B thinking about such scenarios. The left in Syriza often cited the work of Costas Lapavitsas, a Greek Marxist economist who was a professor in London and close to Syriza, as a source of their theoretical and strategic thinking along these lines. This trend believed that no viable solution would be found with the foreign lenders. So a Syriza government should be prepared for a break with the EU when the circumstances made it necessary and appropriate.[9]

Continuing Engagement

There was much to think about when I returned to Dublin after these intense days in Athens. I continued my engagement with Greece from a distance. In fact, the next day a Syriza MP was scheduled to give a talk in Dublin. It was an ill-fated event, organized by the ULA, in which nothing went right. The time, date, and venue had been changed several times over. The speaker missed his flight. A poster announcing the talk had cropped the KKE logo from the iconic photo of protesters at the Acropolis calling for the people of Europe to rise up, which caused controversy, first in Dublin and then abroad, when an attack on Syriza by the KKE was translated into multiple languages, even though Syriza had no part in the design of the poster and the ULA had apologized to both Syriza and KKE. The speaker, Ioannis Stathas, an industrial worker, who had formerly been in Pasok, was first elected to parliament in May. He spoke of the crisis and the need to resist. Having seen monuments of the Easter Rising and other such events in Irish history that day, he told us that we were not living up to our revolutionary history. The Irish left needed less beer and more history, he preached. He was asked serious questions about unity amidst diversity in Syriza, about issues of sabotage and security if they came to power, about what intellectual resources were being drawn on, questions on which he failed to shed much light. He showed little regard for theory and indicated that praxis was all. He felt compelled to say that revolutions were not made by people with gray hair. I felt that I had to stand up for the role being played by critical Marxism in Syriza, as well as for its exponents with gray hair. The encounter underlined for me the diversity of Syriza, which included attitudes I contested.

During the following days, I kept up with what was happening as best I could through the Internet and the telephone. I frequented various Greek portals using computer translations, which were sometimes enlightening but sometimes bewildering. I was continually grateful to those blogging and tweeting from Greece in English. I followed the general strikes and big marches via live stream video in one window and Twitter feed in another. I was riveted to it on November 7, as the second memorandum was being voted on in parliament and massive crowds gathered, shouting and singing, with much drama both inside and outside the parliament. At one stage Syriza MPs came out of the parliament and stood with a defiant banner above the square, while the crowd down in the square went wild with affirmation. Despite the fact that the supreme court ruled the latest austerity measures unconstitutional, the parliament passed them anyway, although in a close vote, losing MPs on the government side along the way.

I learned the important days on the Greek protest calendar: October 28 is Oxi Day, a national holiday to mark the day Greece said no to Mussolini in 1940, but now a big day to say no to the troika. November 17 celebrates the polytechnic uprising of 1973 that led to the end of the junta. December 6 commemorates the death of Alexandros Grigoropoulos in 2008, which led to a youth-initiated uprising. This year Exarchia was in flames once again. In between, there were many protests and strikes and occupations of factories, town halls, and universities. Left students at the University of Athens occupied the central IT system for several days in November. Not much of this made mainstream international news. When I heard people saying that things had gone quiet in Greece, I knew that it was only because they were not listening.

Left Intellectuals in London

From November 8 to November 11 I spent four very intense days at the ninth annual Historical Materialism Conference in London. Most of those participating in it were both academics and activists, combining critical thought and research into the historical process with a sense of responsibility for moving history forward. There were more questions than answers and openness to a variety of positions. The atmosphere of orthodoxy and denunciation that once characterized the relations of different factions of the left was absent here. There were ten simultaneous sessions going on through the days and packed plenaries in the evenings. The eight-hundred-plus attendees were from all over the world, various political traditions of the left, and different stages of the life cycle. In my own presentation, I attempted a historical materialist analysis of the Occupy movement. There were people at it who participated in this movement elsewhere, and it once again became clear that the same patterns played out in many parts of the world. The relationship of the Occupy movement to the Movement of the Squares in Greece, the *indignados* in Spain and the protest movement in Russia was a theme across various sessions. Another big theme of the conference was interrogating the history of the communist movement, although the central focus was the current crisis and the left's response to it.

I had occasion to speak with comrades from around the world, as well to further my engagement with the Greek left through Greeks presenting at the conference. Most of them seemed more inclined toward Antarsya than Syriza, but I found them well worth hearing. Eirini Gaitanou gave a paper on feminism in Greece and highlighted the effects of the crisis on the lives of women. Giorgos Kalampokas gave a very Gramscian analysis of the struggle for hegemony in Greece, arguing the need to set in motion institutions for transforming everyday life and for providing counterpower, even to a left government. Other Greeks too spoke from platform and floor on crisis, resistance, and alternatives. I was pleased to meet Panagiotis Sotiris, who had been assiduous in informing international audiences of the struggles in Greek universities. He noted a new flourishing of theoretical debate and production by students and academics being forged in the combination of political activism with theoretical work.[10] I was very happy to meet Michalis Spourdalakis again. We spoke at various intervals and then had a long talk on the metro before exiting for different terminals at Heathrow to return to Athens and Dublin. He spoke at the conference on the strategy of Syriza that accounted for its rise and its potential to bring real social transformation to Greece and to Europe.

There was a Syriza branch in London. Among their other activities, they held seminars that were made available on video, which I watched with appreciation. There was one on December 7, where speakers included Stathis Kouvelakis and Costas Douzinas. Douzinas, professor of law at Birkbeck, said, "You're never ready to fall in love or have a revolution." He described an emerging scenario where popular will, political agency, and catalyst were coming together, bringing Syriza to a rendezvous with history. Kouvelakis, reader in political theory at King's College in London, analyzed such forces more concretely.

PIIGS: Portugal, Italy, Ireland, Greece, and Spain

On November 14 there was a day of coordinated general strikes and protests in Europe, organized by the trade unions.; This was a big step forward for the left. There were massive turnouts elsewhere, but not in Ireland. The Irish Congress of Trade Unions (ICTU) said they supported it but had nothing planned for the day, because they were mobilizing for a November 24 march. The ICTU had failed to organize appropriately during the crisis, particularly since the Labour

Party entered government. The Dublin Council of Trade Unions (DCTU), with a more militant history, did get twenty thousand out on November 24. The ULA organized a demonstration in solidarity on November 14, which I attended. It was sad to see so little from Ireland on this day. In the evening I gave a talk on Greece at a ULA meeting. The big question on everyone's mind was: How can we build a Syriza here?

On the day someone tweeted "This little piggy didn't come out to strike." I had been noticing that PIIGS—referring to the five EU countries with the most unstable economies—was increasingly being spelled PIGS. It seemed that the narrative of Irish exceptionalism, promoted by both the Irish government and the troika, was prevailing, even among the international left, who sometimes didn't rate us as part of a common struggle. We were trying, even if we failed to mobilize in such numbers, partly because our fellow citizens did not see that what was being tested in Greece was what is in store for the rest of us. The lowering of wages, the shrinking of social welfare, the privatizing of public assets were not meant to be temporary measures. They were core to the restructuring of capitalism that was well underway in Ireland and elsewhere.

I noted for some months the call from Alexis Tsipras for solidarity of the southern periphery. More specifically, he put forward a proposal for an EU conference on debt, calling for a write-down for the southern periphery.[11] Why did he never mention Ireland? What about our debt? Our debt was perhaps the most unjust of all, as it was based on forcing private debts on to us as public debts. In fact, Ireland, while only 0.9 percent of the EU population, had paid 42 percent of the cost of the European banking crisis.[12]

The Syriza Conference

On November 30 and December 1–2, the Syriza conference was held in the Peace and Friendship Stadium in Athens to move forward the refoundation of Syriza as a unified party. Prior to this, over thirty thousand people had registered as individual members and elected over three thousand delegates in sectoral and thematic areas. There were around five hundred branches in localities and workplaces. Previously unaffiliated members now formed the majority of Syriza. Alexis Tsipras addressed the conference, saying, "History is calling us to be the new party of twenty-first-century socialism. . . . All of Europe is looking to us to be the spark that starts the fire." Aristides Baltas presented the manifesto he had been drafting while I was there, which had been subjected to widespread discussion and which passed "almost unanimously."

I followed it all as best I could through Skype, texting, web portals, and so forth. I especially enjoyed a slideshow of the conference showing formal speeches and informal conversation, pensive faces and happy faces, of male and female, young and old, participants. On the soundtrack was Bob Dylan singing, "The times they are a changin'," setting off strong resonances of the convergences of old and new in a left fit for these times.

There were two lists for the 301 central committee members, the Left Platform and a heterogeneous other list. I recognized names on both. The Left Platform articulated a left critique of the majority position gathered around Tsipras. The result was 25 percent–75 percent in favor of the Tsipras majority. Despite some readings of this on social media, it was my understanding that relations between the Left Platform and the rest were characterized more by healthy debate than by hostile contestation at this time. The Left Platform put a strong emphasis on seeking allies to the left, specifically KKE and Antarsya, and not to the right, and on reversing austerity by all means necessary.

The KKE responded to the declaration by accusing Syriza of taking the positions and even the terminologies of KKE, instead of recognizing their common traditions and positions. In his conference speech, Tsipras expressed what many expressed to me, that this hostility from forces of the left was hard to understand and caused them grief. This was especially the case with those who had come out of the KKE, as Tsipras and many others had. I watched most of a three-hour video of an event celebrating the ninety-fourth anniversary of the KKE. There were lots of red flags waving and thousands singing the songs of

Theodorakis. There was a rousing rendition of "The Internationale" at the end. I was moved by it all and felt such a longing for them to step up to play the historic role that they could play at this crucial juncture in the history of the great Greek left.

What Next?

What would be the next act in this consequential drama? Greece would continue to be a cauldron of class conflict, for sure, but would it climax in a breakthrough in this high-stakes struggle for power? Would it move on from critique and resistance to transformation? How long would the present government last? Would a left government succeed it? Would it be able to withstand the monumental, even terroristic, pressures that would be brought to bear upon it? Would it be able to stand against the global plutocracy? Would it be able to resist the cyclone ripping through our world? Would it be able to break the power of there-is-no-alternative and bring forth a real alternative? Would it be able to forge a new path to socialism, not only for Greece but for us all?

As I saw it at the end of 2012, Greece was the crucible, where the best and worst of our civilization were in high-energy collision with each other. This was not some local battle. These cuts to pay, pensions, and public services, this privatization of public property, this redistribution of wealth from below to above: these were not temporary contingent measures. These were integral to a systemic restructuring of capitalism. It had advanced through Europe already from east to west. Where there were once experiments in socialism in the east, there were now oligarchies. Next on the agenda: advances achieved by the labor movement in the west were to be stripped.

Greece showed where the process was going, but it also offered an alternative: an example of critique, resistance, and preparation for reconstruction. We needed to stand with them for their sake as well as for ours. Haris Golemis, elected to the central committee of Syriza, put it to us: "No political success in a single European country can be sustainable if it is not followed, within a short time, by similar successes in other countries. A progressive island in a reactionary archipelago is a thing of the past."[13] It had echoes of the socialism-in-one-country debate all those decades ago. The tasks seemed monumental, both for them and for us. Yiannis Tolios, an economist, also elected to the central committee, articulated the problem starkly, but with a different stress: "If having socialism in a single country is considered hard, having socialism is all countries at the same time is nearly impossible."[14] Greece needed to forge ahead, whether the rest were ready or not, but it was a perilous path.

In Athens I felt at the edge of history. I saw Dublin more clearly as a result. It was time for a new initiative on the left in Ireland and I felt a responsibility to pursue that. The ULA was unraveling. There was need for something broader and better than anything we had created so far. I wanted to see if we could rise to that. I would return to Greece to continue to feel the pulse of the global process and to try to convince others in Ireland and elsewhere that we could not continue to live as we were. Capitalism was killing us. Only socialism could save us.

CHAPTER 2

2013: Preparing for Power

Recurring Resistance

Things have gone very quiet in Greece, haven't they?" So many people said that to me in 2013. I responded that there was a lot going on, even if international media weren't covering it. There were civil mobilizations of teachers and transport workers, as well as rising unemployment, emigration, and impoverishment, being met with continuing protests, strikes, and occupations. Even so, I sensed a lull in the rhythm of resistance since the big demonstrations opposing the passage of the memorandum the previous autumn. Obviously people couldn't keep going at that pitch all the time, but how many were succumbing to exhaustion, despair, defeat? How many were quietly going about their work in solidarity networks, policy development, political education?

The year began in turmoil with police raids on squats and fire bombings and shootings, whether in retaliation or distraction from ongoing debate on the Lagarde list and from legislation enabling public property to be seized by the nation's creditors.

On January 8, as I was taking my daily look around Greek websites, I learned that Thanasis Anapolitanos had died. I had written to him and wondered why I hadn't heard back. It was cancer. He was sixty-one.

On January 19, 2013, an international mobilization against fascism was initiated in Athens, with a march from Omonia and a big concert in Syntagma Square. I was honored to be asked to be one of the artists and intellectuals sponsoring the call for it. Dublin was among the cities that answered the call. We marched from Stephen's Green to the Greek embassy. I spoke there, connecting the rise of fascism to the global economic crisis. I was not impressed by the presence of a number of participants wearing hoods and masks, including those who were carrying the leading banner while objecting to being photographed. I thought the public demonstration was an act of bearing witness and taking whatever risk that involved. I raised the matter on social media, which met with some controversy. One older anarchist cast a wry eye on "toytown activism."

Also in January, I was involved in founding Left Forum in Ireland to discuss the state of the Irish left and to address how we might up our game. I was especially concerned about gathering the unaffiliated left, those who felt that none of the existing parties of the left fit them, to be a more effective force along with the existing parties of the left. Left Forum set out to be a political education project and think tank which might affiliate to the Transform network. We also had proto-party ambitions: to lay the groundwork for a broad left party like Syriza. We had a number of national events with broad participation about the state of the Irish left and the question of whether Ireland needed a new left party as well as smaller debates on reform and revolution and seminars on left theory. Greece came into every discussion.

One afternoon I went to Lanigan's pub. where *The Great Couch Rebellion* by Philip Doherty was playing in the theater upstairs. The two main characters were Irish Adam and Greek Eve, and the dialogue was about the current crisis in Ireland and Greece. "The whole economy is a pyramid scheme," said Greek Eve, taunting Irish Adam to act. So he went on a protest. On Facebook, four thousand said they were coming, but only a hundred came. Therefore, they concluded, more drastic measures were needed. They taunted a bank worker, who was also a friend, as if he were responsible for it all, tied him up, went on YouTube, and threatened to kill him unless the government lowered the tricolor and raised a black flag. The play ignored the existence of the actual contemporary left, while it harkened back to the heroes of 1916 and saw only stupid stunt politics as a worthy successor. Well intended but very immature. It was the mentality of many of the Occupy campers in Dublin in 2011.

The first of my articles on Greece was published in *Irish Left Review* and then republished in *Links, Counterpunch, Greek Left Review,* and *Left Unity*.[1] It was translated into several languages. There were many responses in those publications, on social media and in emails from all around the world, testifying to how much the international left felt it had at stake in Greece. The response was overwhelmingly positive, but not entirely so. One commentator jeered at "marginal middle-class pipe dreamers" who deluded themselves into thinking that anything further left than the Labour Party or Pasok was ever going to go anywhere.

In February, a trade union march against austerity mobilized one hundred thousand people on the streets of Dublin. Not for the first or the last time. Not that all our large and small mobilizations stopped the constant repetition of the mantra that Irish people didn't protest. There was some tension between political activists and trade union leaders over demands for a general strike. The general strikes in Greece added to the pressure for one in Ireland. There was also an anti-union hooligan element appearing regularly on the streets at this time. They attracted modest numbers at events they organized themselves but created havoc at events organized by others. Discussing it on Facebook, one of these "independent protesters" asserted his right as a "sovereign man of Eire to walk this land," even at the head of the ICTU march.

Soon after, MEP Paul Murphy organized an EU Countersummit in Liberty Hall. I spoke at the session on Greece along with Andros Payiatsos, the general secretary of Xekinima, the CWI party in Greece, the Socialist Party's sister party in Greece. They had been part of Syriza but decided to support it critically from the outside. It was not easy to speak on Greece in the presence of Greeks, who knew so much more, but I was putting in the effort to inform myself. Andros asked me how I kept up with it. There were shades of difference about Syriza between us. I was more affirmative, but I had to concede that Alexis Tsipras, especially when abroad, could sound too accommodating. Still, I insisted that there was a strong determination in Syriza not to become the new Pasok. I stayed for other sessions and took issue with Paul Murphy about smashing the state. I was for affirming and transforming it. It was a genial argument. Richard Boyd Barrett, another Trotskyist politician, came in and asked how many Trots it took to change a light bulb. None, because they smash it. We all laughed.

On February 20 there was another general strike in Greece, which I watched on livestream. I then went to see the Costa-Gavras film *Le Capital*, which showed the transformation of a French banker after he became CEO of a bank, parallel to the transformation of French banking and international finance capital in recent years. It showed people proud to be reverse Robin Hoods, making the rich richer and the poor poorer. It examined the process but indicated that the system was so total, so inevitable, that there was no way out of it. Costa-Gavras was present, and I asked him during the Q&A if this was what he intended. He said yes and no. He didn't want an easy, morally righteous Hollywood ending, but he didn't mean that there was no hope either.

In March, there was a brief flurry of international attention to Cyprus. The left-wing AKEL had lost power in the recent election and the right-wing government was negotiating a troika program. I was stunned at the move to expropriate bank deposits, as the "bailout" moved to a "bail-in." Resistance on the streets and in the parliament, where the left was still an effective force, won a modification of this move, but it went ahead.

Through these months, I kept my eyes on Greece while continuing to organize left meetings, attend protests, write another book, deliver lectures and papers on various topics, supervise a doctoral thesis, and participate in 1913 centenary events.

In May, there was a Subversive Festival in Zagreb, which I watched on video. I was especially interested in the session featuring Alexis Tsipras and Slavoj Žižek. Tsipras mentioned Ireland, which he rarely did. Asked what he learned from his recent trip to Latin America for the funeral of Hugo Chávez, he responded that it could be necessary for the left to go into government with the right to achieve its aims. Žižek veered from an ultraleftist and irresponsible remark about sending people who don't support Syriza to gulags to reformist arguments that Syriza should settle for running capitalism better than capitalists, jerkily pulling on his nose and T-shirt all the time. He also said that it was time to go from Marx back to Hegel. I didn't think so. I didn't think Tsipras should be appearing on platforms with him either, especially since Srećko Horvat as chair had introduced him as an adviser to Tsipras.

Grecovery? The Success Story

The international media story on Greece circulating in May, promoted by its government, was that Greece had stabilized and protest had subsided. Grexit had given way to Grecovery. Antonis Samaras, who was most actively articulating this, was touring the world with the good news, even heralding a Greek "renaissance." The feeblest of economic indicators were offered as evidence, although international commentators, even ones who wanted to believe this story, found it hard to get past the fact that most indicators still pointed in the opposite direction. In other statements, Samaras conceded that they hadn't really changed the numbers yet but insisted that they had eliminated the "negative psychology."

Many Greeks were scathing, pointing out that tiny shifts from rating agencies and bond yields paled into insignificance aside the continuing free fall of the economy and the still deteriorating conditions of life for all but the Greek oligarchs. Among indicators being trumpeted were lower wages, which might be good news for investors but hardly for workers. Calling the Greek success story the "latest Orwellian turn of the Greek crisis," Yanis Varoufakis laid the economic facts on the line.[2]

At this point, Ireland came into the story. Enda Kenny arrived in Athens on May 23. On the basis of a few hours in Athens and conversations with Samaras, he endorsed the Greek "success story" and praised Samaras for changing international sentiment toward Greece. Samaras declared that Greece was following Ireland's example to exit the crisis and return to the markets next year. This "return to the markets" was presented as the great utopian aspiration of our time. In Ireland we were told that we were set to enter that promised land soon. So all that evolutionary striving was for this.

At the press conference of the two prime ministers, Samaras said, "Ireland has shown us the way back to growth and to the markets." For the Greek elite, Ireland was a model during the boom and it remained so in the bust. Kenny soaked up the flattery and smugly advised Samaras that the secret of our "success" was to establish "trust" with the troika. RTÉ news opened the report with images of the Acropolis and the ceremonial changing of the guards at the Greek parliament. It was all reported without a hint of skepticism, regarding both Irish and Greek "success" as somehow self-evident. They did not see fit to mention statements by Syriza or KKE calling attention to Ireland's debt, emigration, cuts, all on the road of advancing oligarchic interests at great social cost to the rest of the population. It was not considered newsworthy to note that the Greek left did not see Ireland as a model for Greece. Even beyond the left, there were many voices in both Ireland and Greece who queried whether either country was a success story. Tony Connelly, RTÉ correspondent in Athens during the Kenny-Samaras visit, nevertheless parroted the preferred plotline of the plutocracy.

Return to Athens

A counternarrative was in order. I had been following events, but I had some questions to answer to clarify my sense of where the story was now. Could it be that the time of possibility for the left had passed? Despite the reality that all problems persisted, had even intensified, were the powers that be prevailing after all? Could this be one more chapter in the tragic history of the Greek left, who had been so strong, who had fought so fiercely, but had always been bitterly defeated?

While I kept up as best I could from afar, there was nothing like walking the streets and talking face-to-face to take the pulse of the scene. I returned to Greece in June and spent fifteen days, primarily in Athens, finding out what was happening. I met people I had known previously, to hear how their lives and thoughts had moved on, and I met new people too.

I was with my son Cathal, who was discovering Athens for the first time. We walked the streets, ancient and modern. In the ancient ruins with Wi-Fi hotspots, I tweeted my fascination with the ways classical culture resonated in the present conjuncture. Not that you could say much in a tweet, but my brain was still buzzing with the philosophical discourses that had captured my imagination so long ago. Cathal was better on the historical detail, but I was again reflecting on the relationship of the big philosophical ideas to the sociohistorical forces of the times.

I was also struck by the strength of ancient myth in the contemporary detective novels I was reading. The Alex Mavros novels traced missing persons through the layers of Greek society, from the oligarchs to the communists, set in the last decade with storylines reaching back into the political history of the previous decades and even further back to myths of Demeter and Persephone, Hercules and Cerberus. Near the agora, I noted the street in Monastiraki where the detective lived and the street where his communist sidekick ran a café. The author, Paul Johnston, was now a Facebook friend. I was hoping that he would get on with writing the next one and that someone would translate the crisis trilogy of Petros Markaris, because I had already read all the Alex Mavros and Costas Haritos novels currently available. I learned a lot about Greece from such fiction too.

Walking from Metaxourgio to Monastiraki on the first day, we stopped near Omonia to look at a poster for the Alter Summit, which we would be attending. A man stopped to look at us looking and drew us into conversation. He said that politics was hopeless, that it was all about power and money, that it would never change. He was active in left politics when he was young, he disclosed, but he was now sixty-three and no longer a student and could see no point in it. I told him that I was older than that and still active in left politics. He looked at me quizzically. Afterwards, I thought that I should have pointed to Manolis Glezos, Syriza MP, who was still full of fire and hope at ninety-one.

We proceeded down Athinas and took in all the sights and smells of meat and fish, both raw and cooked, and noted all the goods on display hanging in the shop front displays. Most clothes and accessories were of a sort you might find anywhere, but what was distinctive here was all the different sorts of gas masks on display. Should we buy them? The last time I was in Athens, people asked me if I had a gas mask when I showed up for protests and lent me one when it was needed. On balance, though, I didn't expect to need one this time. I didn't think that the European left march into Syntagma would be gassed.

We walked many streets, particularly around Metaxourgio, Psiri, Omonia, and Exarchia. Cathal went for shortcuts and back streets, often at night, which didn't always look as dangerous as they actually were. Somehow normal life continued in shops, apartments, and offices, but desperation was also apparent in the begging, scavenging, and shooting up, the people wandering homelessly, even crying and crawling. Some things were puzzling: for example, coming across a pile of abandoned clothes that looked like a person had undressed there and walked away. So many sights on the streets made me wonder what story was behind what I was seeing.

Even those who looked prosperous had their problems and were not as prosperous as they seemed. I spoke to a number of people in employment, in several cases people with PhDs working as lecturers or journalists, who had not been paid in many months. How did they live? They lived off others in their families who were being paid. In most cases, those who were earning salaries had had their pay drastically reduced. I met one woman, well-groomed and middle-aged, who broke into floods of tears because no one in her family was working now and they had nothing. Another young woman, articulate and attractive, told me that her life was over and she was only fighting now for a better society for her son. She had been a physiotherapist, and then a waitress, and now she was unemployed. So many people serving in hotels and restaurants were once physiotherapists or journalists or teachers or graphic designers. I met one young man, who did a master's thesis on the EU, who told me that he wished that he could have it back and write the exact opposite now.

An essential port of call was the Syriza head office. We chatted with Costas Isychos, Dimitra Tsami, and Yiannis Bournous on many topics, from expectations of the Alter Summit to protests in Turkey to the breakup of the ULA to preparations for the Syriza congress. They did not believe that the time of the left had passed. They did not believe in the accuracy of the polls. They were still preparing for power.

Alter Summit

We met again over the next days at the Alter Summit. It took place at the Olympic Village on June 7–8. Most sessions were in or around the velodrome. Outside were stalls where various parties, projects, and groups displayed their wares—books, bags, balloons, pamphlets, posters, pens, T-shirts. For meals, there were pop-up kitchens offering various ethnic cuisines on paper plates. The system for paying for food and drink reminded me of the USSR. Queuing for chits and queuing again for products was not one of the most attractive aspects of these experiments in socialism. Milling around and chatting in the outdoors was fine at first—until the second day, when it rained.

People from various parties, movements, and trade unions came together to explore grounds for shared analysis and activity. It was a convergence of forces from the European Social Forum, the parties within the Party of the European Left (Die Linke, Syriza, Izquierda Unida, Front de Gauche, etc.), and major European trade unions. The six Irish people attending it were from diverse sections of the left: MEP Paul Murphy of the Socialist Party, Mark Malone of the Workers Solidarity Movement, John Bissett of the Spectacle of Defiance, Cathal Ó Murchú of Sinn Féin, Sarah Brennan of Debt Action Coalition (and a former student of mine), and myself of Left Forum. A Trotskyist, an anarchist, a shinner (republican), a Eurocommunist, and hard to label—all interacting harmoniously—although Paul Murphy came and went quickly, so as to join in the action on Taksim Square. Not that we always agreed. At one point, John said to me "Žižek is very good on Greece, isn't he?" and I launched into a tirade about how incoherent and irresponsible Žižek was. Another night, Cathal and Mark talked long into the night over many beers in Exarchia Square, exploring the differences in their political philosophies.

At the Alter Summit, proceedings began with a feminist assembly, which concentrated on the effects of the crisis on women. There followed fifteen thematic assemblies over two days on education, debt, health, migration, housing, employment, welfare, environment, the commons, fascism, economic policy, and international relations. The emphasis was on proposals for common international initiatives.

On the evening of the first day, there was a plenary. As a thousand people assembled, there was rousing Greek political music creating an energetic and expectant atmosphere after a much delayed start. Then the manifesto was launched. It had been drafted over many months by activists in many countries. It began: "Europe stands on the edge of a precipice, looking into the abyss. Austerity policies drive the people of Europe into poverty, undercut democracy and dismantle social policies. Rising inequalities endanger social cohesion. Ecological destruction is worsening while acute humanitarian crises devastate the most affected countries. Women and young people are hardest hit."[3]

There followed hours of speakers from many countries, movements, and unions, all saying more or less the same thing: how objectionable and oppressive neoliberalism was and how we needed to combat it together. There were some multimedia intervals on various struggles and sometimes groups burst into song. It was great to be there with so much harmony of analysis and commitment to common action, but as the hours went on, the energy dissipated, as it was repetitious and exhausting. The Irish were tired and hungry, and it was approaching 11:00 p.m. On the metro, we agreed that such repetition should be banned. When we settled into a café in Metaxourgio, someone said,

"Sorry, what exactly is wrong with neoliberalism?" and we all wearily laughed. Unfortunately, we missed the speech of Alexis Tsipras, the finale, and the concert that was to follow.

We were up bright and early and back the next day, participating in assemblies, making contacts, conversing informally. I spent a lot of time talking to Greeks. In search of a hard-to-find session in the swimming area, I asked a man, "Are you Greek?" to which he responded, "Are you Helena?" It was Yiannis Tolios, an economist on Syriza's central committee and part of its Left Platform. We had a long talk after that session. We covered many aspects of politics in Greece and Ireland as well as episodes in our back stories, discovering that we had both studied in the USSR. Costas Isychos came up to talk with us and told Yiannis: "Her life is like a Hollywood movie."

In the evening we took the metro into the center of Athens, where the participants reassembled to march from the National Archaeological Museum into Syntagma Square. It was a lively and colorful march, with street theater and singing and chanting in many languages and styles. We were not teargassed.

Overall, I found the experience of the Alter Summit a bit underwhelming, although I wasn't altogether sure why. I assumed that it was because I hadn't been part of the whole process leading up to it and didn't participate appropriately. However, others found it a bit disappointing too, as attendance from abroad was not what was expected, and attendance from Greece, despite posters all over town, was far less than hoped. This was attributed to a sense of downturn on the Greek left. Nevertheless, it did strengthen the bonds between the different sections of the European left and built networks for ongoing practical initiatives.

In the days after it, the Irish people coming and going were discovering other delights and difficulties of Athens. John, Mark, and Cathal climbed the Acropolis in the heat of the summer sun, while I walked in the shade of the National Garden. In the various cafés, where we met to compare notes at intervals, we were interrupted as usual by a stream of people begging, selling, performing. It was impossible to deal with all of them. However, one little boy with a toy ukulele, who sang Theodorakis songs, won us over completely, and we reached into our pockets.

Life Stories: Next Episodes

What had been happening in the lives of those I met when I was last in Athens? Although I had remained in contact with some of them, there was nothing like a few hours face-to-face in a café to find out how their lives were moving on. Unfortunately there wasn't much good news. Aristides Baltas was in hospital, although I got regular health reports, and prospects for his recovery were looking up by the time I left.

I met my contact in the KKE for another long talk. In addition to having no hope of secure employment commensurate with his high qualifications and receiving no pay for six months from his insecure employment, he had his political troubles as well. There was a move to expel him from the party on the grounds that he gave an academic lecture in a space occupied by anarchists—"enemies of our party." People he had known all his life, some even members of the same family, debated and voted on this in his branch. In the end, they decided to censure, but not to expel, him. He felt politically disarmed and depressed. He said that the discussions coming up to the party congress were very rich, although decisions were unanimous. I had heard from others that this happened by controlling the election of delegates, even expelling critics, so this story fit the pattern. The primary point of controversy was the question of alliances. Before the congress, he argued, there was an inconsistency between the party program and its political practice on this question. Now the inconsistency was resolved, but in the wrong direction. They were still denouncing Syriza and others on the left and refusing to discuss alliances.

As to Damian Mac Con Uladh, when I was last in Athens he was working as a journalist not being paid by *Athens News*. Now he was working and not being paid by *Eleftherotypia*. He worked on *EnetEnglish*, which had become one of my daily sources for keeping up with Greek news. *Athens News* had ceased to publish, as its publisher, Petros Kyriakides, was under indictment for embezzlement.

Kyriakides escaped Greece, dressed as an orthodox priest, leaving debts and unpaid wages, but with perhaps €80 million in his possession as he fled. We discussed many stories that Damian had chased or broken, including his April fool's story on the troika targeting the Greek alphabet as too costly.[4] I raised the question of whether Syriza's moment had passed. He didn't think so, but he thought that the downward spiral was such that, by the time they got the chance, they could be in charge of ruins.

We spent many evenings in Exarchia. The other Irish people in town were impressed by the lively atmosphere in the square. One night it was packed with people watching a film projected on a sheet strung across a clothesline. Left posters were on display, although the mural proclaiming "Our Streets" was gone and had been replaced by a new taverna with almost no customers. Cannabis wafted in the air. According to Cathal's guidebook: "Exarchia may seem a little worn around the edges, but this is the place for all your liberal intellectual café sipping needs." This didn't really capture it. I had some good left (not liberal) café conversations there, but there was a rougher side to it, not covered by "a little worn around the edges." I was long past being impressed by the strut of black bloc macho. A smoke bomb, the kind they hurled at riot police, exploded near us one night. It was possibly aimed at us, although I had no idea why, except that there was a lot of inchoate rage.

In contrast, we also explored the southwestern suburbs by the sea, where city dwellers who couldn't get to the islands went to swim. The water might look clean and clear, but scientific tests indicated otherwise. It was also where other stadiums built for the Olympics were rotting. It was also one of the areas where rich Greeks lived. When I looked at the map and saw how much space the Glyfada Golf Club took up, I thought it was obscene.

Calm before the Storm?

My intensive discussions of Greek politics continued. Everyone was scathing about the Greek "success story." Everyone admitted that resistance had receded, but no one thought this was more than a temporary lull. Too many people had too many problems for the status quo to hold. Whether Syriza was the answer to those problems was a question that met with various responses. Whether Syriza would get the chance and whether they would use it to initiate a radical transformation of the society was also a matter of contention. On the issue of the social democratization of Syriza, the danger that Syriza would become the new Pasok, including the comparison of Alexis Tsipras to Andreas Papandreou, I got a whole range of responses, even from within Syriza. Some brushed it off, dismissing it as the ultra left never being able to get real or to cope with proximity of power. Others admitted they worried about it, but argued that there was no space for a social democratic solution to the problems of Greece. Still others, and not only left activists, but people I met in casual conversations on the street, in hotels or cafés or at demonstrations, put it more strongly, pointing to compromise positions taken by Alexis Tsipras, especially when abroad, and by those around him speaking to the media in Greece.

I had particularly searching conversations on these issues during meetings with Michalis Spourdalakis and his colleagues, Costas Eleftheriou and Chrisanthos Tassis, political scientists at the University of Athens, and with Haris Golemis, director of the Nicos Poulantzas Institute, and his colleagues, Theodora Kotsaka and Vagia Lysikatou. All spoke as political persons, not as detached academics. Many of the controversies coming up at the party congress came into the conversations, as did the changing nature of the party and its relation to the ever-changing wider movement. I was impressed by the seriousness of analysis of forces in motion and determination to chart a new path for Greek society and for the international left. At NPI, we also discussed the possibility of our Left Forum affiliating to the Transform network.

The Storm: ERT

The situation was so volatile in Greece that changes could come very quickly and you never knew what the day might bring. Tuesday, June

11, 2013, was such a day. During the previous week, so many of my conversations had probed the withdrawal from the streets, the lull in the movement, but always these conversations indicated that it was the calm before the storm, that anything could happen. That very day we had such a conversation. Yet by afternoon, a storm had broken. Something utterly unexpected had happened.

When I saw the first announcements that ERT (*Ellinikí Radiofonía Tileórasi*), the public broadcasting service, was going to shut down by midnight, I found it hard to absorb. The first tweet seemed like a chimera, but then the Twitter stream was full of it. I turned on the television, where the station was covering its own closure, first with disbelief and then with defiance. It was a nonstop stream of denunciation of the government and the troika, whether talking heads in studio or politicians speaking to the crowd gathering outside the station. Alexis Tsipras, Manolis Glezos, and other Syriza MPs were breathing fire. New Democracy was making this momentous move by ministerial decree without reference to the parliament or even the cabinet. Two of the three government parties were not supporting it. Only Golden Dawn supported New Democracy, because it was not happy with its treatment by the station. The troika had decreed that 2,000 public-sector jobs were to go by July, and this was a way of doing that in one fell swoop. In fact, there were 2,650 employed in ERT, putting them ahead of the game. It was so reckless and destructive. People I met kept calling it a coup d'état.

There was a call to come to the ERT station at Agia Paraskevi on the outskirts of Athens at 7:00 p.m. Cathal and I agreed immediately to answer that call. At that point, we thought that we were going to a protest, although I realized that it would be a long night. I thought that the riot police would come in at midnight and forcibly close down the station. It was a balmy summer evening and people were streaming through the gates to join others, who were waving flags, listening to speeches, talking to friends. There were thousands eventually. I was very moved by the singing of some of my favorite Theodorakis songs. One moment I would be on my feet with my fist clenched singing the phrases of the songs I knew and thinking in a world historical way of how beautiful and tragic it was. The next moment I would be sitting on the grass in my summer dress and sandals and wishing for one of the gas masks that I didn't buy or wondering how long I could go without sleeping or charging my phone. Later I ran into Lila Mambregianni, who told me she had everything in her bag that I might need—Maalox, crackers, water, umbrella, gas mask, etc. As the darkness fell, there was more apprehension about what was going to happen at midnight. Around 10:00 p.m., word went around that the transmitters were going down all over Greece and by 11:15 ERT was off the air in Athens too. So midnight was something of an anticlimax.

The protest turned into an occupation. New territory was being charted now. The journalists and other employees of ERT decided to keep broadcasting. Various Internet sites carried the broadcasts. The European Broadcasting Union gave its moral and technical support. The KKE gave over the frequency of its television service to ERT for long periods. One remarkable feature of this occupation was that KKE-PAME stood in the same space as Syriza, Antarsya, anarchists, and other leftists, offering hope of a more cooperative relationship between these forces. Theodora Oikonomides @IrateGreek tweeted "Is *The Life of Brian* over?" I hoped so.

After a while, I found my way inside the station. I discovered that many people as well as ERT employees were in there, including Syriza MPs, who were on a rota to be sure that there were at least twenty of them there at any given time. I spoke to many people about why they were occupying the station. Some of those who were its sharpest critics were now its fiercest defenders. They knew it was stuffed with political appointees and gave government too easy a ride, but they were defending public broadcasting as it could be.

Public broadcasting as it could be was what it became during those days. It was riveting television at times: splendid music, political satire, alternative documentaries, talking heads telling the truth about the government and the troika, even about the pressures on ERT that made it other than what it should have been, as well as constant coverage of the occupation itself. The scene outside was like a festival at times. There were memorable moments when people who gathered waved their flags, danced, clenched their fists, sang traditional anthems of the Greek left, enacting a continuity of struggles of past and present, evoking memory of so much that had been won and lost, stirring hope of taking back the world being taken away from us. The continuing broadcasts on ERT were true public service broadcasting, a sustained expression of democracy, as well as a political humiliation of the government.

As I was frequently updating on the social networks, I began receiving calls requesting media interviews in Ireland. In the early hours of the morning, exhausted but still not wanting to leave, I decided to return to the hotel to charge my phone and do the interview for *Morning Ireland* on RTÉ by landline. I emphasized that ERT was the equivalent of RTÉ and tried to get the audience to imagine what it meant in that way. I said that I often felt that RTÉ spoke with the voice of the masters of the universe, but I would come to defend it if there was such a move against it. Indeed I would be delighted to see RTÉ do the sort of broadcasting that was being done on ERT during the occupation.

I was pleased at the response of some journalists in Ireland, who wanted to organize a solidarity demonstration at the Greek embassy in Dublin. Emma O'Kelly of the National Union of Journalists broadcasting branch asked me to get them a direct contact with ERT journalists. When I made my way back to ERT, I was tempted to lie on the grass with the thousand others listening to speeches and songs, but instead I made my way to the newsroom to make that contact. I was directed to Yiannis Fasoulas, who announced on air that I was there. Then they asked me to go on television. I agreed to do that. I spoke of the sudden and shocking closure of ERT in a wider context, situating the immediate events within longer trajectories, seeing the closure of this public broadcaster within a larger and longer dismantling of the public dimension of everything, even an erosion of a public service ethos within the public service. I did four broadcasts that day, later adding interviews on *Newstalk* and *The Late Debate*, all after a night of no sleep, running on adrenalin with a mobile charger for my iPhone. Damian arrived on the scene during the day to cover the story for the *Irish Times*.

During the afternoon, it lashed rain, putting a damper on the atmosphere outside the station. Nevertheless, many stayed out there under umbrellas, while many more streamed inside the station. One man started screaming about the lack of organization and security. Although it was crowded and potentially dangerous, it was a remarkably harmonious self-organized community. People stood around a grand piano and sang songs, including "Imagine." They sat around and told their stories and shared their food.

There were rumors of the government falling and a new election happening soon. The date of July 14 was doing the rounds. There was a lot going on in parliament and government buildings as well. At night I returned to the hotel for a few hours to power up again. I turned on the television to channel 1, where the screen had gone black the night before, and was shocked to see ERT there and then channel 902, the communist channel, and then the color card, and then black again. It was surreal at times. The Greek word for black, *mavro*, was uttered often, as if in incantation.

The third day was a general strike, which was called to protest the closure of ERT. On the way back to Agia Paraskevi, it was hard to gauge how many shops were closed for the strike, because so many shops had closed down in Athens anyway. So many thousands arrived for the rally at ERT that it was impossible to get into the grounds of the station at first. We were with the crowds that filled the street. I met Kostas Skordoulis and Christos Kefalis and we went to a café for a catch-up chat. Later we got into the grounds and milled around for some hours listening to the music and speeches and occupying the space.

An Island Interval

With so much happening in Athens, I was tempted to cancel our plans for a weekend trip to Evia. However, I had arranged to visit friends I hadn't seen in many years. Moreover, it might be good to see how it all looked from there, and perhaps to unwind a bit. I was getting a bit old for the barricades. We arrived in the village of Politika, where we explored the island, probed its politics, swam in the sea, sampled its tavernas. We caught up with Mario and Marta Bunge, both emeritus professors at McGill University in Montreal, Mario of philosophy and Marta of mathematics. Mario and I had a flourishing correspondence about philosophy and science and politics in the early 1980s, when we could explore areas of agreement and disagreement in a way that was no longer possible in 2013, when his attacks on Marxism and my defense of it were going nowhere, except to make Marta and Cathal uneasy. Much more fruitful was asking questions about Argentina and their views on the Peróns and Kirchners. Marta was enthusiastic about Evita and Cristina. Mario was writing his memoirs and focused on Argentina in the 1950s.

I had a long early swim, alone in the sea, as far as I could see. I reflected on how peaceful it seemed, but how there could be no peace in this beautiful country being stolen from its people. We explored the island and were struck by the relative absence of a tourist industry compared to other islands I had visited. It is the second biggest island in area and population and full of good beaches and vistas, yet least known to tourists. The mountain roads were full of dangerous drops, with no guardrails. It was hard to see how anything serving the public good would be built now under troika rule. We saw well over a hundred dollhouse churches that were built on the side of the road commemorating road deaths. At lunch in the port of Loutra Edipsou, we overheard a vigorous argument about Syriza at the next table.

On our final night in Evia, we attended a Syriza rally in Chalkida. This town, where Aristotle died, was alive with people chatting in the cafés and walking along the promenade by the sea. There was an information kiosk there about Vio.Me, the occupied building materials factory in Thessaloniki. On the main square, Syriza was showing ERT on a big screen as a protest against its closure. Much of the broadcast was the concert taking place at Agia Paraskevi. We mixed with Syriza activists and discovered that Syriza came first here in elections in May and June last year, with 19 percent and then 29 percent of the vote. Evia had six MPs in parliament: one each from Syriza, the KKE, Dimar, Pasok, New Democracy, and Golden Dawn. Syriza had five hundred members on the island.

Last Night in Athens

For our final night in Greece, we returned to Athens to attend a Syriza rally in Syntagma Square. I ran into Mary Fitzgerald of the *Irish Times*, who was in Athens for a conference, and we went to a café for a quick chat. After that, I found the crowd too dense to find anyone I knew, even Cathal. There was a big stage and screen. There were lots of colorful banners. The music ranged from operatic choruses to national and international protest songs. "Which Side Are You On?" was one. The high point was a speech by Alexis Tsipras, somewhat in pre-election mode, bidding Samaras *kalinichta* (good night), as it still seemed as if the government could fall and a new election would come soon.

That night the news came that a court ruling had ordered that ERT transmissions be restored, pending restructuring, an order that the government did not implement. Over the course of the crisis, it had been remarkable to see how the oligarchic class, which has made the laws and dominated such institutions, had blatantly defied them and gone for naked authoritarian rule instead. It was the same when a court ruled substantial sections of the memorandum unconstitutional and they implemented them regardlessly.

After fifteen days, so intense and eventful as to seem much longer, it was time to go. In the weeks that followed, I checked out ERT transmissions several times every day and watched the concert every night. I did my best to remind people, especially journalists, that the struggle was still ongoing, even though it fell off the international news agenda all too quickly. I especially had to make the point to journalists, because one NUJ member, who had passed through Athens on his way to a wedding and visited ERT, posted on Facebook as if it was over and a great victory had been won, with the suggestion that his intervention had played a part in it. I had to correct his account.

ERT Open carried on in legal limbo, on an oppositional basis and without pay. They continued to broadcast television from Athens and Thessaloniki and radio from many regional centers and to update on their website and social media. The prospect of election receded, because Pasok would put up with anything to stay in power.

Yanis Varoufakis, the Greek celebrity economist then based in Texas, had also been on ERT and talking with Tsipras in Athens. In late June, he wrote (along with James Galbraith) an article in the *New York Times* making the case that Syriza was not only the best hope for Greece and for Europe, but also for the United States. He reassured the United States that Syriza didn't intend to leave NATO or close US bases.[5] I knew that this was not Syriza policy, even if they wouldn't necessarily move on this on day one after an election. I queried this with Varoufakis on Twitter and he affirmed it even more strongly. This was one of many signs that there was an element in Syriza, certainly including Tsipras, who wanted power and were willing to be very flexible about policies and principles to get it.

IAMCR in Dublin

Immediately after I arrived back in Dublin, I was scheduled to speak at the conference of the International Association for Media and Communication Research in Dublin. It was a big conference, with 1,500 people presenting at many parallel sessions. The international audience was quite wowed by Ireland having such an intellectual left president in Michael D. Higgins, who opened the conference in the Helix at Dublin City University. I was to speak at a special session called "The Eye of the Storm," focusing on the framing of the crisis in the PIIGS countries. I was asked to do a comparative analysis of Ireland and Greece. In the briefing notes for the session, Paschal Preston, the conference organizer, asked for the crisis to be addressed by "situated intellectuals," although he didn't necessarily mean occupying a television station. My paper was called "The Compliant and the Defiant: Dominant v. Dissident Narratives of the Crisis in Ireland and Greece." Sophia Kaitizaki-Whitlock from

Thessaloniki was also speaking at this session and laid out a chronology of the crisis in Greece.

I outlined how the crisis had been framed in Ireland and in Greece in the dominant discourse, which cast Ireland as the compliant and Greece as the defiant. It suited the troika to showcase Ireland as the good debtor, as meeting its targets and blazing the trail of "reform," the code word for lowering wages, raising taxes, downsizing the public sector, paying private debts from public resources, and doing so without protest or disruption. It also suited them to point to Greece as the bad debtor, where everything got worse when they failed to meet their targets and were beset by protests and strikes and moreover had the threat of a left government in the shadows. The lesson: Greeks protest and all gets worse; Irish don't and all gets better. Now Greece had seen the light and was following Ireland to exit the crisis.

The problem was that it was not true—not in Ireland, not in Greece, and on so many levels. I had reached the boiling point at the constant reiteration of the idea that Irish people didn't protest. An Irish academic had repeated it at another session, where I launched into a tirade against it. I spoke as an activist who was run ragged from protest and I didn't care if it was the appropriate tone for a professor emerita at the host institution or not.

The syndrome was epitomized in an *Irish Independent* ad campaign, which I showed on my slides. It showed Syntagma Square full of protesters and O'Connell Street empty. However, there were days when Syntagma Square was empty of protesters and days when O'Connell Street was the site of protests, sometimes massive ones. Irish people did protest. It was hard enough to be involved in constant protest without having it discursively obliterated. I gave some indication of forms and levels of protest since the start of the crisis. There was hardly a day without protest of one sort or another. Some were small, but some brought out tens of thousands. There were a hundred thousand at the GPO in 2010. Our general election in 2011 saw the greatest overturning of Dáil Éireann in its history and a significant rise in representation of the left. The government formed by Fine Gael and Labour, parties that excoriated the previous government from opposition benches, proceeded to implement the same polices and could not have been more compliant with troika demands. In the same year, the Occupy movement saw occupations on every city on this island, with many expressing their disdain for successive governments and the whole international financial system. The RTÉ phone-in show *Liveline* seethed with rage, as citizens told stories of their lives laid waste in this crisis. Public-sector workers overturned the recommendation of their unions in a "deal" cutting their wages and downgrading their conditions, although they subsequently accepted out of fear of a revised version of this. High numbers refused to pay new taxes and charges, either because they couldn't pay or resented that our taxes were going to pay bondholders, while our health, education, and welfare services were being cut. We did protest. We did resist.

Moreover, Ireland was not a success story unless you were of the class whose interests were served by lower wages and pensions, by privatization of public property, by subordination of the state to the market, etc. Nor was Greece by following this road.

So who were the compliant and who were the defiant? I argued that it was not the case that Ireland was the compliant and Greece was the defiant. The governments of Ireland and Greece, all who voted for them, all who failed to protest against them—these were the compliant. Those who rose up against them in Ireland and Greece were the defiant.For the right and center, Ireland was a model for Greece. For the left, Greece was a model for Ireland. Of course, it was a matter of which Ireland and which Greece.

The IAMCR also offered occasions for drinks and dinners with leftist thinkers in town for the conference and I had especially good encounters with John Bellamy Foster and Jodi Dean. We had Jodi speak at a Left Forum event at Connolly Books. In conversation later we explored our different positions on the communist movement. Speaking on communicative capitalism at a plenary session of the conference, she said suddenly: "What is missing now is the communist party." I found it jarring, although oddly refreshing. It was as if the Communist Party was a Platonic Form, which I found hard to relate to any of my actual experience of actual communist parties. While I found more to defend than to denounce, I thought that she had a romanticized view of the communist movement, which had a lot to do with her lack of actual involvement with it. We walked through the center of Dublin and talked into the late hours with other activists, who also found her very engaging.

Syriza Congress

Although I was invited to attend the Syriza congress in Athens in July, I couldn't do so. I followed it from Dublin as best I could and spoke to Syriza activists about it before, during, and after it. I also noted such response as there was to it among the international left, much of which was divided between those who wanted to believe in Syriza no matter what and those who were too ready to write them off as reformists who had moved to the right and defeated their internal left.

The congress, which ran from July 10 to 14, consolidated the transition from a coalition to a unified party. Membership was around 35,000 and they were represented by nearly 3,500 delegates. Membership on an individual basis became possible. Many members were never a part of any of the components of the predecessor coalition. At the congress, there was controversy about if and when all components should disband. Synaspismos, by far the largest, with 10,000 members, had dissolved itself just before the congress, but several smaller ones were reluctant to do so. The most powerful voice against dissolution at the congress was Manolis Glezos, a heroic figure of the Greek left, who argued for continuing diversity and against being a "party of applauders."

There were other procedural issues surrounding the methods of electing the party leader and central committee. At issue was a tension between a mass party dominated by a charismatic leader and a small group around him, with a more passive membership and more flexibility about policy, versus one with an active membership and stronger collective accountability. There were also debates and divided votes on amendments regarding leaving the Eurozone, canceling the debt, and considering alliances to the left or right. While components would dissolve, platforms would not. The most powerful was the Left Platform, which got 30 percent of the vote in elections for the central committee and up to 40 percent in some votes on amendments. Some international commentators decided that mainstream Syriza was reformist and had moved to the right and cracked down on its internal left. I did not see it this way. I had strong relationships with both Left Platform and mainstream Syriza. I had great respect for people on both sides. I did not believe that the left was confined to the Left Platform. A party of this size was necessarily diverse and held ideological positions along a certain left spectrum. All of us looking at it had our own ideological positions and affinities to those closest to our own positions. My strongest ties were to ex-Synaspismos and to a position stemming from the tradition of left Eurocommunism. These ties crossed the Left Platform versus Left Unity divide.

There were real tensions. There was worry about a tendency toward social democratization of Syriza, too great a willingness to bend in order to be acceptable to international centers of power and wider sections of voters. There were accusations that Syriza wanted to be in government at any cost, that it was more preoccupied with winning than with what to do when it won. There was unease about concentrating power around the leader and his inner circle. On the other hand, there were demands to "get real" and accusations that some would rather not be in government than compromise their radicalism. There were people both inside and outside Syriza who did conform to this type, but most active members of Syriza that I knew were serious about finding a viable path to exit the crisis and transform the society in a radical way. They believed that capitalism was the problem and socialism was the solution. They wanted to organize systematic political education, which Syriza lacked, so as to have a critical and active membership. However, unlike those who called themselves revolutionaries and denounced reformists, they had stopped dreaming of storming winter palaces and bolshevizing the twenty-first century.

They were not holding out for an all-encompassing insurrection, which would destroy capitalism one day and inaugurate socialism the next day. They were planning for a protracted process, which would include winning multiparty elections, entering into difficult negotiations, agreeing to unattractive alliances, undoing damage done, building the new inside the shell of the old.

On alliances, the preference was for alliances to the left, but Antarsya lacked numbers and KKE rebuffed all overtures. If only it were otherwise. So what was to be done? If Syriza won the next election with 28 percent or even 30 percent of the vote, even with the fifty bonus seats, where would they get the numbers to form a left government? As undesirable as it might be, should making up numbers with elements from Dimar or Pasok or Anel not even be discussed? Or should Syriza roll over and let ND form another government to wreak further disaster?

I had to admit to having my worries about Syriza becoming the new Pasok. I had seen parties and movements I fervently supported blatantly betray the hopes and needs of those who put them in power. I had seen it particularly closely with the ANC in South Africa. Some of Tsipras's speeches seemed too compromising. Some acts, such as speaking at an event to honor conservative prime minister Konstantinos Karamanlis, seemed too ingratiating to the right. In his last appearance with Žižek in May in Zagreb, Tsipras took no issue with Žižek's lurching from right to ultraleft, inciting Syriza to manage capitalism better than capitalists as far into the future as anyone could see. There were other instances I could cite.

However, I did not think that anything I had seen or heard so far constituted decisive evidence of a move to social democratization of Syriza. I still thought that they were the best hope for Greece and the European left.

ERT Carried On

Meanwhile, the government didn't fall, but was reformed after Dimar left. A number of politicians who failed to be elected became ministers. A channel called DT appeared to hold the place of ERT until one called NERIT was launched. It ran old dramas and documentaries. One filmmaker announced that he would sue for bringing his work into disrepute on this "despicable channel." ERT workers were offered the prospect of short contracts at reduced wages, which they rejected. ERT carried on broadcasting. The whole operation was more organized than in those first shocking and frenetic days. Whatever happened next, it would go down in history as a formidable example of workers' control of the means of production and true public broadcasting with broad democratic participation. On August 19, I was sorry to learn that the European Broadcasting Union was deserting ERT and supporting the government's replacement service.

In August, the World Congress of Philosophy took place in Athens. Although I participated in previous congresses, I didn't go to this one. When I saw a photo of the opening concert held at the Odeon of Herodes Atticus at the foot of the Acropolis featuring music of Manos Hatzidakis and Mikis Theodorakis, I couldn't help wishing that I was there. When I saw an invitation from ERT workers to the two thousand philosophers to engage with their cause, I was even sorrier that I wasn't there to stir it up. I wrote to ERT Open to ask if there had been any response and was told that there was not. Knowing the species all too well, it was obvious to me that many of them were more inclined to bland and abstruse iterations on various subjects, including civic engagement, than to actual civic engagement.

Back to Zakynthos

In September, Sam and I returned to Zakynthos. As usual, I began my days with a long solitary swim in the sea at sunrise. I walked around talking to locals in the town and hotel. There were strikes on in the universities and schools. I solicited opinions on this and the wider situation. Sometimes I was astonished at the lack of interest in politics and the lack of sympathy for strikers. One British man I met, who had been living there for ten years and working on the street in Tsilivi booking boat trips, told me he was once a union rep in London. Now he thought that each person should just do what they needed to do to get by. He saw no reason why anyone should do anything else. I was getting that from Greeks too: a refusal to engage with the bigger picture and a longer time horizon discourse in favor of a here-and-now, me-and-my-family, getting on with whatever, never mind about the rest. They tried not to turn on the television, because it was just too depressing and they didn't want to know. As to strikes and strikers, they were dismissive, saying that they were lucky to have jobs at all. I spoke with a barman, who thought that they might as well all commit suicide as see Syriza come to power.

Meanwhile, in Perama near Piraeus, thirty KKE members were out putting up posters when they were attacked by fifty XA members with metal pipes and wooden bats. A few days later, Pavlos Fyssas, an antifascist rapper active in Antarsya, was killed by XA. Crowds gathered outside XA offices in different parts of Greece. These attacks led to a groundswell against them. There were many demonstrations around Greece and abroad. Only days before, an ND-XA government was seen as a realistic, even likely, outcome of the next election.

Once more, Nikos Potamitis was our guide to the politics of the island. He brought us to ERA Zakynthos, the ERT radio station on the island. We met people running and occupying the station as well as people there for a meeting of the teachers' strike committee. They asked if we would go on air, so we did. Marina Mandzou interviewed us and Anastasia Liveri translated. It was, predictably, about the crisis in Ireland and Greece. The studio, attractively decorated with big colorful panels, was full of camp beds for those occupying it during the nights. As in Athens, no one knew when the riot police might arrive to forcibly shut it down.

Nikos said that he would pick me up at 6:40 a.m. the next day, if I was willing, to picket a school with him. I hated to give up my dawn swim, but it was for class struggle, and Nikos gave so much of himself that it was hard to refuse anything he asked. We went to a high school in Zakynthos town. A few parents dropped off pupils, who lifted the banner blocking the gate, as did a few teachers. Picketers tried to convince them not to do so. I just added to the bodies and let the locals do all the talking. Participation in the strike at this school was high: 73 percent. I talked for a while with Antonis Kassimatis, a cardiologist in Syriza. I asked if crisis had led to an increase in cardiological problems. Yes, he said, to every kind of health problem, first psychological and then physical. Word came that some pupils were arrested during the night for attempting to blockade the entrance to the school. We then marched from the school to the police station, along with about thirty pupils, to protest. Nikos and others talked to police. The riot police arrived, but did not attack. After a while, Nikos and a few others went to the prosecutor's office to intervene on their behalf and got them released.

In the evening, I attended a meeting of teachers, parents, and activists to discuss how to proceed with the teachers' strike as well as a two-day general strike that had been called. The meeting was in a music school in a large lecture theater. There were about 150 people present. It went on for hours and only ended after midnight. Nikos asked me if I would speak. I agreed to do it, but then the atmosphere turned really contentious and it didn't seem appropriate. Passions became inflamed over the relation of KKE to other forces, especially to Syriza and Antarsya. The immediate issue was about the next day, whether to have one or two marches. According to the usual pattern, KKE-PAME would have its own separate march and everyone else would unite in another one. One person after another, whether in Syriza or Antarsya or no party, would say "Why can't we all march together?" The position of most was that there should be one march. KKE fought back, even bringing up things that Synaspismos did twenty-five years ago. Nikos, who spoke several times during the meeting, asked, "What will you do if we come to your demonstration? Will you fight us or march with us?" The KKE people said the others could come, but with no banners and no right to speak. The KKE guy chairing the meeting told Nikos afterwards that he was very clever to put it that way: to have others coming to the KKE rather than the KKE coming to others. The meeting ended inconclusively. On the way out, a young KKE woman was putting the case to me about Syriza going the way of Pasok and not wanting to be corrupted by that. Nikos then brought me back to Tsilivi, while we discussed what happened at the meeting and what might happen the next day.

We arrived the next morning at the town hall where there was tension about what would happen on the streets between the different factions of the left. Nikos arrived with newly made banners to replace ones that had mysteriously disappeared from the school and took soundings about how to proceed. The Syriza-Antarsya-and-others demonstration marched to the place where the KKE-PAME demonstration was happening. Eventually we all marched together through the whole town and back. This was a significant, if still fragile, breakthrough. It was great to be on that march. Sam, although struggling with mobility issues, did the whole thing with his new rollator, but he was struggling toward the end. As usual, at the end of a Greek march, I had that sense of anticlimax, when everybody just dispersed without a proper finale.

The next day got off to a bad start and never got better. I woke suddenly at 6:00 a.m. and noticed that the hotel room door was open. I went to close it and found a man on the balcony. He jumped over the railing with my bag, wallet, iPhone, and iPod and escaped while I screamed. He took my phone from a table just inches from my face where I was sleeping. I reported it to reception and thought that the police might arrive. They phoned the police, who said that I must go into town and bring someone to interpret. At the police station, they had no Wi-Fi to deal with find-my-iPhone, nor did they have an email address where I could make further contact. I spent hours giving a statement to a young female detective and then went searching the town for Wi-Fi and a way to make a copy of the location, but in vain. I was told that I must return in several days to get a copy of the statement, which couldn't for some reason be copied then and there. CSI it was not. They never asked for the number of the mobile phone, but they did want to know my parents' names and my religion (under an icon of Saints Cyril and Methodius). I noted that tourist information had for years given a phone number to contact tourist police. Indeed, I noticed when I was at the police station demonstrating the day before that there was a sign indicating tourist police.

However, there were no tourist police, presumably because of public-sector cuts, despite the fact that this island lived from tourism. The police said that the perpetrator was probably Albanian, not Greek. I felt somewhat disconnected and disoriented without my phone. I also fretted over the memory stick that was in my wallet. It had everything for identity theft and more. I also started to ask: Why me? The hotel said it was the only robbery there in eleven years.

The holiday dimension of this trip was over for me. Or maybe not. On our final weekend, Penelope Vlamis came and drove us around the beautiful north end of the island for many hours. Nikos invited us home for a long lunch and political discussion. Nothing could put me off the political discussion. Efi was home for the weekend and as gracious a hostess as ever. She told me of the difficulties of her life going back and forth to Patras to teach. It wasn't even worth it for the pay, considering the child care and transport expenses. She was putting up with it in the hope of being transferred to Zakynthos. It was crazy. Another teacher in drama education was doing the same in reverse, from Patras to Zakynthos. Requests to do the right thing to the ministry were not getting a result.

Every day was a drama. The University of Athens announced that it was closing. It was terminating all functions, because it was unable to carry on with all the cutbacks and layoffs. I phoned Michalis Spourdalakis, who said that the pressure came from the five hundred administrative staff—out of thirteen hundred in total—who were being laid off. He thought it was the right decision and one that would also be made in Crete, Thessaloniki, etc. Immediately after that, the National Technical University of Athens (formerly the Polytechnic) also made an announcement of suspension of all activities.

As we were leaving, another forty-eight-hour general strike was underway. There was a sense that the public sector was being decimated. Sometimes it even felt like civilization unraveling. I was feeling exhausted and overwrought from the many forms of dispossession raging in Greece, including the minor one inflicted on me. I needed to restore my emotional and material equilibrium to keep going, to keep struggling against these terrible forces that were wreaking havoc with all that had been earned, with all that had been built. Not that Ireland was a haven from all this. It was only that the dispossession was less naked and less severe. Greece was showing where the whole process is going. We all needed to do much more to stand against it and to set the world on another trajectory.

Also I needed a new iPhone. Vodafone showed no mercy. I knew of young people who had lost their phones when they got drunk in nightclubs who were treated better than I was as an old woman with a crime report in hand. They wanted €700 for an iPhone 5. On the plus side, I was happy to discover that the information on my phone was still there on the cloud.

A few days after arriving back, I received an early-morning call from Nikos with news that leaders of XA had been arrested for forming a criminal organization. He was also caught up in a week of action in defense of the public health system.

Contentious conversations on social media continued. One was a response by a friend of mine to a *New York Times* article about Greece turning the corner and how Greeks had to go back to the land and reduce their standard of living in order to go forward. This American professor agreed with it and insisted that she would be proved right. All those years coming to Greece on holidays and engaging so shallowly with it. It was also the phenomenon of wealthy people approving of austerity for others but not for themselves.

Autumn in Greece and Ireland

I tried to generate solidarity with Greek universities back in Ireland. The timing was good, because the union at my university was into a campaign to defend public universities. I was asked for a quote for the press release, so I wrote: "Globally the public sector is being decimated. What remains is increasingly only what serves the immediate imperatives of the market and the class interests of the global plutocracy. All that is public—health, culture, knowledge, space—is under attack. Universities are being starved of resources. What resources remain are diverted from broad knowledge and systemic scrutiny into shallow and short-term commercial goals. In Greece, major universities have suspended operations indefinitely. In Ireland, academics either play the game and build compliant careers or stare helplessly like deer into the headlights of oncoming destruction. Wake up and take responsibility for the future of knowledge, indeed the whole future of a public sphere."

In late October we had a Left Forum event on "The Greek Crisis: Will It bring Barbarism or Socialism?" I spoke at it, along with Aggelos Panayiotopoulos. We were in harmony in our analysis of crisis but differed in our estimation of Syriza. It was a serious audience and a good discussion. There were a number of Greeks there, also raising questions about Syriza and how radical it could be trusted to be.

On Oxi Day in Greece, I watched a documentary on women in Greek resistance on ERT. So much tragedy, wave after wave of it, even now. I kept reminding people via social media that ERT carried on.

On November 7, I woke up to news that riot police had invaded ERT at Agia Paraskevi and evicted those working there. This dominated the whole day for me. Although I knew it was coming, I still felt such a sense of shock and loss. I followed it on social media all day. They were still broadcasting outside the gates. On November 10, I watched the debate in the Greek parliament on a no-confidence motion in the government related to ERT, in which Syriza said all the right things, but the government survived. There was still television broadcasting from Thessaloniki and radio from other centers. ERT Open continued on the Internet. They set up a new office across the road in Agia Paraskevi in order to be in sight of what they had lost and to what they intended to return. Nineteen regional radio stations remained open. There were still 700 of the 2,650 workers working without pay.

Left Forum held a debate at Connolly Books on "Revolution, Reform, and Everything in Between," featuring two Jameses, James O'Toole and James O'Brien. Both gave stimulating talks. The response from the floor was dominated by the revolutionary position, as SWP members turned up in numbers. I came into the discussion and made a number of points, including taking issue with OToole's remarks on Greece, especially the word "Syrizamania."

In December, I went to a DCU School of Communications seminar, where Eugenia Siapera gave a presentation on the landscape of journalism in Greece today, with most emphasis on alternative media, especially ERT Open, Radio Bubble, and the Press Project. I was skeptical about the concept of "post-democracy" but agreed with her on everything else. On a day-to-day basis, it was wonderful having someone in my everyday life in Dublin with whom I could discuss Greek politics as it unfolded.

At the end of the year, I remembered that I had other plans for these past two years, but Greece had forced itself into the center of my focus in a way that I couldn't escape. It was at the cutting edge of both the crisis and the alternative. Greece was nearer to the eye of the storm, but the same winds were blowing on us all. The devastation wreaked there was so much greater, but the defenses were also stronger. It was my hope that this might also be where a rainbow would appear.

CHAPTER 3

2014: Holding Pattern

Waiting, Watching, Working

It had been a year and a half since Syriza almost won the election, became the main opposition, and positioned itself as the next government of Greece. The party continued preparing for power, strategizing about how to get the necessary numbers to form a government, how to run ministries, how to negotiate with creditors. As the year went on, Syriza became increasingly impatient with the preparations and wanted to get out of the waiting room and into office.

Meanwhile, my life in Dublin continued in its usual round of protests, meetings, commemorations, seminars, lectures, correspondence, books, launches, and social media. Left Forum flourished and then faltered. I was angry much of the time. In academe, I lashed out yet again at a visiting academic giving a lecture at DCU, speaking on uprisings and the Internet. He was making lazy generalizations about the left but not seriously bothering to know what the left was saying or doing. In the trade union movement, such as an occasion at the grave of James Larkin, I found it hard to encounter those I once considered comrades who were trying to have it both ways, pretending (even to themselves) that they hadn't crossed over to the other side. In my conversations with trade union officials and

Labour Party politicians, I held out Syriza as an example of what they should be.

In March, there was a convention of the European People's Party in Dublin, which nominated Jean Claude Juncker as the EPP candidate for president of the European Commission. It was the first time there would be such an election. The Party of the European Left had nominated Alexis Tsipras as its candidate. Paul Murphy proposed a broad left march to the National Convention Centre. Left Forum was a cosponsor, along with a wide spectrum of left parties. Despite the unity of the serious left for this event, there was hostility from the lumpen element, who cast scorn on people who would only show up at 6:00 p.m., while they would be there all day. These were people who went from stunt to stunt, denouncing everyone else but building nothing. On March 6, we gathered at Liberty Hall, where there were several speakers, including Sabine Wils of Die Linke, Des Derwin of the Dublin Council of Trade Unions, Padraig Mannion of the Workers Party, and myself. I spoke of the EPP as a party representing plutocracy and stressed the need to meet class struggle from above with class struggle from below.

We then marched along the river to the EPP venue. When we arrived, there was a barrier and a line of police with dogs and batons at the ready. There were a group of twenty-five or so protesters already there, some with red and black flags and hoods and masks, who taunted us and then charged at the police. The police then charged at them and us. We proceeded to go to the side and continued our own protest. Among others, Sean Edwards of CPI, Brid Smith of SWP, and John Bissett of Spectacle of Defiance made speeches. The other protesters concentrated on protesting against us rather than against the EPP. One of them, Steven Bennett, charged at Paul Murphy to take the microphone from him. Then there were scuffles between groups of protesters and police. I reported it on social media, which attracted hundreds of comments, some of them extremely vitriolic. The black bloc, who also called themselves "little ninjas" on this occasion (although they towered over me), issued a statement saying that the police attacked first and brutally batoned all in sight. It was not true. They were living in a macho self-romanticizing cartoon fantasy. Through the crisis, there had been a cycle of these small lumpen groups constantly forming and fragmenting, generating momentary messiahs competing with each other, full of inspirational quotes and self-glorifying behavior and street stunts and provocative stances to the left and the trade unions. The worst were middle-aged males, who had never been politically active before this and denounced those who were.

"Challenging Troika Rule" in Dublin

During this period, I was involved in organizing the visit of Alexis Tsipras to Ireland. In February, I was asked by Haris Golemis of Transform Europe and the Nicos Poulantzas Institute if I could get an Irish university to host a conference on "Challenging Troika Rule, Transforming Europe," with Tsipras as the keynote speaker. Trinity College Dublin would have been the best for getting a wider audience, because it was in the city center, but there was no one senior enough who was left enough inside TCD to make that happen. So I tried my own university, Dublin City University. I wrote to the dean of my faculty, John Doyle, and held my breath. The answer came quickly and affirmatively. So it was on, scheduled for a month later. Whatever plans I had for that month were put on hold, and I went about organizing this conference. This involved working on the program and inviting Irish speakers to participate along with professors, MPs, and MEPs from Greece, Cyprus, Spain, and Portugal. It also meant booking rooms, publicizing the event, making catering arrangements, organizing live-streaming and various logistical matters, including hiring a driver for Tsipras and his entourage.

On the day, March 10, I concentrated less well than I would have if not distracted by organizational responsibilities, but the level of presentations and discussion was good. I opened the conference and chaired the first session. Irish speakers were Michael Taft, trade union economist, Professor David Jacobson of DCU, Paul Murphy MEP, and Mary Lou McDonald TD (member of the Irish parliament). The morning concentrated on an analysis of the crisis and speakers were mainly professors. The afternoon was pitched to exploring alternatives and speakers were mainly politicians. These included Euclid Tsakalotos, Syriza MP; Mariana Mortagua MP; and Marisa Matias MEP, both of Bloco de Esquerda in Portugal.[1]

The politics of this were a bit tricky: because it was an academic conference cosponsored by DCU, there could be no political campaigning. It sailed a bit close to the wind in this respect, because EU elections were on the horizon and several speakers were candidates. The Syriza agenda in Ireland was to consolidate its political contacts in EU countries and support for Tsipras as the lead candidate for the Party of the European Left. I made sure that the dean was fine with the program and speakers. Another tricky aspect of it was the fact that Syriza was hedging its bets vis-à-vis Sinn Féin and the Socialist Party, the two left parties that were serious players in this election. Tsipras spent the day of the conference meeting with SP and SF and only arrived at DCU for his own speech. It was clear that Syriza was leaning toward Sinn Féin because of its more favorable showing in the polls.

Tsipras arrived forty-five minutes after his speech was to begin. I was tearing my hair out as several hundred waited. If I had realized it would be this way (and I should have, considering other events I attended in Athens where Tsipras spoke), I would have organized for someone else to speak first, or even to play Greek music. When he arrived, I began the session by stressing the new energy and organization in the European left in responding to the crisis and introduced Tsipras as the forward face of this movement. I found his speech disappointing. It was somewhat bland, making a moral appeal to opt for a "social Europe" over "Mrs. Merkel's Europe" in a way that seemed voluntarist and oblivious of ideologies, class interests, and sociohistorical forces. His handlers had asked that he speak and take no questions. I said that this would not be acceptable. It was part of a university conference and people had waited and then listened and should be able to raise questions. They conceded, but it was agreed that Haris Golemis and I would be there to mediate in case his English made that necessary. His English was okay, but he answered every question using far too many words to say too little. I assumed that he was a politician reaching to wider sections of the population than those who usually looked to the left. Indeed, his speech did go down well with such people. Peter Matthews TD, a politician on the right of the Irish political spectrum, told me he was very impressed by Tsipras and later that night spoke of him in glowing terms on current affairs television.

The presentation didn't go down well with sections of the Irish left, however. The Workers Party issued a statement saying that the Tsipras visit was against the interests of the Irish working class. The CPI publication *Socialist Voice* ran an article attacking Tsipras, Syriza, and the Party of the European Left and siding with the KKE. "The portrait of Che Guevara in his office, or his lack of a tie, cannot cover the fact that Tsípras is devoid of class analysis and if in government—much like Obama—would merely manage capitalism in a superficially less offensive way," wrote the author, who signed it as NL, although they were not the real initials of the author.[2]

I was happy about this visit as a step in binding the Irish left ever closer to the European left. I was glad to meet the speakers from abroad. Of course, I was glad to meet Tsipras. I told him that I was pleased that he finally took Ireland into consideration in his analysis, because I had sent him several emails noting occasions when he had glaringly omitted us from his analysis. It was an exchange in good humor. I found Tsipras to be pleasant and polite. He thanked me several times for organizing the event. His personal assistant, in contrast, who had made various requests to me by email, never even spoke to me. However, nothing about this encounter lessened my worries about Tsipras and elements of Syriza being too bland and populist in present discourse and too compromising in future practice. Nevertheless, I chose to let my hopes outweigh my fears.

EU Elections

The elections for the European Parliament attracted more attention in 2014 than any time previously. I think this was because of an increasing awareness of how much power the EU has over us. They were held at the same time as local and regional elections, which also increased the turnout. They were conducted in all countries during the same period, but with different electioneering rituals and electoral systems. I was in Sicily during the last week of April and didn't see too much electoral activity. I saw posters for Forza Italia and Partito Democratico, but I looked in vain for ones of Rifondazione Comunista or L'Altra Europa con Tsipras. Perhaps they went up after I left. About L'Altra Europa con Tsipras, an electoral front formed in March 2014, I wondered about the wisdom of calling a political formation by the name of one person, let alone a young and untested leader of the opposition in another country. When I arrived back in Ireland, there was a profusion of posters. There was hardly a vertical structure without them.

In May, electioneering intensified, particularly manifested in media debates. In Ireland, there was a lot of door-to-door canvassing too. A new feature this time was the election of the president of the European Commission by the European Parliament. There were television debates featuring the five candidates for this position, with the left of the spectrum being represented by Tsipras but also by Ska Keller of the Greens. These debates never really sparked. A bland centrist discourse about European values and social inclusion prevailed and ideological differences were not clearly articulated.

The count was on May 25. The EU election was good for Syriza in Greece, Podemos in Spain, and Sinn Féin in Ireland. More eyes were focused on the composition of groups within the European parliament than ever in my memory. After this, a domino theory began circulating, projecting victories for the left in coming general elections in Greece, Spain, and Ireland.

The GUE-NGL (European United Left-Nordic Green Left) group in the European Parliament was up 17 seats, to 52 (of 751).[3] It would have been higher, but KKE left the group. The biggest party in the group was Die Linke in Germany, with 7 of 96 seats. Syriza came first in Greece and won 6 of their 21 seats. Podemos in Spain won 5 and other left forces won 6 of 54 seats. Sinn Féin won 4 seats in this group, including one from Northern Ireland. The candidate I supported in Dublin, Paul Murphy, got a decent vote, but lost his seat. L'Altra Europa con Tsipras won 3 seats. It was also a good election for these parties at the regional and local levels. In Ireland, commentators were saying, "Dublin is red" because so many left councilors were elected. Also the SP won a national by-election on the day, and a few months later Paul Murphy won another by-election. In Greece, Rena Dourou became prefect of Attica, a position never before held by the left. Nikos Potamitis was elected to a council for the Ionian islands.

Syriza were buoyed up by this election and increasingly impatient for a national election, strategizing about how to bring the existing government down instead of waiting out its full term.

On June 11, ERT Open celebrated a year of continuing to broadcast after the government moved against them. They too were keen for an election to come so that they could be paid for their work. So many had hopes of setting their lives on a new path.

Meanwhile, I got on with other tasks in Ireland. As far as the future direction of Greece was concerned, it was in a holding pattern. Syriza projected a sense of being ready to take over and being frustrated at not being able to get at it.

Zakynthos Again

In August, Sam and I returned to Zakynthos. We stayed in Argassi and not Tsilivi this time. I did go back to Tsilivi to meet Andreas Pylarinos, an eighteen-year-old medical student, who wrote to tell me that he found my stolen wallet in a field near his home. Naturally, the money (€400!) was long gone, but I was glad to get back my memory stick with so much of my information on it.

On our second night, we went to an artsy taverna with Nikos and had one of our normal world historical conversations, focusing on the continuing crisis and on what sort of counternarrative the left needed to construct and project. A few days later, we had a splendid Sunday with him. We headed for the southwestern coast of the island. Throughout the day, there were many conversations with people discussing their problems with Nikos as a public representative. We met a man who had once supported the junta but now looked left. We went out on a boat for a while amidst beautiful scenery and perfect weather. Then we went inland to a traditional village that was not benefiting much from the tourist industry on the coast. We visited the home of an artist-craftsman struggling to survive. Three generations were living under one roof, and they discussed the problems presented by their daily lives.

All the while in our comings and goings through the day, we grappled with all the big issues, ending with the tricky one of how to wrest power and wealth away from those who had it to give those who needed and deserved it. Nikos was feeling frustrated, not only over the odds against us in doing that on a global scale but wanting to make headway in Greece. He was simultaneously keen for the election to come and Syriza to win it and worried about whether Syriza would do what needed to be done. He was much less trusting of Tsipras and those around him than he had been previously. He was worried about assertions that there was no plan B in play. He said that he would rather go back to being a 4 percent party than to be so compromising to troika demands as he thought some might be. The next morning, however, he phoned all excited about a poll that put Syriza at 35 percent.

The next day I was back on the air, on ERA Zakynthos. It was interesting to note the differences from the year before. When I was last there, it was all hands on deck, even with camp beds in the station, where it was being occupied 24/7 in case the riot police came to close it down. It was now a scaled-down, but still determined, operation. The camp beds were gone and they only broadcast for an hour a day. Petros Pomonis, the manager of the station, interviewed me, Aspasia Liveri, translated and a young lad, the son of an ERA worker, did the sound engineering. The interview again focused on the crisis in Ireland and Greece and the global forces underlying it. Petros then locked the station and drove us back to Argassi, while we continued our conversation. Although he was in Antarsya, he was very hopeful about what a Syriza government might do.

Every morning, I had a two-block walk to the sea for my dawn swim. On the way, I saw a big bag of bread, presumably what the supermarket didn't sell the day before, tied to a pay phone (yes, still a pay phone!). On the way back, it was always gone. A small symptom of the crisis up close.

On our last night, we were again guests of the Potamitis household in Akrotiri, where we were served many courses and drank much wine and struggled with the problem of how to expropriate the expropriators. We were only there for a week this time, so we took our leave and wondered what would happen before the next time we would meet again.

Autumn Intervals

I was not long back in Dublin when I was off again to Prague in September for the general assembly of Transform. It was an opportunity to talk with Haris Golemis, who was ebullient about the prospect of a coming election and what would come next. However, I focused more on Prague and on its transformations in the past decades, especially as I had experienced them myself. I stayed for a week and spent a lot of time walking the streets and reflecting on the life stories of those I knew here and the conversations I could not have with them, because they were dead. I did have the chance to talk with living Czechs, mostly communists, who saw themselves in critical continuity with the socialist past. On the evening before the assembly, I went on a political tour of Prague, along with others from Transform, which enunciated a counternarrative to the dominant narrative in other tours of the city. After the two-day assembly, I accompanied Jiří Málek and Walter Baier to attend the *Halo Noviny* press festival. As I walked the streets alone over those days, I noted so many palaces and churches. Although the monarchies and aristocracies were gone, although this was one of the least religious countries in the world, the visual impact of the city was dominated by tributes to monarchs and saints. Where were the monuments to the people who built it all? I got my answer when I visited the Museum of Communism over a McDonald's and next to a casino. Here the photos, statues, banners, posters, and films of the communist past were dumped together in too small a space and treated with contempt. The narrative was unremittingly hostile. I asked who owned it. It was privately owned by two Americans and one Czech. I asked how these things were acquired, but the person working there could not tell me. I said that it was all wrong. These things belonged to the state and to the party. There should be a proper museum of communism in Prague, but it should be publicly owned and it should also give scope to a counternarrative. This was contested history in the Czech Republic, where the Communist Party of Bohemia and Moravia is the third largest party.

During the autumn, although I kept up with Greece on a day-to-day basis, it slipped from the center of my focus; it felt like a lull before a surge and coincided with other demands on my time and attention. There was an upsurge in anti-austerity mobilization in Ireland, because water charges proved to be the last straw in a burden of cuts in pay and pensions and public services along with new taxes and charges. This was bringing people into the streets, a hundred thousand or more.

Also I had promised to give a series of lectures at the National Autonomous University of Mexico in November, so I spent much of October both preparing my lectures and giving myself a crash course on Mexican history and politics. Although I spoke with Mexicans about the crisis in Ireland and Greece, and they were interested, they were preoccupied with their own crisis, as was I during my days there. The disappearance of forty-three students in Ayotzinapa brought to a boiling point long-simmering rage about so many dead and disappeared as a result of the rampages of the narco-state. Several of my lectures were canceled, because universities were on strike, and I joined in the assemblies and protests. I took part in one massive march of over a hundred thousand people from Reforma to Zócalo. I had time to see many murals of Rivera, Siqueiros, Orozco, and O'Gorman and to explore the UNAM campus, which was nearly a city in itself. One of my lectures was on philosophy of history and was a defense of grand narratives. I felt in the presence of grand narratives here, because of the world-historical sweep of the murals, the scope and seriousness of knowledge at UNAM, and the historical materialist narrative running through the magnificent museums. A worrying feature of the political landscape was the weakness of the left. Many radical left forces, including the Mexican Communist Party, various Trotskyist parties, and other left formations, had dissolved themselves into the Party of the Democratic Revolution, the PRD, which had so disappointed expectations that even its leader, its presidential candidate, and many members had left it. It was also implicated in the Ayotzinapa disappearances.

Thessaloniki Program

Meanwhile in Greece in September, Syriza launched its electoral manifesto, the Thessaloniki Program. It was a national reconstruction plan based on four pillars: confronting the humanitarian crisis; restarting the economy and promoting tax justice; national planning to restore employment; and transforming the political system to deepen democracy. It was criticized by oppositional parties, but also by some within Syriza.

Yiannis Milios, head of the party's economic policy unit, resigned from that position and declined to stand for election, because he discerned an ideological shift taking place within Syriza. He saw the main focus shifting from wealth redistribution, taxing the rich, and building up a social economy toward more neutral goals, such as growth, productive reconstruction, and combating the humanitarian crisis, which portrayed the society and the economy as terrain of common interests, not divided along class lines. This shift manifested itself in the Thessaloniki Program, which dropped many of the original demands and slogans of Syriza and anything that could have been understood as anti-capitalist.[4]

However, there was more and more emphasis on getting into power than on what to do when getting it. Syriza was tired of waiting and knew the time was coming.

In December, the tempo picked up in Greece again. Syriza decided to use the vote in parliament to elect a new president of the republic to bring the government down and provoke a new election. After three votes, where the government failed to elect the ND nominee, the government fell. The election was called for January 25, 2015. It was game on for Syriza.

The international left responded by going into overdrive in organizing international solidarity.

CHAPTER 4

2015: Fighting Goliath

National Election, International Electioneering

Never had I seen so much international activity surrounding a national election. All through January I received a constant stream of requests to participate in solidarity initiatives—from gathering signatures on petitions of support, to taking pictures of people holding messages of support for a video, to crowd-funding to get Greeks abroad home to vote, to all of which I responded immediately and wholeheartedly. Every day there was something to do. Every day there was so much to read. Every day there were demands to write, mostly in social media debates. So many felt that they had so much at stake. It was the horizon of hope for the international left, especially the European left.

Sinn Féin's newspaper *An Phoblacht* asked me to contribute to their "Building an Alternative" series. I argued that to build an alternative we had to imagine an alternative, to win consent to a counternarrative of the crisis, to fashion a force capable of bringing this to fruition. I held out Syriza as such a force, which stood as a challenge to us to build such a force here. I described them as engaged in a titanic struggle that was not just a matter of winning elections but facing down the formidable forces ranged against them, nationally and internationally, as they moved to reverse the cuts, to redistribute wealth, and to engage in radical social transformation. I set out what forces on the Irish left needed to find a way to come together in a front that could form a left government. On the cover was a photo of Tsipras as well as a call for talks on a left coalition. The editorial, entitled "Can Ireland Emulate Greece?" called for progressive forces to come together to discuss how to ensure the future election of a left coalition government.[1]

"Avanti Popolo" in Athens

On the eve of the election, Aristides Baltas, my colleague and comrade, wrote to me saying, "This is the last day of the old era," which brought tears to my eyes.

On election day, I was on edge and at the computer all day. In the evening I went over to the home of Eugenia Siapera and Vangelis Papadamakis to watch the results. It seemed possible that Syriza would not only win but win with the 151 seats it needed to form a government alone. I watched as international leftists sang "The Internationale" and "Avanti Popolo" on the streets of Athens. I couldn't help wishing that I was there. It was a paradigmatic moment for the international left.

In the end, Syriza got 149 seats and immediately formed a coalition with Anel. Already sections of the left were pointing accusing fingers and sighing sellout. I thought this coalition was unfortunate but necessary and I did not think it would constrain them unduly, especially as Anel were committed to an anti-austerity agenda.

A photo of Alexis Tsipras and me appeared on the DCU website with a story about his becoming prime minister of Greece and the international conference where he spoke at DCU. The Connolly Youth Movement of the CPI put out a statement on Greek elections, which was very condescending to Syriza and Irish Syrizans and affirmed the superior wisdom of the KKE. There were others in Ireland and abroad striking notes of negativity, but it was swamped by a wave of affirmation. So many wanted to believe that the left could win, that the left could govern. Even beyond the left, there were so many who wanted to see a force stand up against the oppressive global system bearing down on us all.

The handover from the outgoing to the incoming government could not have been more graceless. Samaras failed to appear at the swearing-in of his successor. Ministers, including the prime minister, entered offices stripped of files, computers, even soap and toilet paper. However, nothing could dampen the initial euphoria of a left government coming to power for those who had wanted it for so long.

I watched the first bold steps of the new government with joy. I was proud of their civil oaths, the honoring of communist resistance fighters executed by the Nazis at Kaisariani, the appointment of people I knew and admired to ministerial positions, the announcement of legislation to halt privatization, to restore the minimum wage, to rehire public servants, to reconstitute ERT, to offer citizenship to the children of migrants, and to alleviate the effects of the crisis on those most in need. There were images of ministers driving to work, including one on a motorbike, and of the prime minister flying economy class. I was delighted at the pro-government demonstrations in Syntagma. One person on a vox pop said, "It's like walking around in a different country." My friend, Marxist philosopher Aristides Baltas, was appointed minister of education, culture, and religious affairs. He quoted the *Communist Manifesto* in his first speech in parliament.

When it came to the election of a new president of the republic, there were rumors about figures who would capture the popular imagination and signal the start of a new order. The list included such internationally acclaimed cultural figures as Mikis Theodorakis and Costa-Gavras. Then Syriza nominated Prokopis Pavlopoulos of New Democracy. I was really disappointed at this. It was a gratuitous gesture to the right. Leftists tended to smooth it over, noting that the office wasn't so powerful and it didn't matter much, but I thought that it did matter and it didn't augur well. One Greek tweeter asked, "Did we go through all this because we preferred Prokopis Pavlopoulos to Stravros Dimas?" Of course, everyone knew it was not about that, but Syriza could have used this appointment to show

how much it was about something much bigger, but clearly some of the party were not.

Other appointments also caused concern. The appointment of Anel leader Panos Kammenos as minister of defense was unpalatable to the left, but arguably a necessary concession to Anel to make up the numbers to form a government. Less defensible to the left and causing disquiet within Syriza itself were those of Yiannis Panousis as minister for public order and Nikos Kotzias as minister for foreign affairs. Panousis was a professor of criminology, who had trained many officers in the police and was considered too close to them to bring the democratic control of policing that Syriza had promised. This did indeed prove to be the case. Nikos Kotzias was highly qualified for the job as an experienced diplomat and professor of international relations and was once a person of strong left intellectual views. In the 1980s, he was in charge of ideological instruction in the KKE. He was an advocate of multidimensional foreign policy, which the government did pursue in many respects. However, he offered little challenge to US, EU, or NATO foreign policy. When he joined hands and clapped and swayed with other NATO foreign ministers on stage singing "We are the world," the left cringed. Other appointments were unpopular with one section or another of Syriza but were recognized to be a necessary balancing of the different positions in Syriza. So the left were unhappy about Yannis Dragasakis, Nikos Pappas, and Alekos Flambouraris and the right were unhappy about Panagiotis Lafazanis.

Nevertheless, I emphasized the positive. I didn't expect to like everything I saw. In fact, I didn't like a lot of what I saw as time went on. I cringed at all the hugging and kissing of right-wing politicians in Brussels. I knew that certain diplomatic rituals were in order, but Juncker and Tsipras kissing was definitely not.

The Floodlit Negotiations

From February to July, I beheld what were perhaps the most floodlit economic negotiations in the history of the world. It was a high-wire act, with the whole world watching, unfolding in a swirl of twists and turns, rumors and counter-rumors, declarations and denials, diplomatic niceties and bruising recriminations, with incessant commentary coming at it from all angles. There were accusations of betrayal, praise for buying time, advice to live in the "real world," gloating over humiliation inflicted. It was riveting drama.

These negotiations were difficult but necessary to secure the material base for all that Syriza wanted to do, at least as the starting point. Its mandate was to push within the Eurozone to the limits of what could be negotiated in the way of debt relief, but also to reverse the trajectory of austerity (which should more accurately be called expropriation). The prospects were not good, because it was not hard to see that these could prove to be contradictory mandates, that they could not take control of the economy to redistribute wealth within the Eurozone. I thought that this had to play out, because the Eurozone was where Greece was and where people wanted to stay, but I believed that, when it came to the crunch and they had to choose, they would choose to end the expropriation. The negotiation was plan A. I always assumed that there was a plan B, or even a plan C or D. It was obvious from the beginning, despite all the glad-handing and confident statements about the goodwill of "our partners," that the aim of the Eurogroup was to force the retreat, capitulation, humiliation, and defeat of the Syriza government. It was not only about the immediate issues, but about policing the boundaries, about warning others who might think they could elect a left government and follow suit.

There was enormous support for Syriza in Greek society, even beyond those who voted for the party. Although there was no solidarity in the negotiating rooms of the EU, there was enormous solidarity in workplaces and on the streets of Europe and beyond. The KKE warned against international solidarity with the Syriza government. "The workers of other countries must in no instance become cheerleaders for negotiations that are alien to the interests of the Greek workers. This is a campaign that is being orchestrated by the 'Party of the European Left' and other 'flotsam and jetsam' of the class struggle, like the CPUSA."[2] This made me more sad than angry.

The drama spilled into popular culture in a way that I had never seen before. Striding colossally across this panorama was the figure of Yanis Varoufakis as the superstar minister of finance. There were cartoons galore, even a video game pitting Syriza Man against Doctor Troika. He lectured fellow finance ministers on macroeconomics, but complained that they only cited rules and regulations. He articulated a devastating critique of the whole "extend and pretend" dynamic of so-called bailouts. Varoufakis gave constant interviews, each providing something new and interesting, always smart and colorful, but not always consistent. There were quotable quotes galore: "Sometimes like Ulysses you need to tie yourself to a mast in order to get to where you're going and to avoid the sirens." I found it amusing at first, glad to see someone on the left so capturing the popular imagination. However, he evoked not only Odysseus or Prometheus but Narcissus. He spoke in a way that was more "I" than "we" and made many contradictory statements. He was ingratiating and defiant in almost equal measure. He played into celebrity culture in a way that was not good for the left. The left paper *I Avgi* spoke of "toxic overexposure," even before a *Paris Match* photo shoot, where he posed in a luxury apartment in the Plaka with a stunning view of the Acropolis. One shot had him reading his own book with his wife's arms around him. He played the piano too and was sure to wear a tight T-shirt to show how fit he was. His wife, Danae Stratou, an artist from an oligarchic background, was keen on the limelight too, with less justification for the attention she demanded.

The mythical references were constant. One cartoon showed Tsipras as Sisyphus pushing the rock up the hill and the troika ready to push it down again. David and Goliath was also an obvious motif, which I used in several of my own speeches to indicate the enormous odds as well as the fragile hope of prevailing against them.

All through these negotiations, I hoped for the best and defended (even if critically) the Syriza strategy. I participated in discussions on social media. I was called upon to speak about Greece in universities and to political and community groups. All of these audiences were eager to engage and full of questions and arguments and expectations.

In London, the SWP organized a debate between Alex Callinicos and Stathis Kouvelakis. In Dublin, the SWP mirrored this in a debate between John Molyneux and myself. I saw it as a Syriza versus Antarsya debate by proxy. I took the side of Syriza. The debate was serious, informed, comradely. It was uploaded to YouTube.[3] Stathis messaged me his agreement with the arguments I was making as he watched it. I got a buzz out of that.

Looking back on my notes for these talks to trace my assessments and expectations, I was struggling to vindicate the trust so many placed in Syriza. I knew that the forces ranged against them were monumental. I knew they could not succeed in everything they strove to achieve. However, I thought they would fight to the end and had a chance to shift direction away from intensified expropriation and toward modest redistribution. I ended several of my speeches with the David and Goliath image and reminded my audiences that David won. I did know that the odds were with Goliath. I was steeled for possible defeat. Even so, I never expected anything as awful as what actually happened.

At first it seemed that they might get a bridging loan, which would mean some compromise and deferral of aims, but would nevertheless give them some degree of fiscal and legislative autonomy. This would give them enough room for maneuver to move ahead with their program. They believed they could pull it off with a complex strategy of polite negotiation, creative ambiguity, and outright defiance. It was riddled with contradictions. The discourse of trust, reason, and persuasion masked the balance of forces at play and the reality of the class struggle in which they were immersed. At other times, the mask was ripped away. In parliament, Nikos Voutsis said, "We are engaged in a brutal class war with our lenders." Wolfgang Schäuble saw this clearly too. He did not think elections made any difference and said so. Designs for a new drachma circulated on the Internet.

On February 20, there was a provisional agreement. The Greek government promised to pay all existing debts, to refrain from unilateral actions, to desist from redistributive measures they had announced, and to implement reforms that went counter to their program. A twelve-hour meeting of Syriza MPs divided two-thirds versus one-third for the deal. At the Syriza central committee, a Left Platform resolution against the deal received 41 percent support. Syriza MEPs and MPs, such as Manolis Glezos, Sofia Sakorafa, and Costas Lapavitsas, publicly disavowed the agreement. Glezos apologized to the Greek people for contributing to the illusion that there could be compromise between the oppressors and the oppressed. Between the occupier and the slave, he insisted, the only solution was freedom. Lapavitsas insisted that they should go ahead and implement their program and face the consequences. Others compared it to Brest-Litovsk and argued that it was necessary to cede ground to gain time. I accepted this, more because I didn't want to abandon hope so soon than for any other reason.

In Ireland, some Labour Party members gloated on social media. Now you see what it's like to campaign in poetry and to govern in prose, they proclaimed. More than ever, Ireland was being held up as an example for Greece. At meetings of EU prime ministers, Enda Kenny condescendingly advised Alexis Tsipras that Greece should win the trust of the troika and meet its responsibilities. Michael Noonan, our finance minister, observed that macroeconomics might be good in theory but bad in practice.

Syriza continued to veer between compromise and defiance. They passed anti-poverty legislation in spite of explicit instructions not to do so. In retaliation, the lenders withheld €2 billion that was due under the previous "bailout." The Greek government received no funding from the troika during this period, but continued making massive debt repayments. It became clear that the noose was tightening. The treasury and banks were draining. The economy was being asphyxiated. The government sequestered reserves of local government, hospitals, educational institutions, and pension funds to pay debt. There were questions about whether wages and pensions could be paid. The tension of deal versus default heightened. It was an emotional roller coaster for all who were rallying to them.

The government enjoyed broad support during this period, up to 80 percent in public opinion polls. At home and abroad, they were in the spotlight and a beacon of hope for those who were unhappy with the way the world was being governed and its wealth was being distributed.

Syriza Spring

In May 2015, I went to Greece, combining political discussion in Athens with a brief holiday with my son and daughter in the Peloponnese. I thought that the public picture of Greece was swamped by the negotiations. Understandably so, because so much depended on them. However, I wanted to see the less visible aspects of what this left government was doing: how ministries were being transformed, how a left government was doing whatever it could do with what it had despite a high degree of paralysis necessarily caused by being starved of funding. I had received an email from Aristides Baltas in February asking me when I was coming to Athens, so that he could welcome me in his new office as minister of culture, education, and religious affairs. I decided to take him up on it and pursue this. What was happening in his ministry was of particular interest to me. I took the metro to Marousi, where the education ministry had been moved a few years back to remove it from protesting students. The building, not far from the abandoned Olympic Village, had been an Olympics administration building. His ministerial office was huge. We sat at a corner of a long table, where he conducted most of his meetings. We spoke for more than three hours, which was more time than I expected. I overlapped with Leo Panitch, who conducted a formal interview with him during some of this time.[4]

He said that he started every meeting by saying, "Look, we have no money, but what can we do anyway?" He spoke of eliminating elitism in education and making schools centers of community life. Quoting from Antonio Machado's poem, he said, "We make the road by walking," and went on to characterize the road since entering government as uphill, full of obstacles, some expected, some not, but also full of possibilities not understood previously. He was interested in opening up the state and changing relationships and everyday life. Even within the ministry itself, he sought to alter the atmosphere, to walk along the corridors and to talk to colleagues about their jobs and their lives. I asked him about the history curriculum and cited criticisms I had heard of the conservative, nationalistic, and religious conceptions of history taught in schools. He admitted they hadn't gone there yet, but would need to address such matters in the future. He found that separation of church and state was proving complicated and difficult, but he wanted to see a new law on it. He was proud of his good working relationship with Archbishop Ieronymos, the head of the Greek church.

We also spoke about the current situation. Much was being held in suspension pending the negotiations. Syriza had lost the chance of a bridging loan and was paying wages, pensions, and current expenses from the budget, but money was running out. The lines that could be not crossed were changing every day, but he insisted that there were areas where Syriza would never give way, such as troika demands for a "flexible labor market." Syriza had explored other sources for funding in Russia and China, but both wanted to see the economy stabilize first and to receive return on their investments. He admitted that they didn't know how to get out of the maze just yet. He thought that Tsipras had shown himself to be a first-class statesman. I expressed surprise at this, but he reaffirmed it, as did Michalis Spourdalakis, who was also there. We agreed to meet again in July to continue our discussions.

I had already been speaking to Michalis Spourdalakis, who had become dean of the Faculty of Law, Economics, and Social Science at the University of Athens. When I arrived at 57 Solonos, it was all boarded up and I doubted that I was in the right place. I called Michalis on his cell phone and he came down to meet me. He revealed that it was that way because there were student elections going on and they didn't want them disrupted by anarchists. He explained that this building had been occupied by anarchists recently. They had thrown computers out of windows and ripped fire hydrants off walls. They had also occupied Syriza offices and the radio station Sto Kokkino. I asked if he thought of them as serious anarchists or as *agents provocateurs*. He thought it was the latter.

We spoke of many matters, including the debates within Syriza. The party-government relationship was a particular point of tension at this stage. The party had recently taken a decision not to make an IMF payment that was coming due, but the government paid it anyway. There were other issues surrounding appointments to cabinet and other state positions. The latest controversy was about ERT and the appointment of Lambis Tagmatarchis as CEO, who was seen as representing the old ERT and not the transformed ERT post-2013. The government minister in charge was Nikos Pappas, who was distrusted by the left. There were also issues about the other stations. Instead of being democratized, the airwaves were being auctioned off to the highest bidder.

Michalis invited me to a seminar one evening where Leo Panitch was speaking on reform or revolution. He traced this debate on the left and posited that a third term had to be added, namely, restraint. Both revolutions and reforms have proved reversible. The resilience of capitalism was such that it has resulted in the commodification of all aspects of life. The left must fight to hold back the onslaught before it can advance. This resonated with my recent reflections about how far we were being forced back to fight for what we thought we had already won. Afterward, the discussion continued in a taverna, where we all shared our thoughts, along with many dishes of amazing food and jugs of wine.

There were so many people I wanted to see in Athens, but I knew I would be back in July to speak at the Democracy Rising conference and I would have ample time to see many more people then. At the seminar, I met Maria Nikolakaki and Creston Davis, who were organizing the July conference. They were full of enthusiasm for this as well as the other projects of their Global Center for Advanced Studies.

I also spoke to non-Greeks living in Greece, with whom I had a lot of interaction on Facebook. Kevin Ovenden's dispatches had been a daily source of information and analysis for many English-speaking leftists. We met in Syntagma and spent a lively evening in a café off Ermou discussing everything under the sun, including his forthcoming book on Syriza.[5]

In Corinth, I again met Damian Mac Con Uladh, still struggling to earn his living as a journalist after months working without pay for *Athens News* and then *Eleftherotypia*. This time I also met his wife, Phaedra Koutsoukou, a teacher, and their two sons, Kimon and Iason. After a long lunch by the sea in Loutraki, we went together to ancient Corinth, which was much more elaborate than I expected and much enhanced by their commentary. Both Damian and Phaedra have PhDs in history. Phaedra's mother had been an archeologist on this site, losing her position when Pasok came to power.

In Nafplio, once the capital of Greece, we spent a long evening eating, drinking, talking, and laughing with Paul Johnston, author of the Alex Mavros detective novels. I entreated him to write more of them, especially to pursue the ongoing mystery of the fate of the detective's missing communist brother, my favorite of his characters. I asked him if the communist aunt in one of his novels was based on Liana Kanelli, KKE MP, and he confirmed that it was.

May is a good month for the sort of trip where you walk around unknown landscapes and archeological ruins. As well as Corinth, we visited ancient sites in Epidaurus, Mycenae, and Sparta and the medieval fortress in Mystras. While I was resting at Mystras, I chatted to a ticket collector, who told me that his politics were to the left of KKE or Antarsya, but he voted Syriza. He lived in Sparta, which was very difficult, because XA were very strong there. Indeed as we drove through the region down into the Mani Peninsula, there was a lot of XA graffiti. There was a strong sense of being descendants of the ancient Spartans there.

The Mani was fascinating to explore with striking landscape and architecture. The driving was difficult, with many narrow roads with sharp bends and deep drops, but Cathal managed it skillfully. The stone towers were especially beautiful, but it was so sad to see so many villages depopulated and so many buildings derelict. We stopped in Vathia, an amazing village perched on a mountain. Only two people live there all year-round. We walked through an abandoned tower house, where the doors were open, and we wondered where its inhabitants lived now. We ventured all the way down to Cape Tenaro. We stayed just outside the harbor town of Gythio and had a beach to ourselves when we went to swim in the sea.

Back home in Ireland, I kept watching. One development that I was especially happy to see was the reconstitution of ERT on June 11, two years to the day that it was suddenly shut down and we received the call to come and occupy it. It was the most impressive occupation in which I have ever participated. It went on for two years: committed and creative broadcasting and worker control of production, all without pay. It came at considerable cost to those involved. Eighteen ERT workers had died in ways that were attributed to the shock and stress of the resistance: suicide, heart attack, cancer, accidents.

However, ERT was not reconstituted in the way Syriza had promised. ERT Open had developed detailed proposals for a new ERT. Syriza in government, instead of affirming and building on what this popular struggle had achieved, disregarded the popular demand for a new model of public broadcasting, based on critical and creative programming and workers' self-management. Instead, they reinstated the old order and hierarchical management. Instead of public broadcasting, it became government broadcasting, as it had been previously, except that Syriza was now the government whose line was privileged. ERT Open, which was to be a temporary project to be dissolved when ERT was reconstituted, decided it had to carry on after all.

ERT back on the air and these and other public-sector workers rehired constituted election promises kept, even if not in the way people hoped. Other measures included food, electricity, and rent assistance for the poorest families; free access to public health care; prison reform; the release of migrants from detention camps; and citizenship for second-generation migrants. There was a more democratic and participatory atmosphere in the government apparatus, although there was also passivity and resistance. The new government could not immediately and automatically liberate the state from decades of clientelism and corruption, but there was little evidence of Syriza tackling it very vigorously either. Zoe Konstantopoulou, president of parliament, set up the Truth Committee on the Public Debt, which declared the debt to be "illegal, illegitimate, odious and unsustainable." Lapavitsas, who had earlier proposed a grass-roots debt audit, criticized this effort for reporting too quickly, without proper evidence and argumentation. Overshadowing all else, however, was mounting tension about deal or default.

Greek Flags Flying on the Streets of Dublin

All through this period, we saw an intensification of solidarity activities in Ireland, coordinated with international solidarity networks. Ronan Burtenshaw, coordinator of our Greek Solidarity Committee, set out to get a Syriza speaker to Dublin in February. A formidable organizer, he went for four speakers instead of one and mapped out a wide range of activities over a week, from addressing community Right2Water activists in Edenmore to participating in an academic debate at Trinity College Dublin. At TCD, Syriza's Ntina Tzouvala, a PhD candidate in law at Durham, got a standing ovation before she even spoke from an audience not normally inclined to the left. At the Edenmore rally, John Douglas, president of the Irish Congress of Trade Unions, who was chairing it, declared, "We need a Syriza and we need it now." That got a spirited affirmative response. I asked how many there would contribute to building a Syriza and most raised their hands.

Our committee's activities ranged from meeting requests to speak to various groups to photocalls in Greek restaurants to occupying EU offices in Dublin. During these months, Greek flags started to appear in ever greater numbers during anti-austerity demonstrations, especially at Right2Water marches. I was on RTÉ television discussing the state of negotiations in Greece and arguing that either Greece should get substantial debt restructuring or it should default. The culmination of these efforts, particularly intense during June as negotiations became even more tense, came during the week of the referendum.

The Resounding Referendum

In a stunning move on June 27, Alexis Tsipras announced a referendum on the creditors' proposals. Every section of Greek society got caught up it in it and felt that their lives were at stake. The media, both mainstream and otherwise, were full of it. All through the week leading up to the referendum, there was a flurry of arguments and counter-arguments and many activities both in Greece and abroad. There were also rumors of Tsipras coming under intense pressure to make a deal, even under threat of being replaced within Syriza. There was speculation that elements within Syriza, possibly including Tsipras, wanted to lose the referendum as justification for making a deal. There was some doubt about whether the referendum would proceed. The banks and stock exchange were closed and capital controls were imposed. Greece defaulted on an IMF payment of $1.8 billion.

We saw pictures of queues at ATMs and heard scare stories of businesses grinding to a halt, medicines running out, food supplies threatened. The withdrawal of liquidity was meant to frighten people into voting yes. Polls were neck and neck, tilting toward yes. I was worried about the result. In the changing room at the university pool, I overheard a conversation in which one woman was telling another that she was going to Greece on holiday. She was a bit worried but decided to look on the bright side. "Maybe we'll do well out of it. They'll be desperate for cash." I had to refrain from ranting at her.

There were yes and no rallies in Syntagma. The no ones were bigger and more vibrant. At the final Syriza rally on July 3, a defiant and almost insurrectionary crowd surged around Tsipras coming from Maximos Mansion to address the crowd in Syntagma. Witnesses say it overwhelmed, even frightened Tsipras, who realized that he had unleashed forces beyond his control, causing him to cut a forty-min-ute speech to eight minutes and emphasize how much Greece loved Europe.[6] On July 4, we had thousands on the streets of Dublin, march-ing and waving Greek flags while chanting *Oxi!*, a word they didn't even know before that week. The lead banner, stating that "Ireland Stands with Greece," was carried by prominent female politicians. Greeks living in Ireland danced in the streets. There were many such solidarity rallies elsewhere in Europe. Everyone I spoke to in Greece during these days said that they had never seen anything like the atmosphere of hope, power, and defiance evident in so many sectors of society. Nikos Potamitis told me that it even pervaded his clinics, as patients he was examining—indeed nearly everyone he met—wanted to discuss it and to declare that they were all for no in the referendum.

On the day of the referendum, RTÉ had an all-yes panel discussing the referendum. We tweeted our outraged critique. I was nervous all day about the result. When the result came, it wasn't close at all. It was nearly 62 percent. The crowds rejoiced in Syntagma and we rejoiced with them from our own places. I spoke to the owner of a Greek restaurant in Dublin, who was constantly telling me that he kept out of politics, but then told me that he had tears in his eyes over the result of the referendum.

What next? A victory had been won, but all the problems were still there.

CHAPTER 5

2015: Dealing with Defeat

From No to Yes

The jubilation did not last. Starting the very next day the no was transformed into a yes. Immediately, Tsipras called in the leaders of the defeated parties to agree on a negotiating position with them. Varoufakis was asked to resign and was replaced by Euclid Tsakalotos. In the EU, it became clear that Greece would be punished for the result. The international media mocked a note Tsakalotos wrote on hotel paper caught by their cameras about not being triumphalist. Although the Greek government claimed the result would strenghten their negotiating position, the reality was the opposite. There was no space whatsoever for triumphalism. They were not the victors but the vanquished.

On July 8, Tsipras appeared before the European Parliament and was berated and booed. I had never seen anything like it. The most brutal and blatantly imperial speech was delivered by Guy Verhofstadt, leader of the liberal ALDE group in the European Parliament. Among those who rose to defend Tsipras was Martina Anderson of Sinn Féin, who declared that Ireland "from Kerry to Derry" stood with him.

Goliath Won

Negotiations became ever more brutal. The government put forward proposals that crossed many lines and went further than the deal rejected by the referendum. On July 10, the social media was full of accusations of capitulation and betrayal, of snatching defeat from the jaws of victory. I didn't want to add my voice to them, but I had to say something, because I had been so prominent in defending Syriza. I could not defend their proposals, but I argued that it was a matter of defeat and not betrayal. I did not doubt their good faith, not then anyway. I put the emphasis on the enormous pressures and the brutal power being brought to bear against them.

Even after Goliath won and David lay bleeding, the combat continued. Even after the Greek government capitulated, the Eurogroup pushed further. On July 12, there were negotiations between finance ministers, and then prime ministers, that went on all through the night. Journalists in Brussels released detail after detail, including a demand for ERT to be closed down again. #ThisIsACoup trended on social media. Many tweets and texts made the point that what was once done by tanks was now done by banks. A serendipitous sound bite with a catchy rhyme, it was nevertheless all too tragically true. I too tweeted it. On the morning of July 13 came the announcement that the deal was done. To all the other expropriating measures was added a demand that €50 billion of public assets be put under external administration for privatization.

Even after watching it unfold, nearly blow by blow, I was still shocked by this outcome. So many thoughts and emotions welled up in me, as in many others. No one would ever see the EU in the same way again. For so long, it had hidden its brutalizing class interests behind a mask of liberal technocratic discourse and seemingly bland legalities. Now the EU was fully revealed, and that revelation was good.

Unfortunately, no one, including myself, would ever see Syriza in the same way again either. This was a grievous loss. There would be severe consequences for the Greek people, for the Greek left, and for the international left. Some were quick off the mark in responding. In Ireland, Paul Murphy, who had a strong relationship to Syriza and had just been in Athens supporting them in the referendum, said that the Greek people were "lions led by donkeys," whereas Sinn Féin's Pearse Doherty, who had also been there, was asked on air if he still believed that Syriza would do what they said they would do, evaded the question. I was glad I was not on air that day.

Trauma in Athens

On July 14, I flew to Athens. I had booked this flight months before when I was invited to speak at a conference starting on July 16. When the time came, I was dreading it. It was hard enough to come to terms with this from a distance, I thought. However, it had always been my way to run at difficulty and to work my way through it rather than to run away from it. Besides, others were far more immediately and severely affected by this. I had to shake off my world weariness and think if I could bring anything to the discourse that would help those abroad who were struggling to come to terms with what had happened and didn't have the opportunity I had to probe it more closely.

On the same flight were Eugenia Siapera and Sinéad Kennedy, academic colleagues who were going to the same conference. Staff at the Hotel Novus remembered me from my stay there during the ERT occupation and sent fruit and water to my room, which was nice.

I phoned Nikos Potamitis to talk through the situation and was delighted to discover that he was in Athens and not Zakynthos. He invited me to a Left Platform meeting that evening in the Hotel Oscar, although I couldn't go, because I had made other arrangements. Nikos, a doctor and public representative for Syriza in the Ionian islands, was furious about the agreement. "If there is no alternative to this agreement, then let New Democracy, Pasok, and Potami implement it and not destroy the left to it." He didn't, however, believe that there was no alternative to it, because he had been arguing for a plan B all along. He was determined to put up a fight for Syriza.

My meeting that night was with a KKE member. He had taken issue for a long while with the KKE's refusal to cooperate with Syriza and wider forces on the left. He was on the verge of being expelled from the party, he told me, because of his support for the no vote in the referendum. The KKE's position had been to abstain, substituting its own ballot, which was equivalent to a spoiled vote. He was deeply disappointed in Syriza for not honoring the result of the referendum and argued that there needed to be a force to represent the 61 percent.

The next day there was a public-sector strike. Nikos called and asked me if I would come to a demonstration against the agreement. I didn't hesitate to say yes. It was hard to demonstrate against a government I had supported until then, but it was easier to do with someone who had done so much to build Syriza, rather than banding together with those who never had. We gathered in Klafthomonos Square and marched to the parliament in Syntagma Square. We were behind the banner of META, the Syriza trade union with a section of Syriza doctors. There were about two thousand there.

After that, I went with Nikos and Efi Lazou to her family's home in Paleo Faliro. Her mother cooked beautiful stuffed vegetables and piled more food on my plate than on anyone else's. A meeting of Syriza MPs was taking place. I heard that Syriza MPs were exhibiting symptoms of severe stress. Nikos predicted than forty or more would not vote yes in parliament. He believed that 60 to 70 percent of the active members of Syriza opposed the agreement. One-hundred-nine of 201 members of the Syriza central committee signed a letter opposing the agreement.

In the evening, Nikos, Efi, and I returned to Syntagma for a demonstration that would take place while parliament was voting on the agreement. I met a number of Syriza people I knew, including Stathis Kouvelakis. There were also international leftists who had come for the conference that would start the next day, as well as members of our Greek Solidarity Committee in Ireland. The largest blocs were from PAME, the communist-affiliated trade union, and Antarsya, the anti-capitalist coalition. The police estimate of the numbers was 12,500. There was a quasi-carnivalesque atmosphere. Angry as people were, it was a celebration of a left that would not die because of this. I had some excellent discussions. I was saying to Shane Fitzgerald how nice it was that the air was not full of tear gas, as it had been on previous occasions when I was there, making it possible to socialize and discuss political philosophy. Suddenly there were loud explosions and a lot of smoke. All around us were men in black, wearing hoods and masks. Then came the tear gas. People moved out of the square in a relatively orderly manner, but riot police pursued some into side streets and arrested fifty people. Calls to the minister of the interior, Nikos Voutsis, met with the response that he could do nothing about it, even though he was the responsible minister. It was hard enough protesting against a government we had supported until now without being tear-gassed by them. This was bitter experience. Nikos kept calling to locate me, but I couldn't follow his directions in the tumult.

I went back to my hotel and stayed up late watching the vote in Vouli. It was so sad. I knew MPs on both sides: some who voted yes and others who voted no. At 2:40 a.m., just before logging off, I wrote a brief message to a Syriza MP congratulating him for voting no and telling him that I had been outside. I asked how it had come to this. "Unfortunately the spirit of the left in Greece seems to be broken," he answered. His reply brought tears to my eyes.

Democracy Rising?

The Democracy Rising conference started the next day, July 16. When the conference was first called in February, it seemed like an appropriate title, but by the time it happened, it didn't seem at all appropriate. The opposite fit the facts before us. Democracy Collapsing seemed like a better name. The conference was called by the Global Center for Advanced Studies, a hitherto unknown group that issued an open invitation, circulated on the Internet. I think that much of the response had to do with the time and place. Athens in 2015 seemed like the center of the world. It was a place of possibility when people decided to come. It was the scene of an experiment that had crashed and burned by the time they arrived. There were many presentations on many topics, but this was the major theme on everyone's mind. Sessions dealing with other topics were poorly attended.

The locus of the conference was the iconic law school of the University of Athens, the site of an occupation beginning the uprising that led to the fall of the military junta in 1973. The building showed signs of crisis and cuts. There was no air-conditioning (in sweltering heat), no Wi-Fi, no toilet paper. However, life on the left has rarely been luxurious, and I have attended gatherings in worse conditions.

There was a buzz as participants gathered for the first session. I encountered Aristides Baltas as he was on his way in to address this session in his role as minister of education, culture, and religious affairs. We embraced and looked at each other intently and sorrowfully as I asked, "How has it come to this?" He held my gaze and then gave a shrug of helplessness. In his speech opening the conference, he justified the agreement in terms of a tension between an ethic of conviction and an ethic of possibility and responsibility. It was necessary, he argued, to sacrifice principles for the sake of the nation. If they hadn't signed it, the economy would have collapsed and there would be no money in the banks and no water on the islands. He admitted they had underestimated the force that would be exerted against them, but they were told that the "game is over" and they had to agree.

After the welcoming speeches from the conference organizers, the dean of the faculty, and the minister for education, there followed a debate on socialist strategy. The first speaker, Paul Mason, high-profile British journalist with a left past, opened dramatically: "Welcome to Stalingrad." In response to my tweet recounting this came a comment identifying the obvious flaw in the analogy: the Red Army didn't surrender at Stalingrad. What have we learned? Mason asked. That there is no democracy in the Eurozone and that debt is violence, he answered. What is the answer? he then asked. Not socialism, he answered. From there, he outlined the argument of his new book *PostCapitalism*.[1] Through technological automation, with labor time less necessary and the price mechanism collapsing, networks of connected individuals can liberate themselves. I did not find this convincing. It seemed to me like a puff of smoke. It was as if materiality was evaporating. Tariq Ali, the next speaker, apparently thought so too, as he began by noting that industrial production hadn't disappeared, although it had been offloaded to Asia. Turning to recent events, Ali stated that the referendum victory was a shock to the European elite and Syriza's subsequent capitulation was a betrayal of the 61 percent who voted no. There was a big clap from the audience at the mention of the Syriza MPs who voted no. He stated that the second Irish referendum on the Lisbon treaty should have been the signal for all of Europe to realize what the EU had become. (On two occasions, EU treaties were rejected by referendums in Ireland and were put to the electorate again until the results were reversed. This happened in 2001, 2002, 2008, and 2009.)

Everyone was in the mood for a good informal discussion of all this over lunch. By the time a big international group was herded together and settled into an excellent cooperative restaurant and food was being served, I had to jump up to return to speak at the next session. I got a fine introduction from Michalis Spourdalakis, dean of the faculty, who recounted a conversation we had several years ago, when he remarked that it was time for a new generation to take over and I argued that this was still our time and we still had much to offer, especially a longer and deeper perspective. He also recounted our conversation that morning about being part of the left being teargassed the night before by a government of the left.

In my paper, which I delivered with sweat streaming off me, I attempted to address the current conjuncture within a larger framework. It was called "Ghosts of Alternatives Past." I asked:

> What echoes and shadows of left experiments of the past haunt us as we embark on a new era opened by the formation of a radical left government in Greece? What is the plot of the longer story in which this new episode is embedded? How has the weight of the wider world, the power of the global system, borne down upon attempts to move from capitalism to socialism, whether in rupturalist projects, stemming from the October Revolution, or more protracted programmes of

transformation, such as those set out by the ANC in South Africa in 1994 and by Syriza in Greece in 2015? What are the dynamics of attempting to forge an alternative in the face of the hegemony of there-is-no-alternative? How to make history in conditions not of our making? How, with so much going for it, nationally and internationally, has the ANC failed to achieve, or even approximate, the society that those who fought and died for it set out to achieve? How could Syriza, in the face of far more formidable obstacles, advance both its immediate programme and a new path toward socialism?[2]

At the end, I addressed the position argued by Aristides that morning, dissenting from it in philosophical and political terms.

Michalis thought my talk was too pessimistic. He said that we should think in terms of a marathon and not consider the race to be finished yet. He asked if I was free to talk further. We went down to his office and talked for several hours. As with many Syriza members, he was struggling to deal with what had happened. He agreed that there was massive opposition to the agreement, both in the society and in the party. If it were not for the liquidity issue, which had frightened some into voting yes, it would have been 80 percent voting no in the referendum. As to the 109 of the central committee, there were others who would have signed if asked. Nevertheless, he still thought that there was scope for Syriza to be a left government, despite the agreement, in connecting with the solidarity networks on food distribution and health care. He wanted the party to stay together. He was against pressuring the MPs who voted no to resign. I asked him how he would have voted if he had been an MP. He responded that he would have voted present, which was what some MPs of the 53+ group (the left of mainstream Syriza) did in parliament the previous night, unlike the Left Platform, who voted no.

I pulled myself away from this stimulating conversation after two hours or so, although I was finding it more illuminating than listening to conference papers. However, I wanted to hear Stathis Kouvelakis and was disappointed that he did not appear. Instead I listened, or tried to listen, to other speakers, but their words did not connect with the current conjuncture as I was experiencing and processing it. All through the conference I was conscious of the difference between left academics and left activists (who might also be academics). Not for the first time was I aware of this disparity. I had long ago adopted a participational theory of truth and believed that activism was epistemologically important in how I think and write. It is not only a matter of knowing things we would not know otherwise, but it is a way of knowing what cannot be known in another way. There is a way of speaking and writing about political subjectivity, about concepts such as the people, the movement or the party that just does not have traction with those who have a more concrete experience of them. That way prevailed at this session.

The absence of Syriza speakers was a matter of disappointment to many participants. Several who were scheduled, such as Stathis Kouvelakis and Yiannis Milios, didn't come, presumably because they were coming to terms with what had happened in a way that wasn't compatible with speaking at a conference. However, others, such as Stelios Elliniadis and Costas Lapavitsas, who weren't scheduled to speak, did so. The engagement they brought to it was much appreciated.

The next day these tensions played out in the most dramatic session of the conference. Several hundred people were packed into an overflowing hall that was unbearably hot. The session was provocatively titled "The End of the World As We Know It," which did not fit at all with the academic discourse that floated above the pressing questions filling the room. It started with Leo Panitch speaking about restraint, reform, and revolution. I missed this part, because I was being interviewed for a documentary at the same time, but I had already heard him speak on the same topic two months earlier. Leo was prominent during these days in defending Syriza for an international audience. He was much respected for his work in political economy, but coming under caustic criticism for his stance on Syriza. Next was Costas Douzinas, professor of law at Birkbeck. I came in toward the end as he was speaking about Hegel and philosophy and theology and whatever in a way with which I failed to engage, even though I am a professional philosopher. Then there was Stathis Gourgouris, professor of literature at Columbia, who delivered a postmodernist paper that seemed neither logically coherent nor empirically grounded. There were several variations of the sentence "Democracy is groundless," which made no sense to me. All three speakers, in more or less convoluted ways, were justifying the strategy that Syriza had pursued and the agreement that Tsipras had signed. Leo at least was straightforward, but the others were far from that. On and on. At one stage, a woman in the audience spoke out and implored, "Please stop talking." Various members of the audience weighed in and spoke for and against his continuing. Sam Gindin, Leo's co-author, was an indecisive and ineffectual chair. Gourgouris continued awkwardly, but the audience was restive and he stopped abruptly.

Finally came Costas Lapavitsas, Syriza MP and economic theorist. The atmosphere was tense. Cutting through the obfuscation of the previous two speakers, he declared, "Sometimes reality is simply what it appears to be." He spoke clearly and directly and addressed what everyone wanted addressed. Everyone, no matter on which side of the debate seething under the surface, seemed to forget how tired, hot, and bored they were and sprang to life. Lapavitsas, who had voted no in parliament the night before, asserted that the deal was a disastrous capitulation. He outlined its recessionary effects and set out an alternative path, involving exiting the Eurozone, with clarity and determination. The euro was a class issue, he insisted, and the EU was reified ideology in its institutions and practices. There were calls from the audience for him to resign his seat. He addressed the code of conduct for MPs. He argued that his mandate was from the people of Imathia, who elected him standing on the party program, and from the people who voted no in the referendum. The atmosphere was electric. The effect was cathartic. Animated interventions from the floor tumbled over each other, whether recognized by the chair or not. Sparks were flying. Douzinas responded in a hostile way, claiming that the position of Lapavitsas would be the longest suicide note in the history of the left. Panitch admitted that much of what Lapavitsas said was correct, but argued that the balance of forces was not ripe for it, because it would split Syriza (as if it wasn't the agreement already splitting Syriza). The video captured much of what transpired, but you had to be there to get the full tension of the scene.[3]

A troubling dimension of this was that it set up a philosophy (nonsense) versus economics (sense) mood, which was very frustrating to me as a philosopher. I couldn't help thinking that someone could have brought philosophy to bear in a better way, a more coherent and more grounded way. I certainly could have. The fact that it was an all-male panel did not escape attention and comment either.

In a subsequent reflection on this conference, Bue Rübner Hansen compared it to the Idea of Communism conference in London in 2009, where, he observed, the absence of political economy was astonishing. He thought that political economy had taken over from philosophy as the leading discipline of the left since then. He noted that such a shift was clearly, even violently, displayed when the audience attempted to cut two philosophers short in order to hear Costas Lapavitsas speak. He believed that this meant that theory had become more profoundly involved with practical problems, with many more presentations attempting to provide concrete analyses of concrete situations now than in 2009.[4]

Indeed a number of presentations I attended did involve concrete analyses of concrete situations. I learned a lot about the strategy and sensibility of the left in various countries, especially Spain, Portugal, Italy, Slovenia, Croatia, and Bulgaria. I listened carefully to many younger left intellectuals. Some saw themselves in continuity with the left of the past, but others did not, even renouncing such continuity. Some gave voice to a generational sensibility. Paolo Gerbaudo, lecturer in digital culture and society in London, announced that populism is the zeitgeist now. Younger radicals born after 1989 are into unity of the people against corrupt leaders and not into class struggle. Others too articulated this appeal to the people, to democracy, to horizontality, not to ideology, not to class analysis, not to mode of production. One slogan articulated in Ireland in recent times is: "It's not about right and left. It's about right and wrong." Much of this is coming from Podemos these days and the Podemos voices at this conference were vigorously sounding this note. However, it is not new. I have heard variations on this since the 1960s, and I have come to believe that retreat from class analysis, from grounding in political economy, is retreat from reality, because there is no life disconnected from the mode of production, there are no classless people, there is no real democracy in class society. I might be old, and the younger generation might think this is old-fashioned, but that doesn't mean that this is wrong.

Another theme underlined for me by this conference and the wider discussion going on at this time, although I have been aware of it for quite a while now, was how much of the intellectual left, even the activist strand of it, was formed more by postmodernism than Marxism. It accounted for much of the obfuscating discourse surrounding Syriza's capitulation. Žižek asked: What space did the Syriza government have to maneuver when reduced to enacting the politics of its enemy? Should it step down rather than enact a policy that was directly opposed to its program? He answered no. Addressing the transition from the no of the referendum to the yes of the memorandum, he deployed linguistic sorcery to twist reality into its opposite: "Syriza engaged in a Herculean labor of enacting the shift from syntagm to paradigm, in the long and patient work of translating the energy of rebellion into concrete measures that would change everyday life of the people." (Yes, they would change their lives for the worse, while implementing the very thing they had rejected.) True courage, he insisted, was to do the very thing you were opposed to doing.[5] A number of other texts by Syriza-aligned intellectuals published during this period strained logic and evidence to justify the unjustifiable. Athena Athanasiou, professor of social anthopology at Panteion University, defended decisions in terms of "the performative dialectics of defeat."[6]

No was yes. Wrong was right. Right was left. Capitulation was courage. It was one thing to allude to a gun to the head and to admit to defeat, but another to turn around and to claim a great moral victory and to aim the attack on anyone who said otherwise. There was much violation of elementary logic, evasion of empirical evidence, and denial of ethical culpability. There was desperate clinging to contradiction. Yes and no to the same proposition, to the same process of expropriation, are not compatible logically, empirically, or morally. The point about conceptualizing contradiction is not to affirm it and to wallow in it, but to struggle to resolve it, to transcend it, to create a new synthesis from it. As if intensified economic expropriation and political capitulation were not bad enough already, they added intellectual obfuscation and moral degradation to the dreadful reality unfolding. The citation of Hegel and scorn for the "beautiful soul" to attack anyone who chose to act consistently with their convictions struck me as especially sordid. I was ashamed of comrades doing that. You cannot build a left when you trash the very basis of our beliefs. It came from a mixture of blatant opportunism, genuine confusion, psychological distress, and postmodernist sophistry.

By no means could it all be blamed on postmodernism, but it facilitated it and added a veneer of verbal sophistication to it. Although I have often engaged in a Marxist critique of postmodernism, I know that there is also a history within Marxism of using the concept of dialectics to justify blatant contradictions. In the sudden and sharp twists and turns of the Comintern line, anyone who alluded to the incompatibility of the line one day with that of the day before was told, "You're not thinking dialectically, comrade." At one point in a plenary session in Athens, someone from the floor said, "We don't care about reality," and to my astonishment, or maybe not, a number of people clapped.

Nevertheless, there was much clear and grounded talk. At one plenary, Stelios Elliniadis of the Syriza central committee spoke very honestly, addressing the question of what went wrong. He admitted that Syriza was unprepared, either to be in the euro or out of it. It had underestimated the enemy. It had evaded democratic processes in the party. It had been shocked by the will of people in the referendum result. The next day I spoke to him at the entrance to the conference, and we pursued these problems in more detail. A small group gathered around, and I thought it a fitting contemporary expression of the sort of dialogues I imagined in ancient Athens. Much of the discussion outside of formal sessions was especially rich, as it is with most conferences. I met various people I knew only from social media or met for first time there and connected with on social media since then.

I was picking up via social media that various leftists were concluding that the strategy of broad left parties participating in multiparty elections had been discredited, and that their own position—the vanguard party, insurrectionism, anarchism, or whatever—had been vindicated. However, most participants in this conference believed that this strategy was still the way to go. I still did. One Brazilian speaking from the floor said that Latin America had been at it for a while and broad left parties always go bad. Most, however, still held out hope and wanted to probe the state of play with Podemos, Sinn Féin, Bloco de Esquerda, Die Linke, etc., as well as whatever formation might emerge from the left of Syriza. Someone proposed a new international. At a very rich session on European left parties, someone from the floor put the question to Podemos and Sinn Féin: Which Syriza do you support? He didn't get a clear answer. It was still one party, but it wasn't difficult to see that its days were numbered. During the conference, there came the news of a cabinet reshuffle: Lafazanis, Isychos, Stratoulis, Chountis, all of Left Platform and all voting no, were out, as was Valavani, who had already resigned.

There was substantial Irish participation in this conference. Ronan Burtenshaw had organized a number of panels on Ireland, with excellent speakers. I chaired a panel on republicanism where Dan Finn, Eoin O Broin, and Bernadette Devlin McAliskey spoke. It was of high quality, although only a dozen or so attended, only one from outside Ireland. Some other Irish panels were also poorly attended, because people were preoccupied with other matters. Then a decision was taken to withdraw these panels and amalgamate papers into bigger sessions. The conference schedule was in any case a somewhat chaotic and ever-evolving affair, so I eventually went to the biggest hall and took pot luck, although I didn't always know who was speaking. I was to speak on a panel on the prospects for left government in

Ireland, but withdrew, because panels were getting too big. Eoin O Broin of Sinn Féin did present on this topic in a session on European left parties, which was good, because there was great interest in Sinn Féin among the European left. He made the point that Ireland had never had a left government, but it might in the election after next. He asked the question: If a government comes up against what the EU will allow, what then? A very relevant question that week in Greece and the answer wasn't inspiring.

Over the course of these four days, I had many conversations on the margins of the conference and over lunch and dinner. It was good both to meet new people and to interact with Irish people, such as Richard Boyd Barrett, Eoin O Broin, and Bernadette Devlin, in that particular way you do when abroad—more relaxed, more far ranging, more humorous, especially in the tavernas at night, aided by the flow of wine. One night in Exarchia extended into the wee hours. I had never seen Exarchia Square so teeming with life as it was that morning at 2:30 a.m., when I finally left.

During these days, I also participated in the making of a documentary called *The Birdcage*. I was told that it was inspired by the Wim Wenders 1982 documentary *Room 666*, which asked twenty directors of the time how television was going to affect cinema. Directors Lindsey Aliksanyan and Manos Cížek were asking prominent thinkers and politicians of our time how economics was affecting politics today. I arrived at an address in Kolonaki, which turned out to be a block of flats. I was taken upstairs and put into a room with lots of cameras, a chair, a birdcage, bookcases, etc. I sat on the chair where all the cameras were pointing and waited for someone to come in to interview me. After a few minutes when nobody came, I remembered something about an envelope. I opened it and there was a question about the relationship between economics and politics. I then spoke about the material basis of existence, distribution of wealth, the struggle for redistribution of wealth. At one point, I said I didn't even keep up the struggle to win anymore, but not to let the system go uncontested. At one point, I was on the verge of tears, which surprised me. (The trailer for this film is here.[7])

Kostas Skordoulis met me after this appointment, and we went to a café in Kolonaki to catch up with each other. He filled me in on debates within Antarsya about current developments, especially about how to respond to a possible split within Syriza. He had been occupied for the past few days with the consequences of the arrests in Syntagma Square on the night we were attacked by riot police. Several of his young comrades had been arrested, beaten, and charged. He asked me to sign a petition about it, which I did.

After the Conference

After the conference, I still had another nine days before my flight home. I had originally intended to spend some of this by the sea, perhaps taking the hydrofoil to Aegina, but I couldn't pull myself away from Athens. I spent most of this time having long talks with Syriza activists about what was happening to Syriza. First I spent a solitary day reading, writing, reflecting, and walking by the sea. In the evening, I took a tram from Syntagma to Vouli and walked back to Faliro. Lots of people were swimming in the warm evening. I looked at the wealthy houses with the best views along the seafront and the yachts along the harbor. I thought about how little had been done to challenge the power of the oligarchs. I saw the sunset through barbed wire outside a piece of prime property that blocked the public's access to the sea. Back in Syntagma, I photographed the scene at night and tweeted, "Goliath won. David lies bleeding. What next?"

The next day I went to see Costas Isychos, who had been alternate minister for defense until a few days ago. We embraced warmly, almost the way you do at a funeral, and went to the parliamentary offices. It was the only building where I went through any security check. I had to hand over my passport for the duration of the visit and give details of my hotel and mobile number. Costas had lost his ministerial office but hadn't yet settled into a new office as an MP, so he was occupying one temporarily, presumably one vacated by someone who voted yes in parliament and had now been promoted. He said that life as a minister was like being in another galaxy, mixing with generals, having bodyguards to protect him, limos to take him anywhere, an open bank account that he never used. It was obvious that he could live without that, but living without the Syriza he did so much to build was something else.

He was still in shock over the events of the past few days. It was hard to comprehend, hard to cope, he confessed. "How could we go from no to yes in one day?" he was still asking. Tsipras said he had no choice, but there were choices all along the way. Tsipras was behaving like someone in the throes of extreme psychological warfare, both from the troika and from the right wing of Syriza. He listened to Yannis Dragasakis and Nikos Pappas and shut out other comrades. This was a violation of congress decisions, of the electoral program, even of national law, whereby referenda results are legally binding. It was social genocide. It was a suicidal mission for the left. Now there was a 977-page law to be voted on immediately as a single act, without even time to read it. These were the tactics of previous memoranda under previous governments of which Syriza was so critical. He said that he was being vilified in the media, along with Lafazanis, Stratoulis, and Valavani. Journalists were searching for bank accounts in Argentina for him. Tsipras was still popular, but his downfall was inevitable. There was no space for another social democratic party. The government had alienated itself from the people. There would be evictions and deprivation. The Left Platform was trying to work out a strategy to save what was left and to represent the 61 percent.

It was musical offices with my next visit too. I arrived at the ministry of development in Kanigos Square, where junkies were shooting up outside the door and there was no security inside the door. I found my way to the office of the general secretary of industry, Yiannis Tolios. He told me that he would be soon vacating his office, because he had just resigned his position, because of the signing of the agreement and the removal of the minister, Panagiotis Lafazanis. "What shall we do?" he asked rhetorically, shaking his head with bewilderment bordering on disbelief. "We have not fulfilled our promises. We knew it would be difficult, but not like this." Then he spoke with determination: "I was in prison for these ideas, and I'm not going to take another path to stay in office." He insisted that there was a plan B, clear in its direction, even if every detail was not worked out. He outlined the basics of it for me. It was along the same lines as outlined by Lapavitsas.

Later I did a radio interview with Stelios Elliniadis on Sto Kokkino. I spoke of my political history, my relation to Synaspismos and then Syriza, and my response to the recent turn of events. I spoke honestly and critically. At this stage, there was still space on the Syriza radio station for a critical discourse about Syriza.

From there, I went to the Nicos Poulantzas Institute, not far away. I spoke to the director, Haris Golemis, who seemed quite stressed. I asked what he thought of the current situation. He said to ask him a more specific question. I asked him how he would have voted in the parliament last week if he had been an MP. He answered that he would have voted yes and then resigned. He could not vote against a left government, but found it hard to accept the terms of the agreement. It was a choice for the government of either suicide or execution. He admitted that the strategy of doing whatever was necessary to stay in the Eurozone was defeated and that it was wrong not to have a plan B. They would need a viable plan now, possibly Grexit. He insisted that Tsipras didn't turn from left to right overnight. He had just come from meeting with Tsipras and advised him not to move against the left. There was need for a congress and the priority should be a new plan. He thought that I should also speak to younger colleagues in the institute and gathered them around a table. He told them to speak freely to me, which they did. They were Sotiris Koskoletos, Stelios Foteinopoulos, Aimilia Koukouma, Maria Chaidopoulou-Vrychea, Vagia Lysikatou, and Aliki Kossyfologou. They were struggling to come to terms with such an unexpected scenario. All saw Euclid Tsakalotos as a really tragic figure and regarded him highly. They were somewhat negative about the Left Platform, saying that Lafazanis was stuck in Soviet times and Lapavitsas was technocratic. All emphasized that opposition to the memorandum was not confined to the Left Platform. One said that she felt homeless.

Then I ran into Fergus O'Hare from Belfast, who had also been at Sto Kokkino, and we had dinner in Monastiraki, discussing our impressions from all the people we were meeting. After dinner, we headed for Syntagma for a trade union rally against the 977-page bill that was being rammed through parliament that night at the behest of the colonizing powers. The riot police were a menacing presence. The government closed the central metro stations, just as the previous government had done to restrict the coming and going of protesters. I was once again impressed by the way PAME mobilized on the streets. I was interested to find that someone I knew who had just been expelled from the KKE was still marching with PAME. We agreed to meet the next night and talk about it. After a few hours, I went back to my hotel and watched the debate in parliament on television. Speech after speech from Syriza ministers and parliamentarians analyzed how awful the bill was and how they must vote for it anyway. I exchanged texts with a minister inside (on the yes side) about meeting. I was up until 4:40 a.m., until the final vote was taken. This time it was 36 Syriza MPs not voting yes: 31 voted no, 5 voted present. Last week it was 39. The Left Platform held firm. Varoufakis voted yes.

Even though I was up until all hours some nights, moving into the early hours, I am an early riser by nature and not able to sleep in the mornings, despite feeling very tired. The early swim in the small pool on the rooftop of the hotel with a view of the Acropolis always revived me for the day ahead. I did take some mornings to catch up on reading and writing, and especially to engage on social media in interpreting what was happening. That evening I met my communist contact for dinner. We spoke for many hours in a garden taverna in Exarchia, about philosophy and politics and about how to be a communist without a communist party, since I had some experience of this. His hearing at the party's office had gone as he had expected, but he was still finding it strange not to be a member of the KKE. His relations with comrades from his own branch were still quite good.

Occasionally I met up with other comrades from the conference, including quite a few from Ireland who were still in Athens. I had lunch one day with Ronan Burtenshaw and Catarina Principe from Portugal. They asked me to arrange interviews for them with Aristides Baltas and Costas Isychos, which I did. Afterward we met others at a demonstration in Syntagma commemorating the deaths in Suruc at the hands of ISIS. Some of them had been making good contacts with the solidarity movements and were coordinating international efforts at addressing the refugee crisis building throughout this summer. I admired their efforts. Caoimhe Butterly would soon be back in Greece assisting refugees in Lesvos. I spoke with Mariya Ivancheva, a Bulgarian postdoc working in Ireland, about Left East and her plans for the rest of the summer pursuing that.

I, however, was focusing on the Greek left, especially on all the different positions within Syriza. There were stories about Syriza members disappearing from their jobs, returning to their home villages, shopping in different districts, adopting multiple measures to avoid being asked to explain and defend to others what they could not explain or defend to themselves. I spoke with Stathis Kouvelakis, who said that Syriza as we knew it was dead. How it would be buried was not yet clear. What was sure, he insisted, was that something new must come in its place. Someone had to represent the 62 percent. He had been speaking to young building workers doing some work on his house during the week, and they were all for *oxi* and wondering what happened. He invited me to a Left Platform rally on Monday night.

Another day I spent many hours with Nikos Potamitis exploring working-class Athens: Egaleo (where he grew up), Peristeri, Nikaia, Korydallos, Keratsini, Perama. There was much personal memory, social history, and current politics in our discussions in various locations. The coordinating committee of Syriza in Zakynthos were all against the signing of the agreement and called on their MP to vote no in parliament. Despite this, Stavros Kontonis voted yes. Nikos was furious. On the radio, Nikos asked him: Was there anything that Tsipras would not sign and for which he would not vote?

In contrast to the Left Platform position was that of the 53+ group, named for a letter signed by fifty-three central committee members in 2014 contesting the concentration of power around the leader and the lack of party democracy. The 53+ group was the left wing of the party's mainstream. Michalis Spourdalakis was in this group. He invited me to meet him in his dean's office at 3:00 p.m. and take me to see Aristides Baltas at 4:00 p.m. We had good discussions coming and going. I detected a shift in his attitude to the Left Platform and even to Grexit. I wondered if the 53+ might be moving closer to LP. The 53+ were somewhat in disarray. It was not clear if they would all go in the same direction at this juncture. Michalis aired many of his misgivings about decisions that were taken and his worries about how events were unfolding. He said that they were like a fish on a hook and they needed to get off it. He was not convinced that a memorandum would actually be agreed. He was wary of a Perónist development. He was also quite critical of the Nicos Poulantzas Institute for failing to provide political education within Syriza and flying around doing international seminars instead.

When we arrived at the ministry in Marousi and I met Aristides again, we held each other for longer than usual. He said, "Don't worry. We will win." I asked how. He replied, "Dual power." I told him that he sounded like a Trostskyist. No, he said. It was about a parallel network of solidarity supported by key government measures. "We are still alive," which meant, he insisted, that there was still hope. About the agreement, he justified signing it, citing Kronstadt, Brest-Litovsk, and Bukharin confessing at the Moscow trials. I argued that Bukharin's action wasn't for the good of the party, the state, or society. As to those voting no or protesting, he asked, "Do you want to save your soul or the country?" He saw it as a necessary evil. "Okay, we signed it, but now how do we get out of it?" His position was that there were still things they could do within the conditions imposed by creditors. He cited new education legislation, government help to solidarity networks, crowd-funding to pay the debts of the people who would be evicted. "Politics is managing the possible. Left politics is enlarging the possible." Has Syriza done that or the opposite? I asked. Both Aristides and Michalis stressed that they wanted to keep the party together, to keep the left in the party with space for credible left positions, and to keep a left government in power. We all departed together after 6:00 p.m., and Aristides went off with his bodyguards. Before he did, we embraced warmly. Referring to all the rumors circulating in Athens about who should or shouldn't be arrested for treason, he joked, "Maybe next time you will be visiting me in prison." I said, "Maybe I'm doing that now."

I was struggling to see the actions by comrades in the best light without abandoning my own critical faculties and moral compass. I was thinking of this more in terms of brutal power, intense pressure, and humiliating defeat than in terms of betrayal, selling out, or breaking bad. However, I could not accept the arguments being put forward by Aristides Baltas, as well as by Alexis Tsipras and others in Syriza. It was a familiar line of argument to me, although I did not expect it from them. I do not believe that you can do bad to do good. I cannot see how agreeing to further reductions in incomes and public services as well as massive expropriation of public property can be interpreted as saving the nation. If it were a matter of keeping the state from collapsing and supplying water to the islands, the right managed to do that. More was demanded of the left. They referred constantly and sincerely to their sense of responsibility. However, how responsible was it to go to the brink, with so much at stake for so many people, with no fallback position, no plan B? How could they have so much trust in the goodwill of their creditors, when they were Marxists, who had the strongest of reasons to believe they were dealing, not with persons of goodwill, but with hostile class interests? This was the truth that should have shaped their strategies, even if it might have been necessary to speak the language of international diplomacy within certain boundaries on certain occasions. How could they justify administering further expropriation?

I am of the left who wants to believe in the possibility of left government. I do not believe, as some argue, that left government is a contradiction in terms. Unlike some younger activists, this was familiar territory to me. I have been aligned with left parties in government before this. I was a member of a communist party, the Communist Party of Ireland, and a running theme of life in the communist movement was how to evaluate "actually existing socialism," particularly the great USSR. I strove to defend what was defensible without ceding my judgment to the party line, while risking being called anti-Soviet every time I articulated a critical thought or narrated an experience that did not fit the standard narrative from my times in Eastern Europe, when I probed further in my adventures abroad or in my research than was the norm. I was also a member of a social democratic party, the Labour Party in Ireland, in government and of the left within it that opposed coalition government with parties to the right of it in one period and supported that in another period. During sabbaticals in South Africa, I belonged to the ANC and the SACP, and mixed with members of government and parliament, as well as forces breaking away from them in critical opposition.

I was the longest and strongest supporter of Syriza in Ireland. I had relationships with comrades in Antarsya and KKE, but I aligned with Syriza. I didn't want to let go of the Syriza that stood as a horizon of political hope and a locus of strong personal bonds. I had good relationships across the spectrum of Syriza, which was no problem until now. During this interval, I felt pulled between them as they pulled away from each other. Not that anyone overtly exerted any pressure on me, but it played out within myself. I could only deal with it by looking at the facts and weighing the arguments, while respecting the good faith and sincere struggle of those making contrary arguments. It did not stop me from taking sides.

On my last weekend, I spent a lot of time walking around Athens and Piraeus thinking about all that was happening and would yet happen. Although the primary reality of my time in Athens was intense political discussion and reflection on the trauma being experienced by those I knew best, I wandered occasionally into tourist Greece and saw that it was possible to come and go and notice nothing of this tragedy. There was still blazing sun, warm sea, striking scenery, good food and drink, and everything you could want in a holiday. Despite economic desperation, there was still relatively little crime against tourists, although I had the misfortune of being a victim of such crime myself. I was glad that the country was getting much needed income from tourism. Yet I resented those who came and consumed and didn't concern themselves with the crisis. I spoke to one person who observed, on the basis on a few days' experience last spring, that things didn't seem so bad. "Not so bad for oligarchs anyway," I observed acidly. When he replied, "Oligarchs are people too. Don't they deserve to be happy?" I lost my temper totally.

On my last day, I ran into a philosophy teacher and student. I had met Thodoris Dimitrakos during my previous visits, when he was finding work but struggling to make ends meet. Now he had three jobs and was earning €800 a month, which he thought was doing well. Such is Greece now. I asked if he had attended the World Congress of Philosophy when it was in Athens, and we traded stories on world congresses of philosophy past and present.

On my final evening, I met comrades from many nations in a café in Exarchia. Conversations took many turns, but they kept coming back to what would happen next in Greece. Unexpectedly, however, I had a pleasant chat with Nantina Vgontzas, who is from Pennsylvania, about the Philadelphia left of the early 1970s. Stathis Kouvelakis spoke to me about his research interrogating the concept of Western Marxism and indicated that my book was what he needed to read on Soviet and Comintern philosophy. We all then left together and proceeded first to Pedion Areos, a park in which refugees, primarily from Syria, were camping, and where Stathis delivered a suitcase full of supplies that had been requested.

From there, we moved on to Panellinion Stadium, where a Left Platform rally was beginning. The sweltering stadium was already packed—two thousand or so, with standing room only. There was a big welcome for Manolis Glezos when he arrived. The theme was "Oxi to the End." The main speech was by Panagiotis Lafazanis. I sat with the younger crowd in the bleachers, where Nantina did a bit of translating for those around her. Later I sat below with Costas Isychos. He notified the chair to announce my presence from the podium. Manolis Glezos spoke and was sharply critical of Tsipras and the agreement. The rally ended with song. Afterward, I met Panagiotis Lafazanis, Petros Papaconstantinou, Yiannis Milios, and Costas Lapavitsas. I had a brief but meaningful conversation with Lapavitsas about the relationship between philosophy and economics. "I take philosophy very seriously," he said, but we both agreed that the philosophy at that session did not make the best case for it. I also spoke with Despina Charalampidou, an MP from Thessaloniki who had spoken in Dublin in 2012. I told her she was still remembered for that and congratulated her on voting no. I also spoke to Yiannis Tolios and Stelios Elliniadis to say good-bye until next time.

The next day, I checked out of my hotel, took the metro to the airport, and flew home to Dublin. It seemed as if I had been in Greece for ages. So much had happened. One day during the second week, Ronan Burtenshaw had asked, "Remember that period just after the capitulation?" I looked askance and pointed out that it was only last week. "Time is so compressed these days," he replied, invoking a mantra being invoked frequently by others. Yes, it was: both compressed and consequential. I thought of how dramatic life in Athens was, more tragic than comic but always alluring. No accident that so many such words originated there.

Back in Dublin on July 29, I was making the transition in more ways than one, not least to the temperature. It was 37 degrees (nearly 100 degrees Fahrenheit) in Athens and 13 degrees (55 Fahrenheit) in Dublin. Mostly I missed being close to the action of the major story in which I was immersed. Still I followed it closely, especially in the ways that the Internet makes possible these days.

I followed the Alexis Tsipras interview on Sto Kokkino that day via the Twitter feed. I found many aspects of it disturbing. There were many contradictions and non sequiturs. Most upsetting was his attack on the left, on people who had built Syriza and given so much to bring a left government into being. He asserted that their dissent was premeditated. Being in Athens during this period and knowing close up how shocked these people were and how difficult it was for them to vote no in parliament, to sign the central committee letter or to assert their opposition in many ways, I thought this was not true. They were right to believe that Syriza was not just his, but theirs. The commitments that they had made to the people had been violated by his actions. Were all these active, intelligent people to follow him wherever he led, no matter what? No.

Another aspect of this interview that grated on me was his comment that fifteen of the people arrested at the July 15 protest in front of parliament were foreigners. He pointed out that they were visitors to Athens, not migrants, and said that he didn't care if they were from international solidarity movements. The English translation of this interview published by Transform omitted the remarks on foreigners. No party in my memory (with the possible exception of the ANC) has requested and received so much in international solidarity. Some of us who have given a lot to this were among the protesters who were teargassed that night by a government we had so ardently supported. So, I asked on social media, were foreigners only to act on their requests but not to have an opinion on what transpired? No. This got a lot of likes, comments, and shares. Some commenters accused Tsipras of being corrupt, mad, or a megalomaniac. It was not that somebody got to him or bought him off, I replied. It was the whole system that bore down upon him, and he was put under almost unendurable pressure. None of us have ever been subjected to anything like that. I still thought of him as a decent man and a tragic figure. Another noteworthy aspect of this interview was that he made mention of class struggle, which was rare for him. That night the third bill of prior measures was pushed through parliament.

This day was also the ninetieth birthday of the internationally esteemed composer Mikis Theodorakis, who took the occasion to issue an appeal, along with other esteemed figures in Greece, to defend the no of the referendum, to repudiate the memorandum and resist the enslavement of the Greek people.

On the next day, July 30, there was finally a central committee meeting, which went on for fourteen hours. Seventeen members resigned before it. The 53+ sided with Tsipras, but only on the basis of an agreement to hold an emergency party congress in September. Zoe Konstantopoulou pinpointed this as the day when she realized what a complete betrayal had happened, when Alexis Tsipras looked for a blank check for capitulation and bitterly attacked those who opposed.[8]

After that, negotiations on the terms of the third memorandum proceeded, and the creditors let it be known that they were finding that the Greek negotiators, led by Euclid Tsakalotos, were being extremely cooperative. Tsipras expressed his confidence that all was going well. I remembered, ironically and sadly, that conference in Dublin the previous year, when both Tsipras and Tsakalotos spoke of challenging troika rule. Now they were implementing it. Greece was colonized and they were the colonial administrators.

By August 13, the negotiations were concluded and the deal was rammed through the parliament in another all-night session; I watched via web television until I dropped sometime after midnight. When I got up the next day at 6:00 a.m.—8:00 a.m. in Greece—it was still going. When the vote was finally taken, the memorandum passed, with 222 voting yes, 64 voting no, and 11 voting present. Of Syriza MPs, 32 voted no and 11 voted present. Varoufakis voted no this time. It was Syriza, Anel, ND, Pasok, and Potami on the yes side and Syriza, KKE, and XA on the no side.

Another Election

The next task, as Tsipras and his circle saw it, was to purge parliament and party of the no voters in their own ranks. On August 20, in violation of their undertaking to hold an emergency party congress in September, they called a general election instead, as a means of accomplishing this. It was also to get an *ex post facto* mandate for the memorandum that had already been negotiated and passed through parliament in violation of the mandates of the previous election and the recent referendum.

The Syriza dissenters, which went far beyond the Left Platform and any organized groupings, had to decide what to do. They had been deprived of the possibility of fighting for their positions within Syriza. They could not go into an election looking for a mandate for what Syriza had done in violation of all their principles and promises. The

Left Platform responded most immediately and decisively. On August 21, twenty-five Syriza MPs left Syriza and formed a new parliamentary group called Laïkí Enótita (Popular Unity). LAE became the third largest party in parliament. After the government had resigned, ND demanded a three-day mandate to try to form a government. Then LAE exercised its legal right to do the same, not with any realistic hope of forming a government, but to make its position known and to give the party more time to prepare for an election. The election was then called for September 20.

I spoke to Nikos Potamitis on August 23. He was on a ferry on his way back to Zakynthos after a meeting in Athens. He was going with LAE. He had been in Synaspismos and then in Syriza from the beginning. "We didn't leave Syriza," he insisted, "because Syriza doesn't exist anymore. We are the continuation of what was Syriza." He spoke of the difficulties of starting again. No money, no office, no newspaper, no radio station. LAE didn't even have time to form a party properly. That would come later. Now it was more of a quickly formed coalition to stand in elections as an anti-memorandum front. I asked if he would be standing in the election. He confirmed that he would, although reluctantly, because he never wanted to be a member of parliament and was happy in his work as a doctor, an orthopedic surgeon in the public health system.

On August 24, the general secretary of Syriza, Tasos Koronakis, resigned. He cited the diminution of party democracy and the dominance of the group around Tsipras in taking all important decisions. He particularly objected to Syriza subverting the decision to hold a party congress by September and calling for elections to override this. In the next days, various MPs, including Varoufakis and some of the 53+, announced that they would not be standing for Syriza in the coming election. A further fifty-three members of the central committee resigned, including MEP Nikos Chountis. News came of resignation after resignation, in many cases the entire coordinating committees of Syriza in certain areas, such as Corinth, Kefalonia, and Paris. Syriza Youth issued a blistering statement and dissolved itself as its general secretary and the majority of its council resigned. Among

the thousands who resigned was Theodoros Kollias, speech writer for
Tsipras, criticizing the government's pattern of ignoring or overrid-
ing the party but also citing the bland, classless rhetoric of Tsipras's
speeches. Sofia Sakorafa, MEP, declared her independence of Syriza,
bringing the number of its MEPs down from six to four.

I was prepared for defeat, but not for such a debacle. I was not
expecting either the desperate capitulation to the troika or the reckless destruction of Syriza. So long to build and so quickly destroyed.
"Hope is coming" seemed so long ago and far away. Now I hoped only
for a decent opposition vote. Others here hoped for nothing. There
was no possible election result that offered any immediate alternative.
This was such a loss for the people of Greece and for us all. Being so
old and so long on the left, I'm experienced at defeat, but I still keep
allowing myself to hope it will be otherwise.

On August 27, a caretaker prime minister was sworn in by orthodox
clerics. Vassiliki Thanou-Christophilou, a judge, was the first female
prime minister of Greece. I couldn't take any feminist pleasure in this
and I didn't like the look of her, with her dyed hair and excess makeup
and jewelry. It was said that she was anti-austerity on the basis of her
opposition to the reductions in judges' pay. A caretaker government
was announced. My friend Michalis Spourdalakis appeared and then
disappeared from the list of ministers in this government.

Antarsya met and split over the question of whether to stand in the
election with LAE. The majority decided against it and stood in the
election under its own lists. However, two large sections of Antarsya
joined LAE and stood on its lists.

Then the election campaign was underway. I scrutinized the lists for
names I knew, of which there were many. For Syriza, Alexis Tsipras,
of course, was the candidate for prime minister again. There had been
some doubt about whether Euclid Tsakalotos would stand again, but
his name appeared prominently on the Athens lists. Aristides Baltas
headed the Attica list. Another colleague, who had not been in parliament before, Kostas Gavroglu, appeared on the state list. Costas
Douzinas was on the Piraeus list. For LAE, Manolis Glezos headed the
state list. The Athens lists bore such names as Zoe Konstantopoulou,

Nadia Valavani, Costas Isychos, Dimitris Stratoulis, Stathis Kouvelakis, Panagiotis Sotiris, Yiannis Tolios. Costas Lapavitsas headed the list in Patras and Nikos Potamitis in Zakynthos. Stelios Elliniadis declined to stand for either Syriza or LAE. He was distressed that the election was set up in such a way that the *oxi* front could not receive proper or proportionate expression. LAE embarked on a national election campaign with no money, no office, no infrastructure. However, as Panagiotis Sotiris reflected, "Left politics is all about building a boat while you're already at sea in rough waters."

I was packing to go back to Greece. Before leaving, on August 29, I took part in another Right2Water mobilization in Dublin. There was a big turnout of eighty thousand or so. In contrast to previous demos, there was a striking absence of Greek flags. There were perhaps a dozen scattered around, whereas there were hundreds previously.

On August 30, I flew to Crete. This was an already planned holiday with Sam Nolan in Adelianos Kampos. When I booked it months before, I had no idea that there would be an election on at the time. As it unfolded, I felt restless, being so far from the action in Athens or Zakynthos, where candidates I knew well were standing. I received a message from Nikos asking me if I could come to Zakynthos and accompany him on his campaign there and speak at a meeting. I really wanted to do that, but the logistics of it proved impossible. Nevertheless, I did my best to see how the election campaign was playing out from there. I combined elements of holidaying, especially the daily swim in the sea at sunrise, with discussion of politics at every opportunity I could contrive. I took the local bus into Rethymnon and walked and talked politics there as well.

A tourist could have come and gone without knowing there was an election imminent. It was necessary to probe beneath the surface. People were hesitant to speak at first. A weary sigh was often the first response. So few had any hope. If they did, it had nothing to do with elections. It had to do with emigration. When learning that I was a professor, students asked for advice about studies and employment abroad. A recurring theme on the elections was: Why vote at all? Quite a few, especially the young, who voted for Syriza in January and *oxi* in July, said that they would never vote again. Either because they would never trust any politician or political party again or because they didn't believe that any political force had any power to change anything that mattered to them. Or both. One young woman said that the only thing to do was to consume less. What to do about those who consume lavishly without ever working, while those who work or want to work consume less than they need? I asked. No idea, she said.

I asked all those to whom I spoke if they might vote for LAE. Lack of name recognition was common. When I elaborated and mentioned Lafazanis, Lapavitsas, etc., they knew the names and often replied that it was about drachmas and only drachmas, which they did not want. Some said that they had stayed in Syriza too long and should have offered an alternative sooner. Some saw it only as a choice between Syriza and ND or even as a choice between Tsipras and Meimarakis. Most said that they preferred Tsipras, because he had put up a fight and nothing more was possible.

One evening I attended the inaugural meeting of Laïkí Enótita at the Labor Center in Rethymnon. There was a monument to a militant construction worker outside. Inside the hall, there were pictures on the wall of labor struggles of the past. There were about thirty-five or forty there, more young and middle-aged than old, more male than female. Most were active members of Syriza, but most did not belong to any platforms or constituent organizations of it. The first part of the meeting was taken up with analysis of the past seven months of Syriza in government. They were bitterly critical of the clique around Tsipras and the strategy they pursued. They then proceeded to elect a coordinating committee and to select candidates.

I was unhappy to discover that there were no Greek channels on the television in my room, so I had to get television election coverage via the Internet. Sometimes Wi-Fi wasn't so good there either, so I had to go to the lobby to get a better signal. I watched the September 9 debate of seven party leaders in the lobby on my laptop, while following the Twitter feed on my iPhone, with badly behaved screaming children all around me. The party leaders said all the expected things and there were few talking points about it afterward. The following week, there was a head-to-head debate between Tsipras and Meimarakis, the alternative prime ministers, which commentators thought was more focused but was still uninspiring. What stayed with me longest was Tsipras saying that Syriza would be able to govern properly now with the Left Platform gone. My attitude to Tsipras was moving from disappointment to disdain.

During the last week, there were intensified activities. There was a plethora of opinion polls, many of them showing Syriza neck-and-neck with ND and correspondingly the support for LAE going down. There were the final rallies. The LAE one in Omonia had a few thousand, chanting *oxi* repeatedly. The Syriza one in Syntagma had a few thousand more. I wondered who they were and how they could demonstrate such apparent enthusiasm after all that had happened. As Syriza became a shadow of what it was, the figure of Alexis Tsipras loomed larger. His rhetoric was so blatantly at odds with reality: "Greece will take its destiny in its own hands." It was surreal at times. There was graffiti picturing Tsipras as an orthodox savior. There were people kissing his hand.

On the platform with Tsipras at the final Syriza rally were Gregor Gysi of Die Linke, Pablo Iglesias of Podemos, Pierre Laurent of the French Communist Party and Ska Keller of the Green group in the European Parliament. Gerry Adams of Sinn Féin had been asked to be there too, as well as at the rally at the January election, but he did not accede to these requests. "Alexis will end austerity," said Iglesias, expressing a "great man" theory of history, as well as a poor reading of history in any respect. Also expressing solidarity with Tsipras and Syriza were such major figures as Gabi Zimmer, chair of GUE-NGL group in the European Parliament, Luciana Castellina, iconic figure of the Italian left, and Walter Baier, director of Transform Europe. I was very disappointed in them. Transform put out a statement of support. Its newsletter published a dossier of links to articles on the European "debate" on Greece. With the exception of an article by Varoufakis, every other article took the side for Tsipras-Syriza. Nothing by Kouvelakis or Lapavitsas. Stathis Kouvelakis had published a consistent stream of articles in *Jacobin* analyzing each turn of events, which were very influential internationally.

International intellectuals, such as Leo Panitch, Chantal Mouffe, Etienne Balibar, Paul Mason, and Slavoj Žižek, weighed in for Syriza. Some of these statements strained logic and ignored evidence. Basically, it was vital to prove that the left could govern. The Greek governemnt was defined as a left government. Therefore the left must support it, no matter what. The Syriza group in the European Parliament rolled out a series of videos by MEPs from other countries endorsing Syriza in the Greek election. When I saw one from Martina Anderson of Sinn Féin appear, I clicked on it expecting the same. I was pleasantly surprised when she asked the Greek people to "vote for parties that will stand up for you." This was quite deliberate, as I have confirmed with Sinn Féin MEP Lynn Boylan and Brian Carty, its group manager in Brussels. It was the practice of Sinn Féin not to call directly for a vote for one or other party in any other country. It had no problem if this was taken as support for Syriza, KKE, or LAE.

There was little expression of international support for LAE. Jean-Luc Mélenchon expressed some support for them, as did some figures within Podemos and Die Linke, who did not agree with the positions taken by Iglesias and Gysi. Jesús Romero of Podemos spoke at a LAE rally. Oskar Lafontaine sent a message of solidarity to the LAE rally in Thessaloniki, stressing the need to continue fighting for *oxi* and quoting the words of Brecht: "One who struggles may lose, but whoever gives up the fight has already lost." Sahra Wagenknecht explicitly took issue with Gysi and called LAE worthy of respect. There were critiques of Syriza among the international left intelligentsia from such respected figures as Michael Lebowitz and Boris Kagarlitsky. John Pilger was scathing. He considered Syriza the product of an affluent educated elite, schooled in postmodernism. In their negotiations with troika, Tsipras and Varoufakis showed themselves to be neither radicals nor leftists, nor even honest social democrats, but two slightly upstart supplicants in their pleas and demands.[9]

Within Sto Kokkino, there was an attempt at fair treatment toward LAE in the days just after the split, but Syriza shut this down during the final week of the campaign. Sto Kokkino became a partisan Syriza station without the scope for criticism of Syriza as had existed when I had been on it a few weeks before that. I did an interview for *To Vima* about the prospects for the European left and addressed the effect of the turn of Syriza on this.

I understood why so many among the international left stood by Syriza. I would like to have done so myself. We wanted to be on the side of winners for a change. We were weary of defeat. We were proud of a left government being elected. We groaned at the idea of one more split and allying ourselves with a marginal force all over again. Moreover, we formed bonds of loyalty. My loyalties, however, stretched to both sides of this split. I had to go with reason and conscience. Although there was a certain scorn for those citing conscience, as if it were an unaffordable self-indulgence, I did not feel I had anything to offer to anybody without my integrity, without my conscience. I sided with those who believed that conscience was the very core of what it was to be left, not some expendable luxury.

I was back in Dublin by election day. The day before, I met with Kevin Ovenden in Dublin and got my copy of his book, *Syriza: Inside the Labyrinth,* which was a good account of the story that far. The next day I was glued to my computer as results came. Syriza won by a larger margin than polls had predicted. It got 35.4 percent of the vote, giving the party 145 seats, whereas ND got 28.1 percent, with 75 seats. Syriza immediately announced a renewed coalition with Anel, which received 3.6 percent and 10 seats, giving the government 155 seats out of 300. LAE polled at 2.86 percent, failing to cross the 3 percent threshold that would allow it to be in parliament. This was the bitterest blow. I found it hard to take that candidates of such outstanding quality would be excluded from parliament. This was a defeat of the open and honest left. I admired their conviction and courage in standing in this election under the most difficult conditions. I believed that they would carry on and build a new force on the Greek left that would capture the imagination of more of the activists and electorate abandoned by Syriza. I heard that their defeat was cheered in Syriza headquarters. The television cameras showed a huge banner of L'Altra Europa con Tsipras, waving their testimony to personality politics and questionable political judgment. The only forces opposing the imposition of troika rule in the parliament would be XA from the right and KKE from the left. I was glad that at least KKE was in there, despite its rigidity and refusal to cooperate with the rest of the left. I was sorry that Syriza would not have to look at the faces of those who formed the soundest judgment on them. The abstention rate had to be taken into account. The turnout in January was 63.6 percent, whereas in September it was 56.5 percent. A total of 898,506 more people voted in January than September. Specifically, 320,074 more voted for Syriza in January than in September.

Reporting on RTÉ, Tony Connelly remarked that Tsipras's post-election speech could have been scripted by his creditors. Paul Mason colorfully commented on Facebook that "the aftermath of the Greek election feels like the last scene of *Lord of the Rings*—everybody going separate ways, having confronted battle, demons, alliances broken up, etc." I felt an awful emptiness, a nearly overwhelming sense of defeat, a bitterness of dreams once more turning to dust.

In reality, it was the troika that won that election. It was the global plutocracy who won. Not only did they secure their domination, but they broke the prime vehicle of left opposition to it and made it the instrument of their domination. The Syriza that ostensibly won this election was a hollow shell of the party that won the January election. The party that had been built in decades of struggle by the Greek left was dead. This Syriza, which admittedly had a thread of continuity with it, was an alien thing.

People began to speak of Syriza 1 and Syriza 2. There were many, especially among the ruling elites, who didn't like Syriza 1 but were warming to Syriza 2. Meanwhile, many on the left in Greece and abroad were going cold on it. Tsipras spoke of putting country before party, but it was more that he put staying in power before country or party. Tsipras and those around him did believe that their being in power, no matter what they did, was best for the country. They spoke of their red lines, which were crossed constantly, but the only red line was to stay in power. These were the results of the election: a mandate after the fact for the third memorandum; a negation of the *oxi* of the referendum; the elimination of a left alternative in the immediate future; the destruction of Syriza as a party of the radical left; a shift to the right of both government and parliament. I did not believe that most of those who voted for Syriza voted to affirm the memorandum, to negate the referendum, or to move to the right, but many of them did accept that there was no alternative on the horizon. They voted for those who at least put up a fight. They did not want the return of those who had brought Greece to the terrible state that Syriza was first elected to change. In January, they voted for hope. In September, they voted for the death of hope. Many voted for the least worst option, as they saw it.

Tsipras made much of not returning to the old order, as if the old order had not continued with little challenge from them during their time in government. Little had changed for the oligarchs, the orthodox church, or the clientelist state. The government did very little to change even what was in their power to change. Indeed, their appointments, starting with the presidency, manifested more of a tendency to ingratiate themselves with the old order than to displace it. Now that they had cast off much of their own left, they would find much more scope for making common cause with the center and right. They seemed so much more comfortable with Anel than they were with the Syriza left.

I wrote to Aristides Baltas with muted congratulations after his election to the parliament and his appointment as minister of culture. I noted that I did not feel about Syriza as I did in January. I thought that the party, parliament, and government were much diminished without those who had left. He wrote back immediately, saying that he deeply appreciated my congratulations, that I was wrong about the left, that we would have to discuss it at length. I wrote to commiserate with Costas Isychos, Nikos Potamitis, Stathis Kouvelakis, and Costas

Lapavitsas. All of them replied with reflection and determination to carry on to build a new front on the Greek left.

Syriza 2

The parliament did not convene right away, because Tsipras was off to the United States for the United Nations General Assembly. He did not cut a very convincing figure there and came in for criticism from both right and left. In his body language, he seemed like someone who had lost his way. In an interview with Bill Clinton, focused on international investment opportunities in Greece, both Clinton and Tsipras faltered awkwardly. Tsipras refused to attend an assembly on ISIS because Macedonia had been invited in the name of the Republic of Macedonia, which Greece insisted on calling the Former Yugoslav Republic of Macedonia, claiming that Macedonia was Greek. This was the latest expression of a very erratic and confused foreign policy, veering right and left, but too often falling in with dominant NATO and EU positions. On this occasion, they rebelled against a dominant position from the right, not from the left. Their relationship to Israel, especially in military matters, has been a source of dismay for the left.

During this week, back in Greece, there was a ceremony com-memorating the battle of Salamis in 480 BCE featuring Kammenos, the Anel minister for defense, walking on a red carpet on pallets right down to the sea. The kitschy character of it was the subject of wide-spread derision in the Greek media. When Tsipras returned to Greece, he and Kammenos attended military exercises, generating a series of official photos of them in battle dress. Tsipras appeared not only in camouflage but also wearing a Bush-type leather jacket with insignia, walking along a red carpet and sitting in the cockpit of a C-130 military transport plane. There were caption contests accompanying the various photos on Facebook and Twitter, with some very funny results.

Meanwhile in Athens, there was a skirmish with the church, when Sia Anagnostopoulou, deputy minister of education, raised issues about compulsory religious education and evoked a sharp and dismissive response from the archbishop. The new minister for education and religious affairs, Nikos Filis, immediately went to the archbishop and assured him that there would be no unilateral action. I wondered if there will be any action on this or on state salaries for clerics or taxation of church wealth. Any action has been in the other direction. Just after that, the government exempted the church from capital controls.

When the new parliament was sworn in on October 3, the religious presence presiding in ceremonial robes was in excess of anything I saw, even in old newsreels of Ireland. True, most Syriza and KKE MPs did not raise their hand to take the religious oath, but the scene looked to my Irish eyes like one that should have long since been anachronistic. The next day there was a small transfer ceremony to hand over the role of president of the parliament. The body language was tense, even hostile, as Zoe Konstantopoulou handed over to Nikos Voutsis and spoke of the work of the Truth Committee on the Public Debt she had established, which declared the Greek debt, including that agreed in the third memorandum, to be illegal, illegitimate, odious, and unsustainable. As she handed him each of three documents, he put each on a table behind him immediately and dismissively. Shortly after that, all mention of this commission disappeared from the website of the parliament. The day after that, Tsipras presented a programmatic statement in parliament consisting of taxes, cuts, and austerity measures of €6.4 billion, along with some promises to negotiate still open areas of agreement with the troika, a possibility of debt restructuring, and some alleviating measures in health.

The Syriza Effect

On October 4, there was an election in Portugal, the first test of the Syriza effect on parties associated with it. Bloco de Esquerda captured 10 percent of the vote and 19 seats in parliament, while the Communist Party bloc got 8 percent and 17 seats. This was a better-than-expected result for the left. Addressing the impact of the turn of events in Portugal, Catarina Principe noted:

During the campaign, political forces hostile to us attempted to paint Bloco as irresponsible, saying that Bloco could not govern because of what happened to SYRIZA. Our opponents said, "Look at SYRIZA, there is no other option besides austerity."

Despite this, Bloco was capable of shifting this narrative. We were afraid that the SYRIZA effect would be very negative for us, but it actually turned out to be minimal. This was because Bloco succeeded in shifting responsibility for what happened in Greece onto the European elites, while at the same time strengthening our critique of the European Union and the euro. For the first time, Bloco said publicly that if we need to leave the Eurozone in order to end austerity and regain sovereignty, we will do this.[10]

Fernando Rosas of Bloco also addressed this:

We have publicly drawn our conclusions from this episode [of Greece's acceptance of the memorandum]: firstly, that it is impossible to carry out an anti-austerity policy in the framework of the euro. Secondly, the Eurozone is a sort of dictatorship that prevents European countries from making democratic choices. We want to renegotiate the debt and, if necessary, we would be prepared to exit the euro. We will not make Tsipras's mistake of getting into negotiations without a Plan B. But we don't want to publicly criticise SYRIZA. Our official position is that we must be ready to leave the euro if negotiations over the debt come to nothing.[11]

Tsipras, however, interpreted it differently. Addressing the Syriza central committee on October 10, he claimed credit for the result: "Our victory on September 20 sowed its first seeds in Europe. The people of Portugal took the baton of hope and change." Tweeting during his speech broadcast live, Zoe Mavroudi thought that Tsipras sounded like someone with no self-criticism and no remorse. Ironically, he said that the party must be the left conscience of the government. She was not the only one to note that most of those who could make that happen were gone. A new general secretary and political secretariat were installed and Tsipras reached out for new people to join the party, no matter for whom they had voted before this. In practice, this meant recruiting to the right. There was certainly no possibility of recruiting to the left.

On October 16, another omnibus bill containing measures that inflicted further deprivation on the population passed through parliament with 154 votes. ND, Pasok, and Potami, although approving the memorandum, did not vote for the specific measures. KKE and XA also voted no. Syriza MP Vassiliki Katrivanou, of the 53+ tendency, was absent. On the same day, parliament appointed 178 new orthodox clerics, to be paid public salaries. Tsipras again expressed relief at being rid of the left who had left Syriza and referred to those who stayed as "the useful left." The question was: Useful to whom? Useful for what? The answer: To implement the expropriation against which they previously stood. To align with the class interests of those they set out to oppose.

The Irish parliament was also dealing with national finances. On October 13, the budget was presented in Dáil Éireann by two ministers, one Fine Gael and one Labour Party. Brendan Howlin of Labour ended his speech with a flourish: "Who speaks of Syriza now?" indicating that the Irish government's compliance with the troika program and prudent management of our finances had delivered far more than the Greek government's defiance and failed radicalism could ever do. Cameras zoomed in on the left. When Paul Murphy of the Socialist Party got the floor, he countered: "Who speaks of Pasok now?" The microphone went off as he added, "Who will speak of the Labour Party a year from now?" referring to the polls predicting poor electoral results for them. Pearse Doherty of Sinn Féin responded to Howlin by telling him that he would be in a better position to lecture Syriza if they were reelected with as many votes. The reference to Syriza was a talking point on media coverage of the budget. Others in Sinn Féin used the reelection argument too. I pointed out on Twitter that reelection didn't constitute justification. Fine Gael might get reelected too.

The Syriza effect hovered around the upcoming general election in Ireland expected in February 2016. Labour Party voices bragged about how their sensible approach accomplished what Syriza 1 had failed to do and gloated over the belated sensible approach of Syriza 2. The left who supported Syriza took a range of positions, from defensiveness to denunciation. The transformation of what was a beacon of hope to a debacle of despair rendered many on the left bitter or silent. Brendan Ogle, trade union official involved in Right2Change, complained of those who first used Syriza to give too much hope and then brought it to bear to extinguish hope.

Further afield, elections in Argentina and Venezuela produced defeat for the left. Nearer to home, in France, Front de Gauche, the radical left aligned with Syriza, was beaten into fourth place and hardly figured in the international media commentary. Stathis Kouvelakis was critical of the lack of radicalism in the French left and believed that the capitulation of Tsipras accentuated a dramatic decrease in the level of expectation, to the point where the role of a patch of social democracy appeared as the maximum the radical left could hope to obtain in the current climate. He argued that efforts at recomposition of the left in recent decades had failed, leading to a sense of impotence on a terrain of ruins.

It was the election in Spain on December 20 that was most in sight, because Podemos was next, after Syriza, in the hierarchy of hopes. Spain was to be the next domino after Greece in bringing down oppressive rule. Predictably, this vision was given a massive jolt by the negotiations and capitulation in Greece. In January 2015, Podemos seemed to be in a three-way tie for first place with the People's Party and the Spanish Socialist Workers' Party—PP and PSOE. Podemos peaked in the polls at the moment of the Syriza victory and declined as Syriza failed to deliver. The rallying cries of "Syriza, Podemos, Venceremos" no longer filled the air. There were internal factors too, as the Iglesias leadership centralized its power, moderated its message, and confronted a challenge from a populist party on the right.

Podemos managed to come third in the election with 20.7 percent, thus ending the two-party system, but it was far from the result hoped.

Exodus from Syriza

Although disappointed by defeat, LAE people tried to pick up the pieces of their lives and politics. They went back to their jobs or looked for new ones. They met to decide what to do next. Would they form a front or a party? If so, what kind? On October 19, LAE organized its first post-election public rally. They filled a cinema in Metaxourgio in Athens, with some not able to get inside. Lafazanis spoke of the need for a left refoundation.

Meanwhile, another grouping of ex-Syriza members formed the Network for a Radical Left. They came mainly from Syriza Youth and the 53+. Their immediate goal, Dimosthenes Papadatos told me, was to recover, to tackle the disappointment, to stop the phenomenon of quitting. It was evident that there needed to be a new party, but he didn't think it could be built immediately. For the time being, they would cooperate with LAE in anti-memorandum mobilizations.

The exodus from Syriza continued. As well as high-profile resignations, there was a disintegration at the base of the party. On October 22, Tasos Koronakis, who had previously resigned as general secretary, resigned from Syriza altogether, stating that the distance between government policy and his own beliefs was constantly growing. On November 19, three government MPs refused to support the omnibus bill of troika-required measures. One was the prominent Syriza MP Gavriil Sakellaridis, from the inner circle of Tsipras, who had been government spokesman during the first Syriza government. He resigned his seat in parliament, because he could no longer vote for the government and what it had become. He was replaced by the next on the list who would vote yes. Another Syriza MP refused to vote for the bill, but also refused to resign his seat, as did an Anel MP, bringing the government majority down to 153.

Many others left without any publicity, including some who had taken the Tsipras line and attacked those who had previously left.

They voted and campaigned for Syriza in the September election and defended them until they could defend no longer. Others didn't even resign, but simply drifted away. One central committee member told me that he was just disengaging and fading away. It took different people different times to realize what had happened and to decide what to do.

LAE, although largely disregarded by mainstream media, used social media and public meetings to build for the longer term. Their national conference on November 21 was attended by 1,500 people representing 250 branches. It was addressed by Panagiotis Lafazanis and Manolis Glezos, as well as by Alekos Alavanos, previous leader of Syriza, on behalf of Plan B, by Themis Symvoulopoulos of United Popular Front (EPAM), and Yiannis Albanis of the Network for a Radical Left. Messages were received from Zoe Konstantopoulou, who was in Barcelona, and Costas Lapavitsas, who was in London. The one from Lapavitsas was most specific about direction. He called for a program for productive reconstruction and for recasting the international position of the Greek state, particularly for redefining its relation to EU. This program, he indicated, should be developed with all social forces battling the memorandum and with democratic procedures and debate. I spoke with Nikos Potamitis after the conference. He thought it was a good discussion of all that needed to be considered. There were many groups, tendencies, and individuals coming together, and much determination, but "we are less than what society needs," he said. Preparations for a founding congress were underway. A press release on November 26 stated, "LAE will persevere until the end. Nothing will be forgotten and will be reimbursed in full, not only the policies, but also the serious criminal charges for unprecedented abuse of public funds and the sale at derisory prices to foreign buyers of public property of strategically national importance."

There were also moves to form a pan-European movement that would put forth a plan B for Europe. Some international media stories about it cast Yanis Varoufakis as the Lone Ranger, but there was a serious initiative in this direction involving Jean-Luc Mélenchon, Oskar Lafontaine, Costas Lapavitsas, Zoe Konstantopoulou, Stefano

Fassina, Mariana Mortagua, Lola Sanchez, Susan George, and others. Whether this could become a substantial pan-European movement remained to be seen, but mentions of it on social media generated much affirmative response. Varoufakis came to Ireland in November for the Kilkenomics Festival and was interviewed in various media, not hesitating to speak of Ireland as well as Greece and of how Ireland played the role of model prisoner. On RTÉ's *Prime Time*, the main television current affairs program, he was subjected to a hostile interview by Miriam O'Callaghan, comparing him unfavorably with the Irish finance minister, Michael Noonan, and implying that Greece failed in negotiations because of his arrogance. Varoufakis handled the situation with poise and pointed to the realities of power.[12]

Interval in London

In early November, I flew to London, primarily to talk to Greeks about how the post-election period in Greece was taking shape. I wanted to speak with Costas Lapavitsas and Stathis Kouvelakis, who were based there, and I also wanted to go at the time of the Historical Materialism conference so I could meet other Greeks who would be there for the conference.

As soon as I arrived and checked in, I met with Michalis Spourdalakis and Leo Panitch. We spent a long and convivial evening talking about many things over dinner and later in a pub. I was happy that this was still possible, given our divergent responses to recent developments. It was not only possible but warm and fluent. Both Michalis and Leo still supported Syriza, but far from uncritically. Michalis didn't shirk from difficult facts and added more of them to the picture. He made a distinction between supporting the government and being in the party, and claimed that the party was still radical. We all probed each other in a way that was honest and challenging. I laid my cards on the table about the book I was writing and where I was going with it.

Michalis was speaking at the conference the next day. I told him that he might be in for a rough ride. He asked teasingly if I would be defending him. I told him not to count on it. I did think it was an important position to be aired, and I respected his integrity in defending it.

At the conference he argued that there were no absolute defeats or absolute victories. After defeat, it was important not to be defeatist. It was necessary to realize that no attempt at radical transformation of society has ever been anything but a painful marathon with numerous retreats, defeats, detours, and short-term disappointments. He compared the situation of Tsipras signing the agreement to that of a trade union leader, who, after a 61 percent strike vote, was confronted by management with a threat to close the business down, so agreed to terms previously rejected by the members so they would not lose their jobs. It was retreat, not a betrayal, he insisted. He put the blame not only on the troika but on the party. After 2012, there was a rush to power by any means, a failure to develop the party, both in its strategy for social transformation and in extending its base. Key figures in the government saw it as necessary to appease the old establishment. His key conclusion was that Syriza must become Syriza again. The road map involved staying in government, building the party and solidifying its relation to its social base, making left appointments, implementing the parallel program, and reconsidering its strategy in the Euozone.[13] Given how controversial this position was, it was surprising that there wasn't much challenge from the audience. I came in and queried how Syriza could become Syriza again after all that had happened and so many had left.

Also speaking at this session was Andreas Karitzis, who had been a member of the political secretariat and central committee of Syriza but had left Syriza. He outlined his task as understanding what were the positive and negative features of the Syriza experience, specifying what was needed to adapt and be effective in the new conditions of doing politics and engaging in a process of shaping the conditions for a new resilient and potentially hegemonic emancipatory political practice to emerge. Syriza had failed to halt the neoliberal stranglehold on Greek society and did not have any coherent strategy or narrative about where to go from here. He criticized the left for being too focused on the transformation of the state and transposed this to the need for a new politics. He saw the raw materials for this in the solidarity networks. He advocated processes that would empower people, such as advancing social economy, cooperative initiatives, community control over functions such as infrastructure facilities, energy systems, and distribution networks. I asked him about LAE, and he replied that it was still too tied to old politics.

We continued the conversation on a bench outside and later on a long Skype call. He explained that he was not shocked by what happened in 2015. He had seen it heading that way already, especially in 2014 when it became clear to him that people he knew for years were using the same words but not meaning the same thing and moving away from what they had meant. They became increasingly blind to what they were doing. Once in government, everyone only wanted to hear good news. Democratic processes were barely tolerated. It was class struggle that divided the membership of Syriza. I asked about ERT and he responded that it was even more indicative of how things had gone wrong, even more so than the agreement with the lenders. He did not believe that Syriza could last for a long period of time. It was the best of what the Greek left had created, but it would be seen as a first unstable step to a left future. He didn't know how it would end, but the solution would be multilevel and long-term.

At the conference, different groups on the Greek left were present and arguing their positions, but unfortunately they were scheduled in such a way that they were in different sessions. Broadly, these were Syriza, LAE, and Antarsya. In one slot, I had to choose between hearing Kouvelakis or Spourdalakis and Karytzis. This was hard for me, but I felt that the Spourdalakis and Karytzis positions were less familiar internationally than the Kouvelakis one, and I should air them. Besides, I had arranged to meet Kouvelakis after the conference. It was a four-day conference with 750 attendees and many parallel sessions and difficult choices to make.

At a plenary session, Panagiotis Sotiris of LAE (previously Antarsya) spoke alongside speakers from Podemos and Bloco. He started by declaring that the whole Greek left bore responsibility for the fact that Greece was no longer a laboratory of hope but a cause for despair. Greece was the country where the most aggressive experiment in neoliberal social engineering was met with the most massive, almost insurrectionary, sequence of struggles. In the September elections, the Greek left failed to contest effectively the left version of there-is-no-alternative. However, an alternative was possible. The moment of the referendum, he argued, was optimal for a strategy of rupture: end negotiations, stop debt payments, nationalize the banking system, return to a national currency. This would have been the starting point for a broader process of transformation. It would have been difficult, but arguably not more difficult than what would happen as a result of the disastrous concessions Syriza made, because of its attachment to the EU and alliances with sections of the Greek elite. There could be no change from within the EU, he argued. Sooner or later, Syriza would face its winter of discontent. A new way forward could come with reflection and self-criticism, recuperation of popular sovereignty, an elaborated anti-capitalist narrative, a program of productive reconstruction. The existing solidarity networks in Greece not only dealt with urgent social needs but were also experimental test sites for alternative forms of production and social organization: indeed, traces of communism. There was a dual-power strategy in self-managed enterprises, solidarity clinics, and popular assemblies. The tragic defeat of the Greek left was not only in signing the agreement but in the way Syriza leadership more gradually detached itself from the party and movements. The process of recomposition of the left needed to be based on a radically new politics.

Another session of the conference was organized around the Antarsya position. Savas Michael Matsas gave a lively analysis of the history of Greece as class war. The failure of Syriza was in class compromise, not only in negotiations, but in constant reassurances to the right since 2012. He was critical of LAE for fetishizing the state and monetary policy. He was for an indefinite general strike. Kostas Skordoulis spoke next, also arguing the Antarsaya line vis-à-vis Syriza, KKE, and LAE, although he emphasized how much the different sections of the left knew each other and talked to each other, indeed to Homeric proportions. He regarded Antarsya as the most successful anti-capitalist formation in Europe. The discussion from the floor was lively. It was dominated by an intra-Trotskyist debate on whether Antarsya was a divisive project. The Fourth International took a position against its own Greek section, advocating that they should have been within Syriza. This had now been superseded by a debate about whether they should be in LAE, as two substantial sections of Antarsya had split and joined LAE. After I spoke from the floor, challenging the revolutionary-reformist conceptualization dominating the session, a young woman behind me tapped me on the shoulder and told me that she had translated an article of mine on Greece into Spanish.

There were also Greek presentations in thematic sessions. One on spaces of dispossession showed a map of Athens highlighting public spaces in the process of privatization, which made the reality of the expropriation especially vivid to anyone who knew and loved Athens as I did. In all, I took in twenty-five presentations over two days. Although I concentrated on Greece, I also attended ones on Ireland, South Africa, Spain, and Portugal. Most participants were both intellectuals and activists, which created a particular quality of interaction. Occasionally there was someone presenting a doctoral thesis in somewhat sheltered terms: "I want to set these two literatures in conversation with each other." Alternatively, and more typically, one person, upon hearing three fine papers on Ireland from Colin Coulter, Sinéad Kennedy, and Angela Nagle, asked, "What can we do?"

In intervals between sessions, I had many conversations. One was with George Souvlis, who is doing a PhD in Florence, whom I met in Athens and connected with on Facebook. He was in Syriza Youth and had joined LAE. He said that many over-fifties in Syriza were in denial. Most of the youth were still energized and wanted an alternative. It wasn't only the signing of the memorandum that turned them against the Syriza government, but the failure to move on essential issues: separation of church and state, the defense budget, cleansing the state apparatus, controlling the police, and welcoming refugees.

I stayed a few days after the conference for further discussions. One morning I met Dimitris Sotiropoulos, an economist working at Open

University, who had been one of the Syriza speakers in Dublin in February. He left Syriza shortly after that, because of the February 20 agreement, in which the government agreed to austerity but gained nothing. He was very interested in the debt issue, but thought that the truth commission had turned debt into a legal issue and the case on odious debt was difficult to make. He thought the euro-versus-drachma debate asked the wrong question. He surprised me by saying that he thought that left government was a contradiction in terms and revealing that he was closer to autonomous groups, making me wonder why he had been in Syriza at all. It showed how broad their reach was coming up to 2015.

After that, I took a stroll around Bloomsbury. I went into the British Museum. It was magnificent in its way, but it raised so many questions. One obviously was: How did these things come to be here? I viewed the Parthenon marbles and wondered if the current Greek government would make any progress in getting them repatriated. Not long after that, I read that Aristides Baltas announced the abandonment of the legal case brought under the previous government and promised to pursue their return by diplomatic means. Another dimension that always occurred to me in such museums is: Whose stories are being told then and now? I always walk through these places reciting Brecht to myself: "Who built Thebes of the seven gates? In the books, you will read the names of kings. Did the kings haul up the lumps of rock?" When I exited, I came upon the Trade Union Congress, where a sculpture testifying to the role of labor was in evidence.

Although I spent most of my time talking to Greeks, I spent a lovely evening with Kate Hudson and Andrew Burgin, founders of Left Unity and active in the Greek Solidarity Campaign in Britain. Kate and I went way back, to the 1970s, when we were both active in communist parties and took the same positions in many debates of the period. I met Kate in the CND office, where she was general secretary, and went home with her. Andrew prepared a lovely dinner for us, and we discussed past and present in Ireland, Britain, and Greece until we were all exhausted.

My next night was in the company of Stathis Kouvelakis, who taught in London while leading a complicated life moving between London, Paris, and Athens. He has become a primary voice for the international left in interpreting events in Greece over the past few years. His articles in *New Left Review* and *Jacobin* were much circulated and discussed on social media. It was good to have this one-on-one opportunity to explore all this further with him. We spoke probingly and passionately for nearly six hours, covering a wide range of themes. We also ate and drank and walked and laughed. It was good to be able to do that, because so much of what we were discussing was defeat. It left me thinking about how much strength we on the left draw from each other in such interactions. Of course, much of it was analyzing the current conjuncture in Greece, about which we and many others were still quite preoccupied. Stathis felt he had to step back a bit from Greece, to reflect, to go wider and deeper and to get on with other things. All the same, he was involved in LAE branches in London and Paris and working on a major article for *New Left Review* on what the international left needed to learn from what happened in Greece. He felt that LAE messed up in the general election, but that it had a future. It had critical mass, social roots, and left commitment. We focused on the political forces, but also the personalities, with fascinating characterizations of Tsipras, Dragasakis, Pappas, Baltas, Lafazanis, and others. Some of the *realpolitik* he outlined was chilling. We agreed on almost everything. He didn't think it would have been good for Syriza to move against the orthodox church too soon. I had my doubts about this. He told me not to worry so much about religious instruction in schools, because it made many people into atheists. We didn't confine ourselves to Greece. We went wider and deeper from there into the atmosphere in universities, various figures in the history of Marxism, such as Engels and Bukharin, and much more. He walked me to the door of my hotel at midnight, and we took our leave, determined to do this again, some time, some place.

The next day I met Costas Lapavitsas in his office in SOAS (a college within the University of London specializing in Africa, Asia, and the Middle East). He had given up his job as a professor there to stand for election as a Syriza MP. After LAE had failed to enter parliament, he came back to London to put his life there back together and was on a new contract at SOAS. I asked about his life as an MP. He said it was hell. He didn't really have a home. He didn't eat properly. He was back and forth between Athens, where he was a national figure and so had media appearances and other such calls on him, and his constituency in Imathia, where he was expected to be a local fixer. His expertise as an internationally respected economist was ignored by the leadership of Syriza, although it was valued by Left Platform. However unpleasant he found his life as an MP, it was also clear that he was furious that he was not an MP still. He exuded a sense of vision and determination that he believed should be brought to bear on the situation and was angry at the process that unfolded that has pushed him out of that arena. He told me that he was calm now, that if I had been there a month earlier, he could not have spoken to me so calmly. The anger was still evident. When addressing certain matters, he took a deep breath and then unleashed scathing critiques.

At the same time, he was funny and friendly and engaging on many levels. He asked me questions about my own work and opinions on various matters. I formed a sense of him that was very different from what I had been led to expect from the way others spoke of him. From quite a few people in Syriza, I heard that he was technocratic, that he understood economics but not politics. From other people, especially during the election, the name of Lapavitsas meant drachma and only drachma. I referred to this characterization of him during this conversation and in subsequent correspondence. He considered this typecasting unfair and it made him very angry. He said that so much of Greek politics was hot air and he refused that style. It was also about marginalizing both him and the position he represented, which had now been effectively banished from parliament and public debate.

While he was still insistent on the key role of monetary policy and the impossibility of controlling the economy within the Eurozone, we barely mentioned the drachma or the euro in two hours. We talked politics primarily, but more than that. In his speech at the Athens conference, he insisted on speaking of what had happened in terms of political judgment and not of personality or morality. In London, when I spoke of the philosophical, psychological, and moral dimensions, he agreed that these were important, and he had a lot to say along those lines. He profiled some of the leading figures in Syriza and said that they had no ideas and no morals and were only interested in power.

As to LAE and why they were not able to break though in the election and be the force they should be, he thought it could be blamed not only on the circumstances in which the government called the election but on the way LAE conducted its own campaign. It went into the election with no strategy and no program and made bad decisions about which figures were to the forefront and other matters. They came across as honest and decent, but musty. He agreed that something needed to be in that space, but it needed to be something more than LAE as it was during the election. He believed it would take time, because Greece was exhausted and defeated and the dust had to settle.

He was keen for something to happen on a Europe-wide basis. He was to speak a few days later at a European Plan B summit, although it had to be postponed because of the murderous events in Paris that weekend. Yanis Varoufakis was to speak at it too. Even now, Varoufakis has a very different notion of a plan B than Lapavitsas. In an interview with Lapavitsas on *Jacobin*, during the time they were both Syriza MPs, Sebastian Budgen, editor at Verso and organizer of Historical Materialism, called Lapavitsas the anti-Varoufakis, referring both to their personal styles and political economic positions. Lapavitsas is not at all flamboyant, but in his stark straightforwardness he is a high-impact personality in his own way. He is definitely more grounded and more consistent.

Not long after that, he delivered his inaugural lecture at SOAS, which was on money. It was a wide-ranging and lucid lecture. Watching it on YouTube, I was struck by how he conceptualized economics as integrally connected to philosophy, history, psychology, sociology, politics, everything. He addressed "the shambles that is called Syriza," which was unprecedented in political history, having come to power with sensible political proposals and moving rapidly to abject surrender. Why? Staying in the Eurozone was given priority over everything else. The power of money utterly destroyed Syriza. Economics alone was not enough to explain it. Psychology was necessary to explain the power of money and the power of fear. It was a case of Stockholm syndrome, whereby the tormentors appeared as the wise. He argued the need for a new narrative other than the one shaped by the power of money, for a story beyond capitalism. A starting place for challenging the power of money was the nation-state and national parliaments.[14]

His experience of being in national parliament was a particularly bleak one, especially during those votes in July and August, when the parliament colluded in the abnegation of the power it had won. He told me that he doubted if anything he did in the past year was worth it, but I thought that being among those who voted no and began the building of an alternative was worth a lot.

What Was the Plot?

Throughout the autumn and winter period, it was one thing after another, all reinforcing my sense that Tsipras and Syriza had lost the plot. There was a new plot emerging, but it was a right-wing one, displaying remarkable contiunuity with what previous Greek governments had done. Every day it was diverging more and more from the path of what a left government might have been.

I recalled conversations where people (including myself) worried that Tsipras would become the new Papandreou and Syriza would become the new Pasok. Now I thought: if only. In their first period in government, Pasok under Papandreou did pursue a left line and bring significant poltical change. It is true that the situation facing Tsipras and Syriza was far more severe and limiting. However, I never expected to see the day where Tsipras sounded like Samaras and Syriza pursued the policies and practices of New Democracy.

The movement that had lined up with Syriza was now marshaling their forces against it. There were many protests and sectoral strikes. High school students, nineteen thousand of them, gathered to stand against inadequate staffing and infrastructure. A placard condemned "killers of knowledge." Seamen went on strike against the privatization of ports and the deterioration of their working conditions and pensions. There was 100 percent support in Piraeus. There was a public transport strike in Athens. Municipal buildings were occupied for assemblies to plan mobilizations against the third memorandum.

On November 12, a general strike was called by unions in both the private and public sectors. Syriza, the party, supported the general strike against the Syriza-Anel government. I asked both Kouvelakis and Lapavitsas (separately) what they thought of that. They both laughed. It seemed to me that it was running with the hare and hunting with the hounds. However, I also realized that this was the position of people who were honestly conflicted and still had not yet fully come to terms with what had happened. The general strike received broad support. Hundeds of thousands did not report for work. Shops, flights, ports, metro, schools, and archeological sites were closed. More than twenty thousand people marched in Athens. A small group of hooded youth threw petrol bombs and rocks, while police responded with tear gas and stun grenades. As ever. On November 17, an important day in Athens for events commemorating the Polytechnic uprising that brought down the military regime, there were protests at the speech of Tsipras. He was surrounded by bodyguards and met with boos, slogans, and flying objects. Representatives of Syriza were prevented from laying wreaths. Scuffles ensued and the wreaths were left in tatters. LAE and other left groups did so unobstructed. There was a heavy presence of riot police and the metro was closed.

A poll at the end of November showed support for Syriza down to 18 percent (in contrast to 80 percent in the months just after it was elected). Other parties were down too, so there was no alternative government on offer. This was testament to the disppointment and alienation from electoral politics in much of the population.

In December, there was another general strike. On December 6, the budget passed, 153–145. One vote after another in this period involved Syriza MPs violating what they had promised. In early December, Manolis Glezos, still a figure of great moral authority on the left, appealed to them to unleash their consciences from the opium of the party line. None did. In mid-December, there was a central committee meeting "to start a great course for the necessary political, ideological, and organizational reconstruction of the party." LAE's statement on the Tsipras speech to the new Syriza central committee spoke of the "tragicomic spectacle of stuttering the vocabulary of the old Syriza."

Much of the Syriza 2 strategy was to implement the memorandum with anti-memorandum rhetoric and to promise compensatory measures in a parallel program. These were social welfare measures to cushion the impact of austerity on the poorest 10 to 20 percent of the population. Tsakalotos argued that they could only justify implementing the troika program if they also implemented radical initiatives in health and education.[15] On December 17, the parallel program collapsed. The bill was withdrawn by the government at the behest of the lenders, who threatened to withhold the next billion if adopted. This was their last justification for being in government. All through the autumn the promise had been that this was what made Syriza different from other parties implementing troika memoranda. This was the memorandum with a human face. Some measures were then slipped through semi-surreptitiously. Once again, the promised debt relief failed to materialize and was kicked down the road. As did the promised battle with the oligarchy, which had failed to get off the ground. The commitment to cut military spending was somehow forgotten, even though it would release much-needed funding for health and other priorities. The recapitalization of the banks in November took the form of handing them over at reduced prices to hedge funds and other specualtive institutions.

Privatization proceeded. Fourteen regional airports passed to the Fraport consortium. Adding to the sting was the fact of it being German, evoking a sense of being reoccupied by Germany.

Anti-German resentment was never far from the surface, as social memory of the occupation remained strong. It was understandable and justified. However, the left has not always done enough to raise the level of consciousness from nations to classes.

The refugee crisis mounted relentlessly. Thousands arrived every day, primarily fleeing civil war in Syria. The response of civil society was more impressive than that of the state. Syriza said the right things and Tsipras arranged a photo-op with Martin Schultz in Lesvos, but the government was caught between the weight of desperate human need from those who had already lost so much and EU pressure to police its borders and stop the flow.

On December 22, a bill allowing same-sex civil partnerships was passed despite opposition from the church, communists, and fascists. A bishop called for a toll of funeral bells in protest. Another spoke of spitting on homosexuals. The vote was 193 (of 300) for it. There were many absences from the right as the vote was taken. On this issue, Syriza held firm, to its credit.

A diplomatic incident also occurred in December. Czech president Miloš Zeman publicly expressed his regret that Greece didn't leave the Eurozone. The Greek ambassador to the Czech Republic was recalled. Meanwhile a Eurobarometer poll indicated that 60 percent of Greeks were unhappy in life. The European average was 19 percent. It also found that 83 percent of Greeks had no confidence in the future. The European average on this was 32 percent.

Meanwhile, Costas Douzinas, now a Syriza MP, was still speaking of Syriza and its "appointment with history" in terms of romance and revolution, quoting Hegel and Lenin and glorifying contradiction. Panagiotis Sotiris on Facebook remarked that Douzinas had found a wormhole in the galaxy where he lived in a different time line from the rest of us, where all this is somehow leading to democratic socialism.

Alexis Tsipras: Tragic Hero or Devious Traitor?

As I do not subscribe to a great man theory of history and I hate celebrity culture, I have tried to focus on forces of history and personalities in that context. As I was making my way through these years, but most intensely in the summer and autumn of 2015, I was acutely aware of the psychological dimension. In July, everyone I knew was experiencing some kind of trauma. I was too. The different ways that people processed this fascinated me. A matter of speculation and discussion through all this was: How was Alexis Tsipras processing all this? Who was he really as a person and as a political leader of the Greek and European left?

I had formed a view of him as an effective face of the European left. I felt that his knowledge of history and much else was thin, but he was surrounded by people whose knowledge was not thin. I didn't care for his blandifying and compromising discourse, but behind him were the traditions of the Greek left with such a history of suffering and struggle and clarity that would not be betrayed. He was canny in his way. He was popular during his first months as prime minister. I knew people who knew him and trusted him.

Even in July, most people I knew were sympathetic to him, even those who opposed his signing of the agreement. There were stories of how ill he became during the negotiations and what an impossible situation it was. They saw him as a kind of defeated warrior. I was inclined this way myself. However, as he veered from articulating it as defeat to a blustering, contradictory, and dishonest justification of it, attitudes shifted. When he turned his fire on the left and treated with such disdain honest comrades who had built Syriza and stood up for the vision that built Syriza, attitudes shifted further. Mine certainly did.

One person, who had spoken highly of him previously, said to me: "He's not in conflict with himself. I thought so once, but not now. Now we know what he is." Another told me of an old man who said, shortly before he died: "Papandreou didn't fool me, but this one, he did fool me." Someone else who stood up for Tsipras and took his line, even into the autumn, sighed and said, "He's an empty suit, isn't he?"

For a time, he seemed to me like someone who had been tortured and won over to the other side, coming back into the movement after being turned while pretending otherwise. Others claimed he was always careerist and opportunist. The people he brought closest to him were a reflection on him. One person referred to Nikos Pappas, constantly with Tsipras and appointed by him as minister without portfolio, as his "dark side." The concentration of power around the leader and his inner circle and the marginalization of party structures has allowed much of the worst to happen.

I don't know about his inner life, although I'm curious about it, but I do know about his public discourse and behavior. Now, when I see him on my television screen with Hollande or Schultz or Renzi or even Juncker, I see him as one of them now, and not one of us. There is often a metamorphosis effected by moving among the masters of the universe and becoming ever more remote from the realities of those who don't. He no longer walks the streets of Athens as he once did and has increased his personal security since September. His face appears on my Facebook and Twitter timelines many times a day every day. So often he is smiling. I can't help asking if he still had a right to smile.

This transformation of the image of Tsipras from left firebrand to tragic hero to centrist politician to devious traitor has been swift and shocking and sad. Not everyone has moved all the way along this spectrum, of course, but many have. Antonis Antoniadis has filed a lawsuit against Tsipras for high treason.

Who Can Speak? Policing the Discourse

There is always a problem about speaking and writing about a country that is not your own. Several years ago, a Greek-Australian journalist let rip at me on Facebook for daring to write about Greece when I did not live in Greece or speak Greek. She was based in Athens at the time and connected on social media with a number of Irish people interested in Greece and seemed to believe she should be their supreme source. However, I had many sources and I listened and read and watched and wrote about how I perceived the situation, while acknowledging the limitations of my perception. I felt I had a mediating role to play because of the way I came and went and the contacts I had consolidated. My writing was praised and criticized, roughly along lines of whether the person agreed or not with my conclusions. How I praised or criticized others also had a lot to do with whether I agreed with their conclusions.

It was not only about agreement and affinity. It was also about how much those expressing an opinion had invested in informing themselves of the situation. So many ignorant people felt so free to express their opinions on the international mainstream and social media and I often felt angry at foreigners being so opinionated about Greece when they had done so little to inform themselves about it.

The atmosphere around foreigners speaking, writing, even protesting, became very fraught in July, because the whole situation was so fraught. The discourse on the right was what I expected, but it was that of the left that concerned me.

A really sharp-edged article by Alex Andreou, UK-based columnist, cook, and actor, appeared in July. It was called "Alexis Tsipras: Hero, Traitor, Hero, Traitor, Hero." He went immediately on the attack:

> We apologize to Marxists worldwide for Greece refusing to commit ritual suicide to further the cause. You have suffered from your sofas. It is revealing of the political landscape in Europe—indeed, the world—that everyone's dreams of socialism seemed to rest on the shoulders of the young prime minister of a small country. There seemed to be a fervent, irrational, almost evangelical belief that a tiny country, drowning in debt, gasping for liquidity, would somehow (and that somehow is never specified) defeat global capitalism, armed only with sticks and rocks. . . .
>
> How easy it is to be ideologically pure when you are risking nothing. When you are not facing shortages, the collapse of social cohesion, civil conflict, life and death. How easy it is to demand a deal that would plainly never be accepted by any of the other Eurozone member states. How easy brave decisions are when you have no skin in the game. . . .
>
> My question to those critics is: What battles are you fighting in your country, city, town, right now? And at what risk?[16]

This disturbed me. I thought it was unfair to disempower any non-Greek voice as not having skin in the game. I was constantly conscious of not being on the front line of what economic consequences would ensue from either memorandum or Grexit. However, those of us on the international left who did align with Syriza had a lot at stake and were doing our best in our own countries. The left is international. We were not expecting the end of capitalism and the beginning of socialism, but we were hoping for the beginning of an unraveling of the terrible expropriation and the empowerment to build along a new trajectory.

Another article, called "Hubris and Humility in Academic Activism" by Heath Cabot, an American anthropologist who had done long-term ethnographic research in Greece, addressed the role of the international left as it played out at the conference we both attended in July. She was disturbed by the impatience of many in the audience with Douzinas and Gourgouris and enthusiasm for Lapavitsas. She described herself as an outsider with insider knowledge of Greece and felt that those visiting for a conference lacked such nuanced knowledge. Even with her insider experience, she felt that she had no right to express an opinion on certain matters. More to the point, she did not feel that "revolutionary tourists" had a right to weigh in on Grexit when they would not have to live with the direct consequences of this.[17]

She might not have weighed in explicitly on Grexit, but she gave an account of this session of the conference at odds with mine, not factually, but evaluatively, portraying Douzinas and Gourgouris affirmatively and Lapavitsas negatively. I had an exchange with her on Facebook after I made caustic remarks about her article being smug, overstating her insider position in a way that was smothering to any other non-Greek having a position. She responded that she did not intend this, and we struck a conciliatory note, while still not agreeing on the substantive issues, which we did not pursue. All the Irish people at that session with whom I discussed it sided with Lapavitsas, with different degrees of support for Grexit, because of the clarity and honesty of his analysis. They were all intellectually serious and politically committed people, who were listening, engaging, and had a right to express an opinion without being dismissed as "revolutionary tourists" (or being teargassed). They were all active in building an alternative in Ireland.

The attack that made me most angry took place in Dublin. The Workers Party organized a seminar on Greece, Ireland, and the EU, where the invited speakers were Conor McCabe and Ronan Burtenshaw. Conor, a precariously employed PhD in history, had been active in the Irish left around political education and economic research. I assumed he was focusing primarily on Ireland and the EU, because, by his own admission, he had never been to Greece and didn't know much about Greek history, the Greek left, or Syriza. The main point, as he saw it, was that Greece had put a Marxist in the Eurogroup and Ireland had not. If Irish leftists had not put a Marxist in the finance ministry, or planned to put one there after the next general election, then they had no business wasting anyone's time with their opinions about what Syriza or the European left should do. Of all the possible targets at which to direct his ire, looking at all that was wrong in the world, he chose to attack Irish activists who went to Athens. Conor had been employed as a parliamentary assistant to Pearse Doherty, for the banking inquiry, and held this up as an example of what the Irish left should be doing. On Facebook the next day, he posted, "Irish lefties don't have a right to post selfies of themselves in Athens, basking in the glory of other people's struggles, until they've put a Marxist in the Irish finance ministry. My bile was directed against radical tourism, which makes me want to vomit." Ronan Burtenshaw, one of those in Athens, didn't respond to the attack and gave a competent talk on the situation in Greece. Aside from the problematic assumption that Varoufakis was a Marxist, there was the assumption that these Irish leftists were not doing everything in their power to build the Irish left and to bring about socioeconomic transformation in Ireland, which could not be reduced to who was minister of finance. I thought this talk was cheap and nasty and had no redeeming value whatever about other work done by Conor.

An attack aimed at me personally, which I took most to heart, because it came from someone who was sincerely immersed in these events, came from an Irish woman living in Greece, who had been elected as a Syriza councilor in Zografu in Athens. Linda Curley connected with me on Facebook in June 2015 at the height of our Greek solidarity activities in Ireland. She was delighted to see such solidarity between her native and adopted countries. We had very positive exchanges. On July 16, when I expressed my respect for those who voted no in parliament the previous night, she lashed out at me. She was shocked at the whole situation as well as at the sudden reversal in Irish left attitudes to Syriza. She expressed her respect for Tsipras going against all his own principles for the sake of the nation. She referred to a tourist ad inviting people to live their myth in Greece. She made the analogy that people like me were living their *oxi* in Greece. She said that things may look a certain way among the elite left in the amphitheaters of Athens, but it was different on the ground, where people would have to live with the consequences of whatever policies were pursued. I felt the force of this critique. I defended my position but with respect for her experience. This went on for a few months. We did not unfriend each other. She took a Tsipras line through the September elections and felt vindicated by the election of Syriza and the defeat of LAE.

In November, I detected a change, although she didn't post anything definite. We then had a number of long telephone conversations. She left Syriza. She couldn't morally defend it anymore. She apologized for what she had said to me, but I thought there was no need because they were points I needed to consider. Looking back at her anger at the reaction from abroad, she now thought of it as the difference between the view of the snake and the view of the eagle. She resisted, because she had invested so much. She said that others were going through this too. Syriza was dissolving at the base. She thought it would take time for Greece to recover. They were no longer looking the monster in the eye. Syriza had taken the fight out of people and sent them home. They feel as if they have been raped. She had contempt for those who were taking over Syriza now. Businesses and shops were going down like dominos. So many people who were once full of talk about politics no longer wanted to talk about it now, because they were so disappointed and defeated. At the same time, there was incredible self-organization in the solidarity networks and she told me of projects with which she was involved: a social pharmacy, an exchange shop, a grocery shop, a people's *frontistirio* (extracurricular school, which is deemed necessary for a good education, especially for university entrance). These conversations, which went on for many hours, could have gone on for many hours more. She was full of perceptive observations about Greek life.

I have struggled through writing this with the issue of what I had a right to say. To the extent that I immersed myself in these events, I could not be detached from them. The fate of the left anywhere is my fate. I have never been able to confine my thinking and my activity to Ireland. I don't only live in Ireland. I live in Europe and the wider world. It is all interconnected. The rhythms of history do not beat only within the borders of the nation-state. Once I was told by a communist editor-apparatchik that I could not write about Lukács, Althusser, or Colletti, because I was not Hungarian or French or Italian. It seemed to be all right for Russians to write about Marx and Engels, however, although they were not German. I was furious at the absurdity of this.

Some Greeks tell me that they can discuss Greek politics with me as they do with other Greeks. They tell me, "You are one of us." Others will say otherwise. I hope I know my limitations. I am very aware as I come and go how alike and different is the crisis in Ireland and Greece. Specifically, I am conscious of things like how many fewer cuts there have been to my pension than to theirs, which is what allows me to come and go.

Among the international left, people like me were subjected to swipes at Syrizamania and then attacked for disloyalty to Syriza, not necessarily by the same people. Those who have stuck with Syriza have not on the whole paid much attention to what has happened to Syriza since July. Many want to be on side with a party that can win elections and not one more party struggling at 2.8 percent. Some of them remind me of members of communist parties who defended the USSR no matter what. I believe that I have been more loyal to the best of what Syriza was by aligning with those who have broken away and begun to rebuild. I have not backed away from Greece when it became so depressing. I didn't end the story with "unhappily ever after" and leave it there.

Receding Horizon

Syriza was a horizon of hope. Now it is a vortex of despair.

This is true not only for the Greek people and the Greek left. It is true not only for the international left, but beyond that, for many people who looked to Greece for a breakthrough. I saw amazing support for Syriza in Ireland that went way beyond the left. The rise of Syriza helped those of us on the international left to build our own movements of resistance and to look toward a prospect of transformative left government. That Syriza is gone. That distant light in the sky has disappeared. Now Syriza stands as an affirmation of the position that there-is-no-alternative. The sky has darkened and there seems only an endless expanse of there-is-no-alternative.

It raises the question of whether there can be left government in an indebted country within the Eurozone. It also raises the bigger question of whether there can be a left government within an ever more powerful global capitalism. It is hard to give an optimistic answer to either question. Yet what should we do? Concede that social democratic reform is the best we can ever do? Hope for an insurrection? Give up on impacting on the global economy or the nation-state and build cooperatives and alternative social structures? I say no to those questions.

Syriza was the flagship project in the strategy of building broad left parties to merge the best of older left traditions with the energies and insights of newer social movements, to challenge for state power, to initiate concrete reforms within capitalism with a view to transcending it in the direction of socialism. The capitulation of Syriza dealt this strategy a bitter blow, but it did not invalidate it. It remains, for me, the way to go. So while I no longer support Syriza, I support LAE, the GUE-NGL, the Party of the European Left, and Right2Change in Ireland. While they are fraught with limitations and imperfections, they have not crossed over to the other side and contain some seeds of possibility.

At the end of the year, Paul Mason's documentary #*This Is a Coup* circulated on the Internet. It was hard to watch those early scenes of Tsipras vowing to defy the troika and the crowds cheering in euphoria. The production did not deal well with the post-July period, but Mason did ask Tsipras what he would do differently. He replied that he would have "made brave decisions sooner." The meaning of this was not pursued, but my guess was that he meant he would do a deal sooner and was not engaged in any meaningful critical reflection. At the same time, there was a trailer circulating for another film called *This Is Not a Coup*. On it, Alan Friedman of the *Financial Times* declared, "I would not call it a coup. I would call it the way the system works."

These are the factors at play as we consider what happened in Greece and what could possibly happen there and elsewhere into the future. We need to assess the power of the global system as well as our own power to protest, to resist, and to transform. We have proved our power to protest and resist, but not our power to transform, not on the scale necessary.

Mason concluded that he did not believe that Greek society had been atomized, and therefore it had not been defeated. "The question is, who will represent them." That is a question I also ask, although there is also a question of whether they will allow themselves to be represented. "Greeks tried the barricades and then the ballot box. Nobody knows what they will try next."

CHAPTER 6

2016: Talking Left, Walking Right

Words and Deeds

The gap between words and deeds grew ever wider. Sometimes the rhetoric veered so far from reality as to seem surreal.

Alexis Tsipras began the new year by proclaiming 2015 as the year of struggle and solidarity and 2016 as the year of recovery and reconstruction. Who could believe this? In contrast, Costas Lapavitsas declared: "Greece is lost in the desert of memoranda without a compass." At Davros, Tsipras announced: "I believe 2016 will be the year that Greece will surprise the world economic community." He promised Greece would be "back to growth soon." In his blog, Lapavitsas asked where this surprise would come from. After showing charts on the decline in industrial production, retail trade, export value, and so forth, he queried prospects of investment or consumption. After six years of destruction and a still deteriorating situation, this was a dance of fire, a virtual reality, he insisted. Only social psychology could explain it, he suggested.[1]

In the realm of social psychology, Tsipras and Syriza had shifted to another dimension. It was often more bluff than analysis. Journalist Nick Malkoutzis observed: "If it could monetise its chutzpah, the current Greek government would be well on its way to solving the country's economic problems. Effrontery . . . is no replacement for strategic planning and clear thinking."[2] "Power can do funny things to a person," *Newsweek*'s Josh Lowe remarked, noting that Tsipras warned of the dangers of populism while speaking to a wealthy audience on a panel with Wolfgang Schäuble. Schäuble insultingly pronounced: "It's the implementation, stupid."[3]

One Year On

January 25 marked one year since the election that brought Syriza to power. This was an occasion for celebration by Syriza, but for critical assessment by a host of other commentators. Syriza staged a rally in a stadium in Athens. They bussed people in to fill the seats, but I wondered where they found people to get on those buses. Greeks I asked told me that many were people who had something to gain from a party in power. In his speech, Tsipras declared 2016 year zero for rupture with the old order and reconstruction of the country. In the next three months, Syriza would lead the country out of crisis. There would be no fiscal gap in 2016. As to all the protests, he said he wanted people to protest, to fight for their rights. There was a video produced for the occasion that was also shown on ERT. It was full of images of Tsipras smiling, waving, and rabble-rousing, crowds cheering, clapping, and waving flags, politicians shouting at each other on air, with the voiceover proclaiming that the government had tackled the elites, delivered social justice, rescued the economy, and made Greece an international symbol of dignity. Reaction to the video and the rally on social media was that it was arrogant, insulting, dishonest, out of touch.

Syriza's evaluation of itself could not have been more at variance with that of others, including its own former members and supporters. In the *Guardian*, Lapavitsas put it starkly: "Syriza is the first example of a government of the left that has not simply failed to deliver on its promises but also adopted the programme of the opposition wholesale. . . . Syriza failed not because austerity is invincible, nor because radical change is impossible, but because, disastrously, it was unwilling and unprepared to put up a direct challenge to the euro. Radical change and the abandonment of austerity in Europe require direct confrontation with the monetary union itself. . . . This is the task ahead for the European left and the only positive lesson from the Syriza debacle."[4]

Yiannis Milios saw it differently. Aligning neither with Syriza nor LAE, he found any idea of left government to be dead for the near future because of what Syriza did. He didn't think that LAE would succeed, because it was too statist and top-down. There was a need to reconstruct from below. He was not for Grexit. He thought that the main tactics should be not against the EU and the Eurozone but against capitalism and for worker's self-management. The question of exiting the euro might arise, but it should be subordinate to confronting class relations in Greece. What should Syriza have done? Tax the rich, stop payments to the troika, install capital controls, build cooperatives.[5] Manolis Glezos declared that Syriza was no longer the force to change the political configuration of Greece. Syriza was humiliating the left. He went to Corinth to support a blockade of farmers. Again, he apologized to the Greek people for trusting Tsipras, who was interested only in power.

In a long interview in *New Left Review*, Stathis Kouvelakis gave a sharply critical assessment of Syriza in government as well as the indicators pointing in that direction in the period before it was elected. As a member of the central committee, he saw power slipping away from the party to its leadership, which shaped its modus operandi in government, culminating in "the worst betrayal perpetrated by any contemporary left wing force." However, it was not as if there was an intention to betray. It was the lack of elementary realism and perception of class antagonism and the radical asymmetry of the situation, which was not captured by the seeming sophistication of game theories. As a member of the Left Platform, he reflected on how they might have been more effective in mobilizing their dissent at crucial points as events unfolded. The defiant upsurge of the referendum produced a situation that was exactly what Left Platform had hoped for, but it came too late, both in terms of the material possibilities after the treasury had been drained and in the sense that Tsipras made it an epilogue to prepare for the final capitulation. He compared Alexis Tsipras to Achille Occhetto, leader of the Italian Communist Party, or to ex-communist apparatchiks, who ceased to believe in anything, who bowed to the power of Wall Street and NATO. "When your inner world disintegrates, you become a bearer of nihilism." He enumerated the lessons the European left should draw from the Syriza experience: (1) It is impossible to defeat austerity within the framework of the existing monetary union; (2) It is necessary to articulate parliamentary with popular mobilization; (3) It is vital to reinvent an anti-capitalist vision of society. However, the Syriza experience is paradoxical: "although it ended in disaster, at some moments it gave us a glimpse of what an alternative might be." It showed a way to combine electoral success with popular mobilization, especially during the referendum.[6]

Journalist Yiannis Baboulias drew five lessons from Syriza's first year in power: (1) Timing is everything; (2) Mice can't roar; (3) It's about politics, not about who is right; (4) Hope is not a political strategy; (5) Party politics in Greece are finished.[7] Nick Malkoutzis thought that Syriza had yet to prove it was much more than the instigator of the most manic and energy-sapping year in memory. It had been a disappointment to those who hoped against all odds. This started from its flawed strategy in its negotiations with its lenders and continued with its inability to stand for what it was supposed to represent: transparency, meritocracy, and social justice.[8] Harvard Law School declared that the Greek government had distinguished itself for employing the worst negotiating tactics of 2015.

Versions of the recent past vied with each other for attention and assent. From the week he resigned as finance minister, Yanis Varoufakis was making statements about what had been going on behind the scenes, especially about plans to introduce a parallel currency. In January, Yiannis Stournaras, governor of the Bank of Greece, revealed that he and Prokopis Pavlopoulos, president of Greece, had a plan to prevent a parallel currency from being introduced if the government had tried to do so. There was a flurry of commentary in the mainstream media about it, but nothing more happened. "In any other context, this would have been considered a nascent coup d'état," observed Panagiotis Sotiris. "In Europe, it's the new normal."[9] Varoufakis kept it going with claims about a plan X and a China deal that was killed by a call from Berlin to Beijing. Dragasakis denied both stories. Lafazanis said he knew of no Varoufakis plan, and whenever he raised the issue of an alternative currency as the only way to implement their program, he met with only negativity, nervousness, or panic.[10] Lapavitsas was convinced that, although there were perhaps a few draft ideas, there was no serious plan B or plan X in those quarters.

Keeping up with what was going on in Greece became increasingly difficult during this period. After July 2015, some of the best Twitter accounts went silent, spirited blogs dried up, and websites failed to update. This was because so much of the robust reportage, commentary, and critique was grounded not only in outrage but in hope. When hope died, so did the flow of words. I had to depend on more mainstream sources and computer translation. I also made better use of Skype.

Winter of Discontent

During the first months of 2016, the tempo of protest built steadily. During this winter of discontent, there were daily mobilizations. On pensions, the government was battling simultaneously with its creditors and its population. Pensions had already been cut eleven times. Several generations often lived on one person's pension. There was widespread resistance to proposals involving increasing contributions while decreasing pensions. Protesting pensioners were teargassed. There were mobilizations of farmers, fishermen, seamen, lawyers, doctors, and engineers, who were marching, striking, blocking roads. The farmers' blockades of national roads were especially militant and disruptive. Farmers seized and burned EU and Syriza flags. One episode of street theater showed farmers in orange jumpsuits being executed by a figure wearing a Tsipras mask. Their tents and tractors appeared in Syntagma, as did the riot police to confront them. On

February 12, there was a major confrontation, which I saw live on Russian TV and Greeks saw live on Skai, while observing that ERT was ignoring it. Agriculture was under attack through overtaxation and inappropriate regulation aimed at opening this market to international agribusiness. It was the same with other small businesses. The situation was so bad that some were relocating to Bulgaria and Albania. So many sectors had so many reasons to be furious. Syriza MPs were said to be avoiding their constituencies.

The February 4 general strike was the biggest in years. There was massive compliance in both the private and public sectors. An estimated hundred thousand people marched in Athens. There were so many on the streets that separate rallies were impossible, as the crowds merged with each other. There was rioting in Syntagma, Omonia, and Exarchia. The march in Zakynthos attracted a thousand protesters plus 150 vehicles, such as tractors. Internationally, the International Trade Union Confederation supported the strike and claimed that proposed measures violated ILO conventions. Syriza too expressed support, saying that such mobilization would strengthen its hands with its lenders. On April 7, there was another public-sector strike in Greece. Airports were closed and all flights were canceled. Ryanair, which had increased its operations in Greece, again called for such strikes to be banned.

Discussion of debt restructuring was still supposedly on the table, but constantly being deferred, pending troika review. A favorable review was dependent on pension cuts, tax increases, facilitating the transfer of distressed loans to vulture funds, establishing an independent privatization agency, and other expropriating measures.

In Skouries, the long struggle of activists in Halkidiki against the environmental destruction wreaked by Eldorado Gold, a Canadian mining company, resulted in the suspension of operations. The Syriza government, under pressure from below, had examined its licenses and fined it for pollution. However, when the company suspended operations, the minister for development, Panos Skourletis, asked them to come back and reconsider instead of claiming the suspension as a victory.

In April, WikiLeaks released a transcript of a teleconference that had taken place on March 19 between the IMF's European chief negotiator, Poul Thomsen, and its head of mission in Greece, Delia Velculescu. During it, they toyed cavalierly with the scenario of another credit event to force Greece to the edge of bankruptcy. It was not as starkly shocking as some suggested, given all that had happened, but it highlighted tensions within the troika and their distance from the consequences of their policies.[11] The Greek government responded with fury and accused the IMF of playing with fire. The IMF released a statement saying that it did not respond to leaks. Christine Lagarde went on the offensive in responding to a letter from Alexis Tsipras by demanding that Greece respect the privacy and ensure the security of IMF internal communications.

The Refugee Crisis

The refugee crisis continued unabated. Even in winter, desperate people set out across the Aegean and hoped to continue to the north of Europe. Around eight hundred thousand did so in the past year. Increasingly other countries closed their borders to stem the flow, trapping tens of thousands in Greece in the open-air camps, stadiums, ports, or other makeshift shelters. There were attempts to militarize the situation through Frontex and NATO intervention. There were arrests of foreign workers assisting refugees with food and medical supplies for "facilitating illegal entry of migrants in the country." There were threats of expulsion of Greece from the Schengen area. The Greek government did try to cope supportively, despite lapses, but their EU "partners" did not, putting a disproportionate burden on Greece. Tsipras spoke out against Greece becoming a "warehouse of souls." Greece recalled its ambassador to Austria in response to a meeting it convened of ten Balkan countries, excluding Greece, aimed at halting the refugee flow.

By March, there were twelve thousand camped in Idomeni, living in squalor, disease, and desperation, unable to cross the Macedonian border. On the eve of flying to Brussels for an EU meeting on migration,

Ioannis Mouzalas, the Syriza minster for migration, referred to the country north of the border as Macedonia, instead of FYROM, the designation insisted upon by Greek nationalists. The Anel minister for defense, Panos Kammenos, called for his resignation, even though Mazoulas apologized for his "mistake." The leader of the opposition, Kyriakos Mitsotakis, did too. The bishop of Thessaloniki considered it a slur on the nation. Others came to the defense of Mouzalas, considering him to be one of the more competent ministers.

The EU summit negotiated an agreement with Turkey to turn back refugees illegally entering Greece, leaving Greece to bear the brunt of implementing these cruel deportations. Tsipras declared it a diplomatic success. The Greek government may have agreed to this, but many citizens didn't. Some branded it a capitulation on the same scale as the memorandum. Banners hung from the Acropolis declaring "Open Borders" and "Safe Passage. Stop Wars." LAE, along with other left and progressive civil society organizations, condemned it. Syriza MP Vassiliki Katrivanou said she felt ashamed that the agreement was treated as a success, but when it came to a vote in parliament, she and Tasia Christodoulopoulou, the previous migration minister, voted against only one article: fast-tracking deportation to fourteen days. They both voted for the bill, as did all the other Syriza MPs, as well as the members of Anel, Potami, and Pasok-Dimar. Paul Murphy gave a damning speech about it in Dáil Éireann, condemning our government for being party to it. The UNHCR and Médecins Sans Frontières withdrew from certain centers so as not to be indirectly complicit with the agreement. Refugees, increasingly desperate, clashed with riot police and even with each other. Several set themselves on fire. Fueling the desperation were stories of refugees being shot in Turkey or deported from there back to Syria. Amnesty International opposed the agreement on the basis that Turkey was not a safe country for refugees.

Nevertheless, Greece implemented the agreement. In Piraeus, dock workers resisting the privatization of the port as well as refugees camping there and solidarity workers assisting them were attacked by Golden Dawn and the riot police. Meanwhile, Kammenos was strutting around in combat gear ordering military maneuvers, provoking Turkey and Macedonia, and frightening refugees in Idomeni. Pope Francis visited Lesvos and broke protocol to speak to refugees who were protesting about being kept away as well as their general plight. Army and riot police evacuated Idomeni in late May and took refugees to centers in remote places with poor facilities. All the tents, bedding, furniture, prams, medical supplies, and equipment that aid organizations intended to recover and recycle were destroyed by bulldozers.

Polls, Parallel Program, Justification, and Opposition

The Syriza lead in the polls began to slip, especially after ND elected a new leader, Kyriakos Mitsotakis, the scion of a conservative political dynasty. He was the son of a previous prime minister and tied by many threads to the oligarchic rule that had brought Greece to near destruction. The lenders looked upon him favorably. A number of polls showed ND ahead of Syriza, while others showed Syriza a few points ahead of ND. An Alco poll for *Proto Thema* saw ND four points ahead of Syriza, with 81 percent agreeing that the government had lost its moral advantage and 71 percent saying that they no longer trusted Tsipras.

The polls failed to show any indication of a breakthrough for LAE. One factor in this was fear of Grexit. LAE tried to advance informed political discussion of Grexit without being reduced to it. To counter the perception that LAE = drachma, LAE made a comprehensive declaration of their positions on an array of immediate and long-term matters. They emphasized their continuity with the whole history of the national and international left and social movements, referencing the Paris Commune, the October Revolution, May 68, Seattle, and the Occupy movement, as well as EAM and the Polytechnic uprising, and argued for a refoundation of the left, especially after six years of memoranda and the "lost spring" of 2015. They stressed the need to assimilate the lessons of the degeneration of regimes who spoke in the name of socialism, including the Syriza government and its humiliation and submission to the liquidation of social wealth. They declared that LAE was not a drachma party, but it was necessary to realize that the euro was the institutionalization of the dictatorship of finance capital. Escape from this monetary prison was a necessary but not a sufficient condition for a progressive program. Difficulties in transition would not be primarily technical but would stem from the reaction of national and international oligarchies.[12] Both Syriza and LAE had earlier announced congresses for February 2016, but neither took place. Both were rescheduled for June.

Syriza trundled on in the performative illogic of its contradictions. It became ever harder to predict what the government might or might not do. It announced that it was reconstituting the hated Delta force that it had previously abolished. The education bill, on which Baltas had spent so many months, was retracted. Syriza did retrieve parts of its parallel program, passing a bill that brought 2.5 million uninsured into the public health care system, recruiting new medical and educational staff, giving free electricity and water to the poorest households, providing school meals for two hundred thousand pupils.

Dimitris Stratoulis, on behalf of LAE, pointed out that these piecemeal measures for relief of extreme poverty under strict conditions did not solve the major social problems created by the implementation of the memorandum. The parallel program was a public relations exercise to distract from the overall picture of demolishing pensions, transferring mortgages to hedge funds and privatizing public property. Linda Curley, however, was impressed by it and felt pulled back to Syriza.

Costas Douzinas continued to provide philosophical apologia for whatever Syriza might do. In an advance chapter of a forthcoming book called *The Left in Power,* he contended that contradiction was the name of the left in power. The first Syriza government was subjected to a postmodern coup d'état. It was like a rabbit frozen by the powerful beams of the incoming juggernaut. It was held hostage to senior civil servants opposed to its policies and to junior officials accustomed to minimal effort. By July, it was a typical *aporia,* an inability to pass through the gaping mouth of Scylla and the aggressive claws of Charybdis. He described the existential difficulty of voting for measures that Syriza had campaigned against in print and action. Yet he insisted that only time would tell whether blackmail had turned Syriza to the right or just forced it into a temporary retreat. He quoted *Žižek:* "The dream of an alternative is a sign of theoretical cowardice, it functions as a fetish, which prevents us thinking to the end the deadlock of our predicament." The key to performance of contradiction was to live simultaneously in three different temporalities, three concentric circles, which were both overlapping and conflicting: (1) the time of the memorandum, of political panic and personal hysteria, full of intrigue and apostasy, full of impending doom and catastrophe; (2) the time of the parallel program; and (3) the time of the ideal. Syriza could reach left governance and socialism only by continuously and simultaneously implementing and undermining the agreement.[13]

It could be called the neoliberal road to liberation or the hypercapitalist road to socialism. It meant implementing and even extending expropriation so as to end it. This was not a creative coming to terms with contradiction. It was denying the direction of the trajectory. It was wading further and further into the quagmire. It was not taking responsibility for the private expropriation of social wealth, for the destruction of the prospects of the Greek left for the foreseeable future, or the despair of those whose hopes were raised.

For Mikis Theodorakis, there were only two positions: either complying or conflicting with what the international institutions were imposing. It was zero hour, both for the government and the people. He called for a united front against the memorandum. He noted that many said that the Greek people were paralyzed. However, he had seen many times before when they were paralyzed and the next day rose up. Alekos Alavanos, who made Tsipras leader of Syriza, spoke of a great betrayal and declared that neither Metaxas nor Papadopoulos had enacted such a sellout as Tsipras.

Gavriil Sakellaridis, the voice of the government for seven months, who was reluctantly reelected in September, resigned in November and went into isolation. He had been living with contradiction until he could do so no longer. Breaking his silence of several months, he said that the night he voted for the memorandum on August 15 was the worst night of his life. He felt as if he had left his body. He was filled with guilt and needed to punish himself. He did not appear in public. Despite being in the Tsipras inner circle, he spoke to them no longer. Yet he felt bound by a code of honor not to speak of what went on inside Maximos Mansion. He watched many episodes of *Breaking Bad, Homeland,* and *House of Cards* and read many books of economic theory to get back to his PhD. He said that he felt more sadness than anger about Syriza. He seemed to have no plans to participate in the left in the immediate future.[14]

The exodus from Syriza continued. Among those I knew, Sotiris Koskoletos left Syriza and his job at the Nikos Poulantzas Institute. There were generational aspects to the experience of departure. George Souvlis spoke to me of breaking from his mentors. He named leading Syriza intellectuals whom he now regarded as disconnected from social reality and delegitimized as figures worthy of respect. He felt that Syriza in power was worse than ND in that it was not only implementing austerity but damaging the left. Not just in Greece, either. He moved around Europe and witnessed the role of Syriza in dividing the European left. He believed that Syriza would dissolve and its leading figures would be afraid to show their faces.

Despite it all, Syriza MEP Dimitrios Papadimoulis had only good news to report. In an article called "The Success of Greek Structural Reforms," he strained to put every negative measure in a positive light, portraying the recapitalization of the banks, for example, as making the Greek banking system among the most stable in the Eurozone.[15]

Beyond the big economic issues, there were other altercations. In the area of culture, there was a controversy over the National Theatre canceling a play called *Nash's Balance,* because it quoted from a book by Savvas Xiros of the urban guerrilla group 17N. The US embassy weighed in, questioning the use of public funds for the art of a terrorist. The biggest flare-up on cultural terrain was the negative reaction when the program for the International Festival of Athens and Epidaurus was announced by the recently appointed Belgian director, Jan Favre, as being a "tribute to Belgium," focusing on Belgian works, including a retrospective of his own work and excluding Greek productions. Artists met, considering it a neocolonial humiliation, and called for the resignations of both Favre as festival director and Baltas as minister of culture. Favre resigned, claiming that Greece was a hostile cultural environment where he could not make artistic choices freely. Baltas then appointed a Greek director, Vangelis Theodoropoulos, but denounced the attack on Favre as a "coordinated attack by political parties, the media and part of the art world." Also the Ministry of Culture moved to evict the Melina Mercouri Foundation, named for the previous and popular minister of culture, from a premises in the Plaka owned by the ministry, meeting with criticism from Pasok and beyond.

Pasok was also uneasy when Tsipras, a vice president of the Party of the European Left, attended a meeting of the social democratic Party of European Socialism. In the official photo, Tsipras appeared in the front row with Hollande and Schultz, while the leader of Pasok, Fofi Gennimata, was barely visible in the second row. At a meeting between Tsipras and Fotis Kouvelis, the leader of Dimar, now allied to Pasok, Tsipras remarked that crises showed the real dividing line between progressive and conservative forces. It would be hard not to agree with this, but not in the way Tsipras intended.

An editorial in *New Left Review* compared the trajectory of Syriza with that of Pasok: "What's striking is not just the speed of Syriza's fall, covering in six months the political distance that took PASOK twenty years, but the fact that Syriza's starting point was so much farther to the right. PASOK had been responsible for real advances in health, education, national development and civil rights in the 1980s, establishing a social compact on the left of the European spectrum; Syriza's highest aim, soon abandoned, was to avoid further cuts."[16]

In March, the University of Athens announced that it was awarding an honorary doctorate to Mario Draghi, the current president of ECB, which had borne down so heavily upon Greece and prevented any possibility of economic recovery. It was decided by a near unanimous vote of the Department of Economics. I was bewildered about why they would do this. I asked Stathis Kouvelakis. "Stockholm syndrome," he replied. We agreed that it was the only explanation.

Alienation from all this took all sorts of forms. "Anarchists" wearing hoods and wielding sledgehammers caused severe damage at Monastiraki and Kerameikos metro stations and sprayed slogans about political prisoners. PAME, the communist trade union, occupied the Department of Finance and burned the EU flag. Another day, workers in public hospitals occupied the Ministry of Health, using chains to bar the entrance. They pointed out that the prime minister promised a year ago that there would be increased funding and 4,500 new hires. Instead funding decreased and employment fell by 2,500. Every day there was something.

Plan B for Europe

Meanwhile, Greeks were involved in various pan-European initiatives. A succession of events seeking a plan B for Europe took place in the early months of 2016. The first was in Paris in January and featured Jean-Luc Mélenchon, Oskar Lafontaine, Zoe Konstantopoulou, Yanis Varoufakis, and Stefano Fassina. Also listed in the call were left figures in other countries. Its declaration referenced the recent financial coup in Greece and asserted that the euro had become the tool of oligarchic dominance, necessitating a break from the Europe of the current treaties and the fiscal compact and opposition to the proposed Transatlantic Trade and Investment Partnership (TTIP). They announced that their plan A was to be a campaign, including civil disobedience, to end the lack of accountability of the European Central Bank and the Eurogroup and to renegotiate all EU treaties. Failing that, their plan B was to create an alternative monetary system involving parallel payment systems, parallel currencies, and/or euro exit.

In February in Berlin, there was an international gathering organized by Blockupy, followed by the launch of DiEM25—Democracy in Europe 2025—on February 9. It issued a call to recalibrate EU policies on debt, banking, investment, migration, and poverty. The figure of Yanis Varoufakis loomed large over the proceedings, featuring the flamboyant inconsistencies of everything he touched. His huge role generated much interest and media attention as well as dissipation and confusion. As usual, he spoke some sense, for example, when he spoke starkly of austerity as class war. Indeed it was. So what to do about it? Demand live-streaming of Eurogroup meetings. It made me remember quotes from Phaedrus about a mountain giving birth to a mouse and from Marx about sowing dragons and reaping fleas. Another issue for me was the gap between staging celebrity-centered events and building movements. There were, however, a number of other people, both impressive and unimpressive, who supported DiEM25: Noam Chomsky, Ken Loach, Susan George, Caroline Lucas, Katja Kipping, Marisa Matias, Ada Colau, James Galbraith, Julian Assange, Srećko Horvat, Toni Negri, Slavoj Žižek. From Ireland, the launch was attended by Brendan Ogle and David Gibney of Right2Change as well as Nessa Childers, MEP, and David McWilliams, economist and journalist. .

In March, there was a further gathering of DiEM25 in Rome. This did not receive as much international publicity, but it did generate interesting discussion on social media. The most coherent account and critique I read was from George Souvlis. He perceived a naïve approach to how easily structures could be changed, an apolitical blurring of right and left, a leader-centered effort without any serious representative structure inside the initiative, in fact, a super-elitist gathering without any social grounding, without a counterhegemonic project, without an institution to enable the initiative to endure. With Samuele Mazzolini, he wrote an open letter to Yanis Varoufakis questioning the ambiguous physiognomy of DiEM25, the disregard of previous experiences of resistance, and the issue of democracy within DiEM25 itself and expressed concern about it being "a one-man show."[17]

Overlapping in attendance, but different in orientation and emphasis, was a gathering in Madrid in February, organized by the Anticapitalistas, on the left of Podemos, and Izquierda Unida. The former slaughterhouse converted into a cultural space was packed to twice its declared capacity. Star speaker Varoufakis strode onto the stage and received a standing ovation before he even spoke. When his time came to speak, he clenched his fist and evoked the international brigades. He announced that Europe was disintegrating and called for democratization of the EU. Lapavitsas also spoke of the disintegration of the EU. In fact, he said it was one step away from death. He put this in a more global and systemic context, arguing that financialized capitalism was hitting its limits. He insisted that there could be no plan B for Europe unless people understood what happened with Syriza. A plan B was needed to deal with monetary policy, debt, trade, tax, production, and employment. He stressed the need to restore popular sovereignty, with the nation-state providing the basis for that. His speech also received much applause and social media attention.

Transform participated in all of these gatherings and was positive about the potential of DiEM25. I couldn't help feeling that its vision was being blunted and its position was being corrupted by its uncritical defense of Syriza after July 2015. In February 2016, Transform issued a statement about the need for the international left to discuss what lessons needed to be learned from the Greek experience. It was subheaded "A Comradely Debate Without Taboos Is Necessary."[18] However, it seemed evident that there were taboos, because any real criticism of Syriza was denounced as "Syriza-bashing." Transform did point legitimately to the unfavorable balance of forces and the relative weakness of the left in other European countries, but it implied that failure to influence the positions of our own governments on Greece disarmed us from taking a critical view of what the Greek government did. The statement concluded that what was needed was a change in the balance of forces in as many EU countries as possible, as well as the development of a broad European movement against austerity and for real democracy. This was correct, of course, but Transform would have less and less to contribute to that unless it faced the reality of what had happened in Greece.

Transform held a conference in Athens in March cosponsored with Syriza, the Nikos Poulantzas Institute, and the Party of the European Left. It was to discuss an alliance for democracy and against austerity. Irish trade union economist Michael Taft took part. There was also a public event where Declan Kearney of Sinn Féin shared the platform with Alexis Tsipras, Pierre Laurent, Ska Keller, Marisa Matias, and Tania González Peñas.

I asked Lapavitsas if he saw grounds for hope in these initiatives. He felt there was a lot of confusion and hot air. He thought the European left was lost in the woods. He moved to shape something more solid, if smaller in scale, informing the European Research Network on Social and Economic Policy (ERENSEP), with a strong focus on alternative monetary arrangements and on reconsideration of the relationship of nation-state to international structures. The general goal of "another world" was not convincing, he argued, so it was necessary to formulate concrete and feasible proposals to move out of the crisis here and now. ERENSEP's first event was a two-day workshop and public meeting in Thessaloniki on April 27, addressing the topic "What is the future for Europe?" addressed by Oscar Lafontaine and Costas Lapavitsas. I watched this via livestream video, as I did with the other pan-European gatherings.

The Syriza Effect and the Irish General Election

The Irish general election was announced at the beginning of February. The date was set for February 26. There was much mention of Syriza and Greece in the election debates, although a good deal of it was repetitive. Basically, the outgoing Fine Gael–Labour government argued that they had saved Ireland from being Greece and the electorate should not risk the recovery by voting for Syriza allies in Ireland. It must have been in the notes given to Fine Gael ministers to say "The choice is Ireland's way or Greece's way," because so many of them said it. Jobs minister Richard Bruton warned of a "motley crew" of left parties and independents being elected as a "recipe for disaster." It was not a disaster that we had to struggle to visualize, he added, because it had already been visited on the people of Greece, where a populist party had destroyed the Greek economy and ordinary Greeks had to pay the price. The Labour Party sang the same tune. At the launch of its manifesto, public expenditure minister Brendan

Howlin said that Ireland had been in a worse position than Greece in 2011 (it hadn't), but the Irish government had turned it around, whereas the people of Greece still faced an appalling vista.

Much of this argument was put directly to left politicians in debates. It was aimed particularly at Sinn Féin and Anti-Austerity Alliance–People Before Profit (an alliance of two Trotskyist parties and their broader fronts). Sinn Féin did its best to deftly distance itself from Syriza without denying it or even criticizing it. Gerry Adams, when pushed about Sinn Féin's association with Syriza, complained that "the Syriza thing is totally exaggerated by sections of the media. We are Sinn Féin. We are not Syriza." He implied that they would come at issues in a different way without saying how.

Some of the references to Greece and Syriza were cheap jibes. At the launch of the Fine Gael economic policy, finance minister Michael Noonan thought it was funny to remark on Greek flags being handed out as spot prizes at Sinn Féin dances. Pease Doherty, in a studio with Noonan, when he was once again heaping scorn, defended Syriza as standing up for people and being reelected. Paul Murphy of AAA, just as often the target of such taunts, was more analytical and critical. He placed the primary blame for the suffering of the Greek people on the troika, but also on Syriza for not defying them to the end. On radio, Alan Shatter, who had been justice minister, accused Paul Murphy of wanting to turn Ireland into North Korea. Mary Lou McDonald of Sinn Féin, who was also in the studio, chimed in with Murphy about the lack of solidarity with Greece on the part of the government, even stabbing them in the back.

It wasn't only the politicians, but journalists and letter writers to newspapers who echoed or contested this narrative. I did a full Lexis-Nexis search of Irish newspapers for the month of February, which yielded many results. Some were reports of the pronouncements of politicians, but others were editorials and columns and letters having their own say on it. The *Irish Independent* was the most vociferous. On February 17, there was a front-page headline screaming "We'll End Up Like Greece If SF, Motley Crew Take Power." Inside, ran stories of Richard Bruton saying that pensions, interest rates, and economic growth were at risk if Sinn Féin and independents were elected and from Danny McCoy of the Irish Business and Employers Confederation warning that a lurch to Sinn Féin and other radical parties would diminish competitiveness and foreign investment. Both referenced Greece as the cautionary tale of what was in store if we did not heed their exhortations.

On February 21, the *Sunday Independent* ran an editorial entitled "10 Reasons Not to Cast a Vote for Sinn Féin." Numbers 1 and 2 were about Tsipras, Syriza, and Greece. "Greece is a basket case looking at decades of economic stagnation. . . . Why would Ireland fare any differently if it heeded the siren's call?" Elsewhere in that paper on that day, Dan O'Brien declared that the election of Syriza "killed Greece's recovery stone dead." Any government of the same hue would produce the same results here, he admonished.[19] A reader, John Wake Harlow, took issue with these articles for not putting the blame where it lay: it was the EU and IMF who were to blame, and not Syriza, who tried to resist draconian austerity, which caused the economy to contract.

Other papers, commentators, and letter writers came in on it too and made similar arguments. Suffice it to say that many were presenting Greece as the dystopian drama that Ireland had escaped but could descend into if we voted left.

The left rarely mentioned Greece, except when it was forced to do so. It would have been otherwise if things had taken a different course. The left too saw Greece as a dystopian drama, but placed it within a wider constellation of forces and stressed the power of capital exerted upon Syriza through the EU and the IMF. Different sections of the left were critical of Syriza to different degrees, but did not want to side with the right's arguments against it. Nevertheless, after July, Syriza was an embarrassment for the left here and elsewhere.

The one time the left took the initiative in bringing Greece into the Irish election was at a Right2Change conference on February 13. It opened with a video collage, which included Greek flags and *oxi* placards raised in Dublin. Yanis Varoufakis was to speak at the conference. He didn't come to Dublin, as he promised, but he did address the conference through video link. He took a rousing tone, declaring that the Irish people were facing a stark choice. The election would either condone or condemn the violation of the Irish people by an unscrupulous local regime and the ECB. Ireland as a model of successful austerity was a lie. Oligarchs used our country to beggar our neighbors. Michael Noonan promised to fight for debt relief for Ireland, but he didn't. He fought tooth and nail to stop Greece from getting debt relief, so he wouldn't be taken to task. Varoufakis urged Ireland to send Noonan packing. He then turned to Howlin, quoting his speech, "Who speaks of Syriza now?" Varoufakis retorted: "This is why they crushed us, to crush your spirits, to lie to your faces and still get reelected on the campaign of fear." He then spoke of the need for a European movement against the anti-democratic practices of the EU and referred to the launch of DiEM25 in Berlin.

This was widely covered on both mainstream and social media. Simon Harris, Fine Gael minister in the outgoing government, tweeted that Varoufakis should mind his own business and that he was the last person we would take advice from, advising the twitterati to compare economic indicators in Ireland and Greece. There was a barrage of hostile tweets in reply. I tweeted that Ireland was his business and Greece was our business. On radio, RTÉ played back the part of Varoufakis's speech about Noonan with Noonan in the studio. Noonan smugly replied that Varoufakis was a failed finance minister who was making excuses for his own failure. He rode off on his motorbike to his holiday island and left poor and elderly Greeks looking through dumpsters for food. Pearse Doherty came into it and said that Fine Gael and Labour were trying to create the impression that Syriza created the financial crisis in Greece, when it was sister parties of Fine Gael and Labour that had done so.

Writing in *Ekathimerini*, Barry Colfer, a PhD researcher in Cambridge, looking at the Irish election discourse on Greece, concluded: "While different groups have sought to develop conflicting narratives of the Greek crisis to advance their own political agendas, no one group has successfully mobilized 'the SYRIZA story' to its ultimate advantage."[20]

So it went. When votes were cast, it was clear that the outgoing government had lost, although it was unclear who had won. The result was all over the place, as was the nation. Significant numbers of voters had turned away from the parties that had governed Ireland until now, but they had not turned to the left in sufficient numbers for there to be a left government. The left appropriately quoted Gramsci about the old dying but the new not being born. It was still a good election for the left. No party had the numbers to form an overall majority. The two parties of the outgoing coalition did not have a majority between them. Labour went from 37 to 7 seats. Sinn Féin won 23 of 158. The AAA-PBP won 6 and there were quite a few left independents elected.

It was obvious that the narrative about keeping the recovery going and not jeopardizing it by voting left didn't have the resonance the government expected it to have, especially among those not experiencing the recovery. To me, the most hilarious quote of the count came from Tom Curran, Fine Gael general secretary, in the RTÉ studio, speaking with bewilderment: "The emotional intelligence of our campaign failed to shine through."

Many commentators connected the mood of voters in Ireland with those of Spain, Portugal, and Greece. Fintan O'Toole in the *Irish Times* analyzed the result as a rejection of the European narrative that austerity was like chemotherapy, unpleasant but effective medicine. Ireland was the anti-Greece that vindicated this story. However, Irish voters said, "We don't believe you." We would no longer conform to the drama that had been scripted for us.[21] Varoufakis responded to the inconclusive election result as confirming a pattern in Europe's periphery, where the "old regime seems to be debased, but there is nothing new to replace it."[22]

When asked about lessons of the Syriza experience, in a special issue of *Jacobin* on Ireland to commemorate the centenary of the 1916 rising, Eoin O Broin, TD of Sinn Féin, replied that it was necessary to think carefully, not only about how to acquire state power, but about what to do with it when we have it. The biggest problem for Syriza, he said, was that they won too soon and were isolated in the EU when the imperative of capital and other governments was to crush them. Meanwhile, "they are still there, hanging on by their fingernails and doing a lot of things that even people like me, who are supportive of them, find difficult and uncomfortable. But the landscape is shifting."[23]

On April 7 I attended a University of Limerick conference on "Journalism in Times of Crisis" and presented on "ERT: Rupture, Resistance and Restoration of Greek Public Broadcasting." I felt furious all over again as I delivered it. The conference was full of talk, too, about media coverage of the election and the Right2Water movement.

April in Athens

In April I returned to Athens. On the metro from the airport, there were the usual beggars in contrasting modes. One of them was melodious, singing and playing guitar, while another was particularly destitute and desperate. As soon as I arrived in central Athens, I encountered the Greek left on the streets. From my hotel, I heard songs of struggle and went out on the balcony to behold the march against unemployment from Patras to Athens as it arrived in Metaxourgio. An hour later, I took the metro to Syntagma to join it for its final rally in front of parliament. It was a KKE-PAME affair, always impressive on the streets. They always had the best music too, the traditional anthems of the Greek left rather than the more eclectic pomo music that characterized Syriza events when they were on the streets, which they weren't anymore.

I then spent the evening with Linda Curley, who had gone back to Syriza. As we climbed Lykavittos Hill and dined in Kaisariani, she put to me all the arguments for sticking with Syriza despite everything. She reiterated all the things she said to me in July and September, after apologizing for them in November. She said: "You don't live here. You want to live your myth in Greece. You can't make the Greek people the sacrificial lamb on the altar of your ideology. We didn't know how to govern. We had to bring in people who did. It's not perfect, but we are trying. It took so long to have left government. We can't walk away from it now." I argued back, but I did more listening than talking. We also spoke about Ireland, our children, her husband's job at the World Bank, her work as a councillor, and the beautiful views of Athens from Lykavittos.

The next day was all in the company of ex-Syrizans. I arrived at the offices of Laïkí Enótita on the eighth floor of an office building near Omonia. I was greeted by Costas Isychos, who was in charge of international relations and foreign policy for LAE, the same position he had held in Syriza when we first met. I couldn't help remembering all that had happened in the four years since then and to contrast these downscaled premises with the Syriza offices. We spoke of many matters in the immediate past—policies, debates, strategies, motives—and the mini-civil-war of comrades parting ways. The left government ceased, as far as he was concerned, when it divorced from the social forces that brought it to government.

Given the efforts he put into developing foreign policy for Syriza as a party, I asked how he felt about the foreign policy pursued by Syriza in government. Sad and betrayed, he replied, with the abandonment of the Palestinians being particularly distressing. Tsipras had indicated that he would appoint Nadia Valavani and him to the Ministry of Foreign Affairs. Instead, he appointed Nikos Kotzias, who was not a member of Syriza and was thought to be aligned with the United States. He sent Isychos to Defense and Valavani to Finance as alternate ministers. Costas spoke of his time as a minister, where he sometimes felt as if he were "in another guy's suit." He found it strange to have military bodyguards standing to attention and saluting him whenever he made the slightest move. Life had changed for him in so many ways.

We explored the question: Who is Alexis Tsipras? He described a battle for the soul of Tsipras. When he was nineteen, Tsipras was sent to Cuba to represent Synaspismos Youth and Costas remembered his enthusiasm for the Cuban revolution. When Tsipras became leader, one strand was pulling him toward Marxism and movements, whereas another was weighing in for pragmatism and polls. He used both at first, but eventually made his choice. He was a master tactician in ridding himself of the left in the summer of 2015, whereas the left was outmaneuvered and not ready to form a new party. Regardless of what he said, Isychos believed that Tsipras knew what he had done and was not at peace with it.

Panagiotis Lafazanis, leader of LAE, came in to talk with me and we pursued the issue of the problems of LAE and its prospects for the future. The party was trying to overcome its marginalization in the mainstream media by going directly to the people through rallies, which were well attended, and participation in wider movements, which were still active. I raised with both of them the complaints of Syriza about LAE members being responsible for thuggish behavior at Syriza events. Linda had complained to me about LAE people disruptively forcing their way into a Syriza meeting addressed by Nikos Pappas in Zografou. It was not their way, they both answered, to disrupt meetings in that way, but people in and out of LAE were angry and betrayed and they could not control it. They recounted numerous other episodes where Syriza MPs were attacked by angry crowds, including one where a minister was detained in a room by three hundred students until police arrived. Some Syriza MPs were afraid to walk the streets in their own constituencies now.

LAE had five thousand members from all over Greece and also some branches abroad. It was planning its inaugural congress. There were problems among different groups within LAE. There was a letter written by Dimitris Belantis, which was signed by fifty-nine LAE activists, arguing that LAE needed to break with practices carried into LAE from Syriza or even KKE. Much disaffection surrounded the leadership of LAE, which had not been democratically elected, in the beginning perhaps necessarily so, because of being formed in such a hurry. There was a pressing need for a constitutive congress that would put democratic procedures in place and elaborate a political program. In many of my conversations about LAE, both with those inside and outside it, there was criticism of Lafazanis as an unsuitable leader, although everyone thought him to be a honorable and hardworking person. LAE was very much still in the making. Antonis Davanellos wrote: "What we've done so far is to regroup our forces in order to continue to be present, within certain limits, on the battlefield, and to not give up on the possibility of victory. . . . The reconstruction in Greece of a massive, radical, and anti-capitalist left in the twenty-first century will continue. . . . Therefore, we do not consider the UP [LAE] 'a finished party,' but 'a political front in the works.'"[24]

I then went to meet Dimosthenes Papadatos, who had been part of the 53+ tendency of Syriza. We met on Panepistimiou and walked to a nearby taverna. He had left his position as a parliamentary assistant last May and left Syriza in August 2015. This meant a plunge in his personal circumstances, giving up a decent professional salary for the dole and leaving his rented accommodation to move back with his parents. He described the collective depression of his contemporaries. He was one of the ones determined to build an alternative. For the time being, this was Network for a Radical Left, which was allied with LAE but not in it. He voted and advocated for LAE, but did not think it was itself the answer to what must come next. He presented me with the book he co-edited entitled *To OXI pou egine NAI* (The No that became Yes) and asked me about prospects of it being translated and published in English.

In the evening, I had a delightful dinner with Stathis Kouvelakis and Pascale Arnaud in the Neo Psychiko house that had been the home of Stathis's mother's family for several generations. It was also the house where Costas Lapavitsas lived when he was an MP. The parents of Stathis were both lawyers. They had been in the same class as Nicos Poulantzas in law school. During the period of the dictatorship they were in exile in Paris. Stathis's father was later a member of the Council of State and minister of justice for Pasok. Stathis remembered Andreas Papandreou and what a commanding presence he was.

We consumed many courses (cooked by Stathis) on the terrace overlooking a garden where lemons, oranges, olives, and lilies were growing. It was quite exotic, being my first time to eat squid with black ink, which was served with more pasta than I could eat in a week and lots of white wine. We talked of many things for hours—families, religions, cultures, politics, and philosophies—but mostly about the immediate past and the path forward for the Greek left. Pascale, although a film editor in Paris, had been coming to Greece for many years and participating in its political life. Stathis recounted discussions and debates on the Syriza central committee and in the Left Platform. He had much to say about what happened and why and what might have been done differently. We explored not only big economic and political issues but educational and cultural controversies. He regretted the fate of the education bill, which would have reversed much of the neoliberalization of higher education, because Syriza was yielding to pressure from the right on it. Stathis was as clear and sharp and outraged as always and often ironic and funny. We also discussed my own writing about all this. I left exhausted but buzzing with thought.

The next day my appointments were with a filmmaker, a journalist, and a novelist. I met with Aris Chatzistefanou over a pleasant lunch at Rozalia in Exarchia. He is best known for the films *Catastroika* and *Debtocracy* by Infowar Productions. He also did those zany political broadcasts for LAE featuring Lafazanis, Lapavitsas, and Konstantopoulou in ironic mini dramas. We spoke of many things, including his latest production, called *This Is Not a Coup*. He told me about his trip to Ireland, where he had interviewed Paul Murphy for it. I had seen a trailer of the film. The punch line was from Alan Friedman of the *Financial Times* saying, "I would not use the word 'coup.' I would call it the way the system works."[25] I would also say that the way the system works is equivalent to a meta-coup.

As I made my way down Panepistimiou, I stopped at a newsstand and bought the paper *Dromos tis Aristeras* (The Road Left), where I found an entire page devoted to my book. A journalist had asked me for an excerpt, but I wasn't expecting a whole page on it, including a photo of me introducing Alexis Tsipras at DCU in 2014. After that, I walked from Exarchia to Syntagma and sat there for a while, watching and reflecting, as aggressive pigeons scraped my hair, until I met Damian Mac Con Uladh, who had recently been reporting for the *Irish Times* from Lesvos. We went together to the British School of Athens in Kolonaki to hear Paul Johnston speak about Greek history and politics in the Alex Mavros novels, all seven of which I had read, and I took the occasion to goad him again to write more of them.

While there, I also met Sofka Zinovieff, author of the novel *The House on Paradise Street*, which I read and liked. There was a nice reception after it with wine and food.

The next day I met Vangelis Georgakakis of Topos Books. I entered the premises in Exarchia and liked the atmosphere of lots of books. I recognized a few, as I had been published here in a volume on the October Revolution and in the journal *Marxist Thought*. Vangelis knew of my connection with South Africa and spoke to me of ANC comrades and his disappointment when a comrade he knew was exposed as corrupt in office. I knew how he felt. I was as intensely involved with the ANC as with Syriza and it had been the same kind of experience for me. I asked about book publishing in Greece these days. He told me that there had been a striking rise of interest in books of the left, old and new, during the crisis, although there was a downward curve since the July 2015 events and the despair following in their wake.

That evening I had a long dinner in a taverna in Exarchia with Stelios Elliniadis, journalist, radio presenter, and music producer. He was a member of the Syriza central committee when I met him. I ran into him on a number of occasions (including on his radio show on Sto Kokkino) during those frenetic days of last July and was struck by his probing sincerity. It was great to have this talk in a slightly calmer climate to explore matters further. He was glad that I was writing about the immediate past, because he thought that a lot of Greeks were blocked from writing about it, because it was so traumatic. He outlined his own way of dealing with it, which was especially complicated, because he worked at Sto Kokkino, the Syriza radio station, where he still had some scope to do decent programs, but was alienated from the actions of Syriza and the overall line of the station. Rather than resigning, he had faded away from both the party and its central committee. He voted for LAE in September. He expressed strong views of the lack of democracy within Syriza, on the dominance within it of those who were part of the system but wore left masks and decided things in the dark. He went back to the sudden imposition of Tsipras as leader when he had not distinguished himself either in activity or theory. He was clever, but he had little experience and no depth. Others, such as Stathis, also raised this with me, again asking why Alekos Alavanos, the previous leader, who was more intellectually astute and politically experienced, resigned in his favor.

I asked Stelios about his background and he told me the basic facts, from his early years in Istanbul until life became too difficult for Greeks in Turkey and his family's move to Athens, to his studies in law, his turn to popular culture, his involvement in left politics. He had been a Maoist, but saw no point in being a Maoist or Trotskyist or Stalinist now. New paths must be opened. He was now working on the paper *Dromos tis Aristeras*, hoping to open a dialogue, especially among those who had supported Syriza. He asked me about Ireland, and I outlined the debates over the centenary of the 1916 rising, the results of the election, and the difficulties in forming a government. He asked me if I would write about it for *Dromos* and I agreed to do that.

The future seemed bleak to him and to most of those I met. By the time the left could reorganize itself, the situation would be different, because almost every public asset would have been sold. To take back the ports, airports, water, and all the public assets that were being priviatized to pay the debt, it would be necessary to confront China, Germany, and France. Where the left should be, there was such an empty space and such a big need now, but the pace could not be forced.

The only person who told me he was optimistic was Kostas Skordoulis, whom I met for lunch the next day, along with Christos Kefalis, again in Exarchia. Kostas pointed to the continuing class struggle in the unions as the source of his optimism, but then he added that Trotskyists were always optimistic. Christos, while quieter, registered his dissent, indicating that Antarsya might have played a more constructive role in the events of the immediate past and even now. We covered many topics, but one fact stood out with me: there were 2,500 refugee children missing in Greece.

Another day I had lunch with my ex-KKE comrade, who still did not want me to use his name, because the party would not approve of his talking to me about it. We walked around the local neighbor-hood, passing the KKE office where he was expelled and crossing a square named after a communist. Although expelled in July, he still voted KKE in September and participated in PAME mobilizations. He was not as active politically now and depressed about the whole political situation, as was everyone else, but with the added layer of being deprived of his party. We discussed whether there was a future for Marxist-Leninist parties. He believed that there was, whereas I believed that Marxists needed to argue for their analysis and play their part within broader left parties. It was harder to make that case now after Syriza, of course, but it was still my position.

That evening I met with Maria Nikolakaki, who had been a prime organizer of the Athens conference in July 2015. She had since parted ways with the Global Center for Advanced Studies and with Creston Davis, her fellow organizer. GCAS was seeking accreditation from a private university in Slovenia and charging high fees, which she con-sidered a betrayal of the commitment to debt-free education. As she saw it, there were two capitulations in 2015, one political and one academic, equating GCAS with Syriza and Davis with Tsipras. I did not think they were proportionate. Syriza was a serious force, whereas GCAS was smoke and mirrors.

Maria had since set up the Cooperative Institute for Transnational Studies. CITS seemed structurally much like GCAS, but she insisted that it would be more democratic and progressive. She was plan-ning another international conference for July 2016 on the island of Lesvos, the entry point for so many refugees in this period. The conference theme was "Crossing Borders." Later we were joined by Anna Holloway and Katerina Nasioka, who were involved with CITS. Anna, the Greek daughter of John Holloway, author of *Change the World Without Taking Power*, said that January and July of last year were the only times she had ever voted, the only times people felt they had any power.

I spoke with Nikos Potamitis by phone. I asked about political life in Zakynthos. He reported that Syriza had almost disappeared, even though it won the election; 70 percent of the members active in the party and in the movements had left Syriza and joined LAE. Now Syriza was recruiting from Pasok and even ND and not only in Zakynthos.

On my last evening, I wanted to walk around and gather my thoughts. I went to the foot of the Acropolis to sit and remember all that had happened since I first came there. I then walked to Monastiraki. When I went downstairs in a taverna, I beheld a glass floor revealing the structures of the ancient city. It always amazed me to come across such unexpected and unmuseumized ruins. As always in tourist areas, there were the wretched of the earth, some with severely deformed bodies, begging, alongside tourists otherwise oblivious to the crisis.

A text from Stelios Elliniadis brought me back to Exarchia. We picked up various threads from our previous conversation for a while. Then I walked to Exarchia Square, where I ran into Stathis Kouvelakis and Eirini Gaitanou, who were just finishing a briefing for the oral defense of her PhD. They invited me to join them, and we again pursued the theme of the Syriza government and how far its own story of itself was from our story of it. "They tell lies, industrial-scale lies," said Stathis emphatically. I asked how constantly shifting red lines, lines Syriza vowed never to cross and then crossed, differed from no red lines at all. The answer was obvious.

There was a concert going on in Exarchia. It was traditional Greek music. People, including children, got up and danced when the spirit moved them. There was more of a sense of community around Exarchia on this evening and less of the scene of strutting macho anarchists ready to pounce. During the week, there were banners protesting drug dealing and "social cannibalism." There was a vigil for a Kurdish hunger striker, and strains of "The Internationale" and "Bella Ciao" filled the air. It wasn't a place where a Syriza MP would dare venture though.

A new party was announced while I was there. It featured Zoe Konstantopoulou in a way that set my "personality cult" alarm bells ringing. The name of it was Plefsi Eleftherias, translated as "course for freedom". The logo was a purple and turquoise sailboat. It was about "sailing into a new future of freedom, democracy, and justice." I searched the photos of the launch for faces I recognized, spotting a few familiar ones, but it was unclear who else was in it. Eric Coquerel from Parti de Gauche in France was there. Nadia Valavani later stated that she hadn't joined it, but attended to support any expression of disengagement from the memorandum. She did not consider PE to be of the radical left. There needed to be a broad front, the heart of which was the radical left, but other expressions were also needed. Costas Isychos saw it in a similar way, telling me that Zoe could bring in different people than LAE. Stelios Elliniadis said that, although he admired Zoe, this was no way to form a party, decreeing it from the top rather than building it from below.

The fracturing of the Greek left continued, not least within Syriza itself. It was not only those who were leaving, whether by public resignation or quiet withdrawal; those who stayed were also divided—between those accepting the party (leadership) line no matter what and those continuing to question it. Those among the 53+ who were still in Syriza posed eleven points for Syriza coming up to the congress. They defined their position as critical Marxism and their goal as socialism. They rejected the approach of arguing that "our" memorandum was better than "their" memorandum, that it was somehow a "red" memorandum. They called for the acceleration of the parallel program. They insisted that Syriza not remain in government at all costs. They opposed the prospect of a national government with ND, Pasok, and/or Potami. They called for democracy within the party. They were trapped in a web of contradictions and they knew it.[26]

The contradictions became too much for the editorial team of *Enthemata*, the political analysis supplement of the Syriza paper *I Avgi*. They had maintained some latitude for critical perspectives, even of Syriza, but found that that balance was ever more stressful and difficult to achieve and less and less related to the overall output of *I Avgi*. Ultimately, they resigned. Stratis Bournazos stated that he knew what Syriza was doing was wrong, but he no longer knew what was right.[27]

The varieties of ex-Syriza left preoccupied me. They had yet to come together in the way that was needed. I looked to them as the most promising force for the future of Greece. I was searching during these months, especially during my days in Athens, for movement forward on that front. I did not find it in any obvious way, but I did see indicators that it would come.

May Mysteries and Miseries

The Orthodox Easter fell on May 1, and even Greek atheists, agnostics, and leftists yielded to the feast of family and food, transferring May Day celebrations to May 8. They did query whether the "holy light" should still be received from a special flight from Jerusalem according to the protocol for visiting heads of state under a left-led government.

Through the spring, there were worries of yet another crisis of state finances. Money to pay wages and pensions as well as debts was again running low. The government once more sequestered funds from public bodies. Creditors were demanding an additional €3.6 billion in contingency measures to be triggered in the event that Greece failed to meet its fiscal targets, which was inevitable with the target set at 3.5 percent surplus by 2018. Not content with the economic capitulation and political decimation of the left, they pushed ever onward to maximal expropriation, escalating the impossibility, tension, and tragedy of Greek life. It was revealed that only 5 percent of previous "bailouts" went to state finances, while 95 percent went to pay debt and recapitalize banks.[28] Another crisis, or crisis within a crisis, was looming, raising again the specters of default and Grexit. It was like the previous May minus the hope.

There was a three-day general strike starting on May 6, as parliament passed a bill on taxation and social insurance worth €5.4 billion in cuts in order to receive the next tranche of funds to pay the creditors. Trade unions, left parties, other groups, and individual citizens gathered outside the parliament to denounce it. Protesting police blocked the entrance to Syriza offices in Athens, while other protesters planted firebombs at Syriza offices in Thessaloniki. Riot police stood against other police, firefighters, and workers of all types protesting at Syntagma. The Greek flag in front of parliament was set on fire. As usual, Molotov cocktails and rocks were exchanged for stun grenades, tear gas, and batons. Riot police beat peaceful protesters indiscriminately. Several members of LAE were injured and hospitalized. Unions representing doctors, lawyers, and others announced that they would expel MPs who voted for the bill. Unions and parties, including Syriza(!), issued statements condemning police tactics. During the debate, Kyriakos Mitsotakis paraphrased Mark Twain and spoke of "lies, damned lies, and Alexis Tsipras." Tsipras replied that he might have had illusions, but he told no lies. Others thought him both deluded and deceitful.

The government had pushed for these measures to be passed on Sunday night, May 8, to enhance its position at a Eurogroup meeting to discuss Greek debt relief on Monday, May 9. The IMF considered some form of debt relief necessary, but powerful players in the EU, most notably Schäuble, thought otherwise. Greece was told firmly there would no write-down of debt, but there might be adjustments of maturities and interest rates. Tsipras and Tsakalotos pronounced the result positive, but the issue remained unresolved. Tsipras, spinning out of control, announced that the Greek people would suffer no longer.

On May 23, parliament passed another omnibus bill of 7,500 pages to qualify for the next loan tranche. This bill brought increases in a wide range of indirect taxes, a new privatization mechanism involving a massive fire sale of state assets controlled by creditors, and the transfer of control of tax collection from the state to its creditors. Syriza MPs begged for sympathy at having to vote against their principles, but the crowds outside were not at all sympathetic. Vassiliki Katrivanou voted for the bill, while taking exception to sections on the privatization fund and the contingency mechanism. She then resigned her seat as an MP, allowing Syriza to fill it with someone more compliant. She said that Syriza was adopting policies in opposition to its core values. She felt the left at a deep impasse and admitted that she saw no credible alternative.

On May 24, the Eurogroup approved the next tranche of €10.3 billion, provided certain further hurdles were overcome, most of which would go to pay the debt. There were reports that the conflict between the IMF and EU on debt relief had been resolved and there would be debt relief for Greece. It was more ambiguous, however, and there was only a vague promise of adjustments of interest rates and maturities and deferral of a decision until 2018. Syriza spun it out as an advance, but the international financial press gave a more accurate account of it, calling the standoff between the IMF and the EU and between them and Greece, more a fudge than a deal. "The end result of Wednesday's breakthrough is not debt forgiveness for Greece; it's the beginning of its relegation to the status of a chronic half-forgotten problem," wrote Leonard Bershidsky in *Bloomberg*. "Like a brain-dead relative hooked up to machines in a hospital somewhere, Greece will continue barely breathing, because no one wants to pull the plug—but neither is anyone interested in arguing out treatments by the bedside."[29]

As summer loomed, commentators predicted a period of calm. The EU had averted a Greek crisis that might complicate the Brexit referendum. Difficult legislation had been passed and bailout funds would be dispersed. Their idea of calm, of course, was not that of those who had to live with the severe consequence of all this expropriation. Mitsotakis, leader of the opposition, accused the government of conducting an undeclared class war in favor of the lower social classes and against the wealthier ones. If only. The truth was the opposite. They had declared it but not conducted it.

In a hard-hitting editorial in *Red Notebook*, ex-Syrizans evaluated the new Syriza. Judging it in terms of the more protracted strategy of the long march through the institutions, it ran a short sprint to a stalemate and ran out of fuel. It stumbled on without discrimination, without ideas for the future, without a compass.[30]

June Journeys

Although the plan was to take a road trip through mainland Greece with Cathal, I set aside time for political investigations in Athens and

Thessaloniki. On the flight, I began reading a newly published and self-justifying book called *Game Over* by George Papaconstantinou, the Pasok finance minister, who signed the first memorandum. What was striking, aside from how absent from it was the lived experience of the Greek people, was how so many of the same things were said and done by all concerned in three successive governments in three successive memoranda. It could make you believe in eternal recurrence, although I didn't.

While in Athens, I turned on the TV to ERT1 and remembered that it was three years since the day it went off the air and one year since it came back on the air. We had to go to a local cinema, however, to see a documentary on alternative health services in Thessaloniki called *Solitude or Solidarity*. I knew of these projects, but it was good to get a vivid visual sense of them. A few days later, we met Dimosthenes Papadatos in Exarchia along with Stavroula Poulimeni, who made the film, and we walked to the Hotel City Plaza. Loukia Kotronaki, a PhD student and solidarity worker, showed us around and explained what was happening. This hotel, bankrupt and empty for seven years, had been occupied by Greek solidarity activists since April 22. Now it provided shelter for 400 refugees, 176 of them children, 4 of them born in this hotel. We learned how this self-organized community of refugees from Syria, Iraq, and Afghanistan, along with Greek volunteers, functioned on a day-to-day basis. There were assemblies three times a week, where important decisions were made, schedules for cooking and cleaning, excursions to outside activities, medical care, education classes, rebetika concerts, protests, etc. The children would start in local schools in September. Those who worked in this hotel, unpaid for two years before it closed, supported the project. It was very impressive, if precarious. In late July, three such squats in Thessaloniki were raided and destroyed by riot police. Syriza, the party, condemned the actions of Syriza, the government, in doing so.

In a contrasting scene, I visited Aristides Baltas, the minister of culture, in his ministerial office, where he gave an account of how the current scene looked from where he sat. He still believed that what Syriza did was inevitable and the best that could be done in the circumstances. There was warm rapport between us, despite the fact that I could not accept this account and had written a strong critique of it and him. He was finding his current job difficult, not only because there was limited budget and high debt, but because he thought many artists were "crazy, all in their own universe." There was limited room for maneuver on any front, he explained. I asked what happened to his education bill and he reported that the government withdrew it in the face of troika opposition. During the first Syriza government, the troika intervened only on financial matters, whereas now they intervened in almost everything. "Greece is in an almost neocolonial situation," he declared. "Why *almost*?" I asked. "Because you can visit me here and we are not in prison," he responded. That was why it was called "neo," I countered. He outlined how each prescribed measure they were forced to legislate and implement corresponded to particular interests in Greece, who transmitted their interests to the EU before they were transmitted from the EU back to Greece again. Greek oligarchs were very effective in wielding international influence on national politics. Syriza were glad that people were protesting against the measures, because that strengthened their hand in negotiations. That wasn't why they were protesting, I observed. Once again, he reiterated that there was no alternative. If they didn't implement these measures, it would be a disaster. They couldn't stop privatization without declaring war, he said starkly. He repeated many of the arguments he had put to me last July. He admitted that there had been losses and honest people had left Syriza, but if their path had been taken, Greece would have been destroyed by the left. That was happening now, I interjected. He disagreed. It would have been civil war, he insisted. Syriza was not up to mobilizing society in a revolutionary situation, he argued, because the vote for them was a passive one and they were surrounded by hostile forces nationally and internationally. I respected his sincerity and commitment, and I could sense how it was possible to inhabit his world and to see things this way, but I resisted and said so as I took my leave. We agreed to meet again.

I also spoke with Michalis Spourdalakis, who was also still in Syriza. We met in his office at University of Athens before moving to a taverna. His duties as dean were preventing him from completing the book he was writing on Syriza's progression from "new radicalism to new realism." The current political situation, as he saw it, was mixed. Syriza did not appear to have a coherent strategy. However, the relation between party and government was better than it was last year. Tsipras was attending and discussing legislation in party structures. He was involved in preparations for the party congress, which had been put back until October. Michalis thought there was a good political document and critical report analyzing the situation since the last congress. I asked how the party was functioning, being so depleted. He argued that it wasn't as depleted as I thought, that only 15 percent had left and new people were joining. What kind of people would join Syriza now, I asked, other than those who join parties in power for preferment. No, it wasn't just that, he argued. He spoke of a new member who joined his branch in Piraeus, an old leftist, who saw the government was under attack from the right and wanted to defend it. When we arrived at the taverna, we met Giorgios Chrondos, also in Syriza, who agreed with much of what Michalis was saying. "Government is hard," he emphasized. True enough, I agreed, but there was still the issue of whether it was on the right track.

Meanwhile, Laïkí Enótita was going ahead with its party congress. I was in the LAE office twice during the week before the congress, and there was much bustle of preparation for it. I spoke with Yiannis Tolios. Over a thousand delegates were expected and all kinds of debates were anticipated: whether to be an anti-memorandum front or an anti-capitalist front, how to constitute this front, how to deal with relations between the various autonomous organizations within LAE, how to participate in social movements. LAE would finally be formally constituted, agree on statutes and elect a central committee, a political secretariat, and a leader.

Since I was so near the National Archaeological Museum, as I had been so many times, I decided to go into it one afternoon, stimulating reflection on the class struggle of ancient Athens and realizing that it was fiercer now than ever, even if the weapons used now were so different from those on display here. When Cathal and I took to the

road, we visited other archeological sites and museums and I continued this reflection.

At Thiva (Thebes), I thought yet again of the Brecht poem, that
great manifesto of history from below beginning "Who built Thebes
of the seven gates?" and was disappointed that it was not displayed in
Thiva's impressive new museum. I thought of ancient Thebans, who
once challenged the power of Athens, Sparta, and Macedonia before
being crushed and sold into slavery.

We proceeded to Delphi, once considered the center of the world.
This impressive site on the slopes of Mount Parnassus built its reputa-
tion on consultation with the oracle, a succession of peasant women
who went into trance states and predicted the outcome of undertak-
ings, such as colonizations and wars, often with ambiguous answers
that allowed much scope for interpretation. I thought of a contemporary question-and-answer: How long will the Syriza government
last? As long as the troika allows. We met an American professor of
history, Gregory Bruess, who was there with his students and very
knowledgeable about Greece, ancient and modern. After a few hours
at the archeological site and museum, we dined in the town in a
lovely taverna overlooking the Gulf of Corinth, where we were the
only customers. We then walked around the town. In a shop selling
local crafts, the owner was blatantly offering customers lower prices
for cash, so as to give the difference to them, not to the government,
"who are assholes." I bought a print of an artistic reconstruction of
ancient Delphi, but insisted on paying tax, using credit card, and getting a receipt. I explained why, although I couldn't put up the kind of
defense of the government that I did last year in these situations. We
talked politics for a while. He was typical of those who were angry at
successive governments for many good reasons but didn't see how
they were part of the problem.

Our next destination was Meteora, a site of monolithic pillars and
mountains, where multiple monasteries were precipitously perched.
We arrived in the rain, but it was still spectacular. The next day we saw
more stupendous rock formations as we traveled through the mountains of Epirus and a stone forest of stratified rock in Zagori. Farther

along this mountain road was Vikos Gorge, the deepest canyon in the world, with every twist and turn leading to another stunning sight. This area was one of great ecological diversity and scientific interest, especially in its near pristine condition. There were no busloads of tourists. We were alone there.

While in Epirus, we explored the town of Ioannina, sited on a large lake with a fortress wall surrounding the old town, and then went all the way up to the border of Albania. We decided to cross it, but then remembered that we had left our passports in the hotel. This was the second time I stood at the Albanian border. In 1990, I had arranged to cross from Yugoslavia, but the crossing was mysteriously canceled "for security reasons."

We then headed across northern Greece to Thessaloniki. Passing through Imathia, I thought of Costas Lapavitsas, because this was the constituency he represented. Arriving in Thessaloniki, we met Spyros Marchetos, professor of the history of ideas at Aristotle University, who had invited me to give a lecture at the university and offered to be our guide to the city. We walked the streets for several days while we talked about the politics of the university and the city. We visited the anarchist book fair in the open air and an anarchist center with a café, shop, library, and kindergarten. We took note of many landmarks, such as the white tower, the ancient agora, and the monument marking the spot where Grigoris Lambrakis, left-wing MP, was killed. The investigation of his death formed the plot of the Costa-Gavras film *Z*. We stopped to remember him. That happened to be the day when left-wing MP Jo Cox was killed in Britain, as I learned when I turned on the news. A few days earlier in Athens, we had met Evi Gkotzaridis, who had just published a book about Lambrakis.

Spyros took us to his apartment high on a hill with a good view of the city, where we sat on a balcony and ate, drank, and talked about many things into the night. I asked him about his father, who was a communist, because my friend Eugenia had told me that he was a close comrade of her father. Spyros said that after his father's eight years in prison, he rarely spoke of politics. He observed that people who have experienced such trauma either talked about it constantly or not at all. On the politics of the present, Spyros was active in Antarsya and ERENSEP and contemptuous of what Syriza had done to the people of Greece. He was very active on the issues of debt and refugees. That evening there were rallies in Athens and Thessaloniki calling for the government to resign and for Tsipras to "go home." According to reports, there were six thousand in Athens and six hundred in Thessaloniki. Many more opposed the Syriza government, but would not join these rallies of the forces who had voted yes in the referendum.

The next evening I spoke to past and present postgrads at the university on the theme of the return of grand narratives. They were very attentive and affirmative. They were most curious about where the politics of the present were heading. I asked Spyros about job prospects for young academics. There were positions opening up, but only six-month contracts paying less than €400 a month. We discussed CITS and he informed me that he and others had dissociated themselves from it and the Lesvos conference, because it was not functioning cooperatively. As we walked around the main campus of the university, we took note of the results of student elections, where KKE and Antarsya outpolled Syriza to the point where Syriza got less than 1 percent.

After the hectic pace of the politics of the cities and even of the mountains and archeological sites, we broke our journey from Thessaloniki to Athens with an interval by the sea in Kala Nera on the Pelion Peninsula. Greeks weekending or daytripping there packed the beaches in the hot sun. I swam early in the morning and again in the evening.

Back in Athens, it was the usual combination of wining and dining and looking for the key to the recomposition of the left that would bring the next wave. We had a stimulating evening with Stelios Elliniadis at Leilim Lei, a Turkish taverna run by political refugees. He was just back from Siberia, where he was working on his documentary about a Greek village in Crimea. I also discussed the panel on Marxism and science for the Historical Materialism conference that I was co-organizing with Kostas Skordoulis, who initiated it, and with Thodoris Dimitrakos, who would be speaking at it.

Brexit came into many conversations during this period. Greeks were very interested in it, especially in terms of what it might mean for Grexit. We arrived home to wall-to-wall coverage of the Leave result, which swamped the weekend news, especially in Ireland. There had also been another general election in Spain. This election brought disappointment for the left. Although the polls, even the exit polls, showed Unidad Podemos coming a strong second, it came third. Meanwhile, the congresses of Laïki Enötita and Bloco Esquerda unfolded in Greece and Portugal. The crashing of the Syriza wave shaped all these events to different degrees. At the Bloco congress, as the list of fraternal delegates was presented, Syriza was booed.

When July 5 came around, marking one year since the referendum, rallies were held by various anti-memorandum forces to indicate that they still said no. Syriza issued a press release saying "The *oxi* vote remains in history as the great reversal," which met with scorn on the social media. The day was also marked by a flurry of controversy over the publication of a book by James Galbraith, unofficial adviser to Varoufakis, called *Welcome to the Poisoned Chalice: The Destruction of Greece and the Future of Europe,* a collection of his articles, speeches, memories, and emails from this period, revealing meetings of the chosen "war cabinet," where phones were surrendered to a hotel refrigerator, while they sketched a Grexit scenario, and plan X, where the Bank of Greece would be nationalized, bank deposits would be redenominated as *nea drachma,* and emergency public order measures would be introduced. ND called for an investigation of government negotiations in 2015, insisting, "This dark period must be fully illuminated."

Conclusion

Nevertheless, the Syriza government continued to negotiate and legislate and Alexis Tsipras continued to give speeches with many words and pose for pictures with many people. In reality, they had lost the plot. They talked left and walked right, but only the confused believed and only the opportunists followed. The others, those who gave this movement meaning, sought another path.

As the arc of this story has continued on its downward curve, a year on from the climactic events of the referendum and capitulation, I have tried to imagine what might come next, but the Syriza wave is still crashing and it is not yet possible to discern the surge that will thrust the Greek left upward again. Nevertheless, I believe that the Greek left will recover, rise, and transcend Syriza.

Meanwhile, as far as the international media and even the international left are concerned, the pulse of this story is flatlining and there is more drama elsewhere. Although the world is no longer watching, there is still much happening in Greece, as the consequences of the capitulation come into play and ever more severe expropriation erodes the possibilities of life for the Greek people. It is true that there is drama elsewhere demanding attention, but it is vital to see how it is all interconnected with the fate of Greece. Brexit and the fallout in the Tory and Labour parties, the US presidential election, the Turkish coup and purge and the whole gamut of wars, atrocities, and struggles for power all require scrutiny and striving from the international left.

Much is happening, but what is most striking is that there is something welling up from below, a massive alienation and anger with the global system and its domination over the fate of the earth and its people. Unfortunately, much of it is confused and inchoate and playing as much to the right as to the left. However, the groundswell erupting around Syriza and Podemos and more recently around Corbyn and Sanders expresses a longing toward what the left has to offer. Much of this mobilization is in the electoral arena, but one of many vital lessons from the Syriza experience is that government is not power. It is worth pursuing as a lever on the power amassed in the global system. The institutions of the public sector—the nation-state, the EU, ECB, IMF, UN—are dominated by private oligarchic interests. Only the left understands that capitalism is the problem and socialism is the solution, but we have a monumental challenge to convince the ever more disaffected masses of that and to find a way from here to there. It is the most complex challenge we have ever faced. Reflection on the Syriza story could be an essential element in moving the global narrative onward.

Notes

Chapter 1—2012: Almost Winning

1. For a good overview of this "cauldron," see Stathis Kouvelakis, "The Greek Cauldron," *New Left Review,* no. 72 (November–December 2011), http://newleftreview.org/II/72/stathis-kouvelakis-the-greek-cauldron.

2. Laurie Penny, *Discordia: Six Nights in Crisis Athens* (Vintage Digital, 2012), http://www.amazon.com/Discordia-ebook/dp/B009HVQ1JW.

3. Hilary Wainwright, "Greece: Syriza Shines a Light," *Red Pepper,* January 2015, http://www.redpepper.org.uk/greece-syriza-shines-a-light/.

4. Antonio Machado, "A Proverbios y Cantares—XXIX (http://comeup-pance.blogspot.com/2008/12/some-poems-by-antonio-machado.html). Translated by Chris Cavanagh.

5. *Red Notebook*'s website can be found at http://www.rednotebook.gr/.

6. See http://www.transform-network.net/home.html.

7. See http://www.poulantzas.gr/.

8. See, for example, Paul Mason, "Love or nothing: The Real Greek Parallel with Weimar," BBC News, October 26, 2012, http://www.bbc.co.uk/news/world-20105881.

9. Costas Lapavitsas, *Crisis in the Eurozone* (London: Verso, 2012), http://www.versobooks.com/books/1155-crisis-in-the-Eurozone.

10. This is discussed in Panagiotis Sotiris, "Hegemony and Mass Critical Intellectuality," *International Socialism,* no. 137, January 9, 2013, http://www.isj.org.uk/index.php4?id=871&issue=137.

11. "Greek Opposition Leader Calls for European Debt Conference," *Guardian,* December 9, 2012, http://www.guardian.co.uk/world/2012/dec/09/greek-opposition-european-debt-conference.

12. Michael Taft, "A Really, Really Special Case Demands a Really, Really Special Solution," Unite's Notes on the Front, January 15, 2013, http://

notesonthefront.typepad.com/politicaleconomy/2013/01/with-considerable
-speculation-about-an-impending-deal-on-bank-debt-with-the-taoiseach-
and-the-german-chancellor-jointly-sta.html.

13. Haris Golemis, "Coping with the Challenge Posed by the Crisis," *Transform!*,
December 4, 2012, http://transform-network.net/blog/blog-2012/news/
detail/Blog/coping-with-the-challenge-posed-by-the-crisis.html.

14. Yannis Tolios, *Eurozone Crisis, Odious Debt, and Default of Payments*
(Athens: Topos Books, 2012), p.157.

Chapter 2—2013: Preparing for Power

1. Helena Sheehan, "To the Crucible: An Irish Engagement with the Greek
Crisis and the Greek Left," *Irish Left Review,* January 21, 2013, http://www.
irishleftreview.org/2013/01/21/crucible-irish-engagement-greek-crisis-
greek-left/. Helena Sheehan, "To the Crucible II: A Further Irish Engagement
with the Greek Crisis and the Greek Left," *Irish Left Review*, July 29, 2013,
http://www.irishleftreview.org/2013/07/29/crucible-irish-engagement
-greek-crisis-greek-left/.

2. See Varoufakis's blog post of May 22, 2013, at http://yanisvaroufakis.
eu/2013/05/22/greek-success-story-the-latest-orwellian-turn-of-the-greek-
crisis/.

3. Full text of the manifesto is available at http://www.socialistproject.ca/
bullet/835.php. The opening of the Alter Summit can be seen on YouTube
at http://www.youtube.com/watch?v=H2dEsbSbByE. More from the 2013
Alter Summit is available at http://www.altersummit.eu/.

4. Damian Mac Con Uladh, "Troika Targets Greek Alphabet," EnetEnglish,
April 1, 2013, http://www.enetenglish.gr/?i=news.en.article&id=485.

5. James K. Galbraith and Yanis Varoufakis, "Only Syriza Can Save Greece,"
New York Times, June 24, 2013, http://www.nytimes.com/2013/06/24/opin-
ion/only-syriza-can-save-greece.html?_r=0.

Chapter 3—2014: Holding Pattern

1. Links to the speeches and sessions can be accessed on the Transform! website,
at http://www.transform-network.net/focus/strategic-perspectives-of-the
-european-left/news/detail/Programm/challenging-the-rule-of-troika-
transforming-europe.html.

2. NL, "A Greek Obama," *Socialist Voice,* February 3, 2014, http://www.com-
munistpartyofireland.ie/sv2014-02/03-syriza.html.

3. A full count of the 2014 elections can be found at http://www.europarl.
europa.eu/elections-2014/en/new-parliament.

4. For an analysis of this shift see Alp Kayserilioğlu and Yiannis Milios,
"Austerity Unbroken," *Jacobin,* January 25, 2016, https://www.jacobinmag.
com/2016/01/greece-syriza-tsipras-varoufakis-austerity-Eurozone/.

Chapter 4—2015: Fighting Goliath

1. John Hedges, "Sinn Féin Leader Calls for Formal Discussions on Irish Left Alternative," *An Phoblacht*, January 29, 2015, http://www.anphoblacht. com/contents/24720.
2. "On the Dangerous and Misleading Campaign of So-Called 'Solidarity with the Greek People'," from the English-language website of the KKE, n.d., http://inter.kke.gr/en/articles/On-the-dangerous-and-misleading-campaign-of-so-called-solidarity-with-the-Greek-people/.
3. For debate, see Nigel Hanlon, *Public Debate: Syriza & Socialist Strategy*, Part 1, https://www.youtube.com/watch?v=v6xMwkKF6WA; Q&A is covered in Part 2, https://www.youtube.com/watch?v=W78OPlfrZT8.
4. Aristides Baltas and Leo Panitch, "Party and Ministry," *Jacobin*, August 15, 2015,https://www.jacobinmag.com/author/aristides-baltas-and-leo-panitch/.
5. Kevin Ovenden, *Syriza: Inside the Labyrinth* (Pluto Press, 2015).
6. Stathis Kouvelakis *New Left Review* 97, 2016 https://newleftreview.org/ II/97/stathis-kouvelakis-syriza-s-rise-and-fall.

Chapter 5—2015: Dealing with Defeat

1. Paul Mason, *PostCapitalism: A Guide to Our Future* (Allen Lane, 2015).
2. Helena Sheehan, "Ghosts of Alternatives Past," *Irish Left Review*, July 17, 2015, http://www.irishleftreview.org/2015/07/17/ghosts-alternatives/.
3. "Lapavitsas Calls for Exit as the Only Strategy for Greek People," *The Real News*, July 17, 2015, https://www.youtube.com/watch?v=8vTTUcaYEWs.
4. Bue Rübner Hansen "Reflections on 'Democracy Rising' and the Need to Organize Networks," Global Center for Advanced Studies, August 24, 2015, https://globalcenterforadvancedstudies.org/ dr-bue-rubner-hansens-reflections-on-democracy-rising-and-the-need-to-organize-networks/.
5. Slavoj Žižek, "How Alexis Tsipras and Syriza Outmaneuvered Angela Merkel and the Eurocrats," *In These Times*, July 23, 2015, http://inthese-times.com/article/18229/slavoj-zizek-syriza-tsipras-merkel.
6. Athena Athanasiou, "The Performative Dialectics of Defeat: Europe and the European Left after July 13, 2015," Open Democracy, August 15, 2015, https://www.opendemocracy.net/can-europe-make-it/athena-athanasiou/ performative-dialectics-of-defeat-europe-and-european-left-after.
7. Global Center for Advanced Studies, "GCAS Co-Sponsors a Film: 'The Birdcage'," n.d., https://globalcenterforadvancedstudies.org/gcas-co-spon-sors -a-film-the-birdcage/.
8. Steve Rushton, "Greece's Former President of Parliament on Why Syriza Party Broke Its Pledge to the People," Truthout, December 13, 2015, http:// www.truth-out.org/newsitem/34014-greece-s-former-president-of-parlia-ment-on-why-syriza-party-broke-its-pledge-to-the-people.

9. "The Problem with Greece Is Not Only a Tragedy. It Is a Lie," JohnPilger. com, July 13, 2015, http://johnpilger.com/articles/the-problem-of-greece-is-not -only-a-tragedy-it-is-a-lie.

10. Todd Chretien and Dan Russell, interview with Catarina Principe, "Why Did the Left Gain in Portugal?" SocialistWorker.org, October 8, 2015, http://socialistworker.org/2015/10/08/why-did-the-left-gain-in-portugal.

11. Dick Nichols, "Portuguese Elections: Surge in Left Bloc Support Puts Socialist Party on the Spot," *Links,* n.d., http://links.org.au/node/4587.

12. Video of the interview can be seen at "Prime Time: Yanis Varoufakis full interview," *RTÉ News,* November 6, 2015, http://www.rte.ie/news/primetime/2015/1106/740096-prime-time-yanis-varoufakis-full-inter-view/. See also "When Miriam Met Yanis," *Broadsheet,* November 9, 2015, http://www.broadsheet.ie/2015/11/09/when-miriam-met-yanis/.

13. Michalis Spourdalakis, "Rekindling Hope: Syriza's Challenges and Prospects," *The Bullet,* no. 1213, January 27, 2016, http://www.socialistproject.ca/bullet/1213.php.

14. Costas Lapavitsas, "Money: The Invisible Bind," video, December 9, 2015, SOAS University of London, https://www.youtube.com/watch?v=dVC1hCr1bIM.

15. "Euclid Tsakalotos: Greek Finance Minister on the Hard Path of Post-Bailout Reform," *Guardian,* December 9, 2015, http://www.theguardian.com/world/2015/dec/09/euclid-tsakalotos-greek-finance-minister-on-the-hard-path-of-post-bailout-reform.

16. Alex Andreou, "Alexis Tsipras: Hero, Traitor, Hero, Traitor, Hero," *Byline,* July 13, 2015, https://www.byline.com/column/11/article/164.

17. Heath Cabot, "Hubris and Humility in Academic Activism," *Analyze Greece!* July 23, 2015, http://analyzegreece.com/topics/solidarity-resistance/item/303-heath-cabot.

Chapter 6—2016: Talking Left, Walking Right

1. Costas Lapavitsas, "The Economics of Fire Dance," *Liberal,* February 1, 2016, http://www.liberal.gr/arthro/31067/apopsi/arthra/ta-oikonomika-tou-chorou-tis-fotias.html.

2. Nick Malkoutzis, "Syriza's Long, Slow March," *MacroPolis,* January 20, 2016, http://www.macropolis.gr/?i=portal.en.the-agora.3565.

3. Josh Lowe, "Syriza Anniversary: What Has Alexis Tsipras Achieved?" *Newsweek,* January 24, 2016, http://europe.newsweek.com/syriza-tsipras-anniversary-418453.

4. Costas Lapavitsas, "One Year On, Syriza Has Sold Its Soul for Power," *Guardian,* January 25, 2016, http://www.theguardian.com/commentisfree/2016/jan/25/one-year-on-syriza-radicalism-power-euro-alexis -tsipras.

5. Alp Kayserilioğlu and Jannis Milios, "Austerity Unbroken," *Jacobin,* January 25, 2016, https://www.jacobinmag.com/2016/01/greece-syriza-tsipras-varoufakis-austerity-euro zone/.

6. Stathis Kouvelakis, "Syriza's Rise and Fall," *New Left Review* 97 (January-February 2016), https://newleftreview.org/II/97/stathis-kouvelakis-syriza-s -rise-and-fall.

7. Yiannis Baboulias, "5 Lessons from Syriza's First Year in Power," Blog post, n.d., https://t.co/JnwANk9La3.

8. Nick Malkoutzis, "One Year of Syriza," *MacroPolis*, January 25, 2016, http:// www.macropolis.gr/?i=portal.en.the-agora.3579.

9. Panagiotis Sotiris, "The Dream that Became a Nightmare," *Jacobin*, February 10, 2016, https://www.jacobinmag.com/2016/02/greece-syriza-alexis-tsipras-varoufakis-austerity-farmer-blockade-protests/.

10. Yannis Palaiologos, "Grexit Choice Explored Last Year but Tsipras Was Not Convinced," *Ekathimerini*, January 24, 2016, http://www.ekathimerini.com/205359/article/ekathimerini/news/grexit-choice-explored -last-year-but-tsipras-was-not-convinced.

11. "19 March 2016 IMF Teleconference on Greece," WikiLeaks, April 2, 2016, https://wikileaks.org/imf-internal-20160319/transcript/IMF%20 Anticipate%20Greek%20Disaster.pdf.

12. Laïkí Enótita, "Declaration of People's Unity," April 14, 2016, http:// laiki-erinienotita.gr/index.php?option=com_k2&view=item&id= 1187:diakiryksi-tis-laikis-enotitas&Itemid=179.

13. Costas Douzinas, "The Left in Power? Notes on Syriza's Rise, Fall, and (Possible) Second Rise," *Near Futures Online* 1 (March 2016), http:// nearfuturesonline.org the-left-in-power-notes-on-syrizas-rise-fall-and -possible-second-rise/.

14. Interview with Gavriil Sakellaridis, *Kathimerini*, March 21, 2016, h t t p : / / anemosantistasis.blogspot.ie/2016/03/blog-post_209.html#ixzz43XjAVtiW.

15. Dimitris Papadimoulis, "The Success of Greek Structural Reforms," Project Syndicate, March 23, 2016, https://www.project-syndicate.org/commentary/ syriza-greek-reforms-success-by-dimitris-papadimoulis-2016-03.

16. Susan Watkins, "Opposition," *New Left Review* 98 (March-April 2016), https://newleftreview.org/II/98/susan-watkins-oppositions.

17. George Souvlis and Samuele Mazzolini, "An Open letter to Yanis Varoufakis," *LeftEast*, March 29, 2016, http://www.criticatac.ro/lefteast/ an-open-letter-to-yanis-varoufakis/.

18. Transform, "A Comradely Debate without Taboos Is Necessary!" Transform Newsletter, February 8, 2016, http://www.transform-network.net/en/blog/ blog-2016/news/detail/Blog/tracing-an-alternative-plan-for-europe.html.

19. "10 Reasons Not to Cast a Vote for Sinn Fein," Editorial, *Independent*, February 21, 2016, http://www.independent.ie/opinion/editorial/10-rea-sons-not-to-cast-a-vote-for-sinn-fein-34471327.html.

20. Barry Colfer, "The Irish Election and What It Means for Greece," *Ekathimerini*, February 24, 2016, http://www.ekathimerini.com/206310/opinion/ekathi-merini/ comment/the-irish-election-and-what-it-means-for-greece.

21. Fintan O'Toole, "The Winner of Election 2016 Is Social Democracy," *Irish Times*, February 29, 2016, http://www.irishtimes.comopinion/fintan-o-toole-the-winner-is-social-democracy-1.2552917?utm_source=politics-

digest&utm_medium=email&utm_campaign=digests.

22.   Damian Mac Con Uladh, "Yanis Varoufakis: Electorate Has Rejected 'Dead-End Policies.'"

23.   Eoin O Broin, "The Red and the Green," *Jacobin*, Spring 2016, https://www.jacobinmag.com/author/eoin-o-broin/.

24.   Antonis Davanellos, "Reflections on Our Experience with Syriza," *International Socialist Review* 100 (Spring 2016), http://isreview.org/issue/100/reflections-our-experience-syriza.

25.   See Infowar Productions, http://thisisnotacoup.com/.

26.   Nationwide Initiative of 53+ Members of Syriza, "Eleven Points for Syriza", April 15, 2016, *Commonality*, http://commonality.gr/enteka-simia -gia-to-syriza/.

27.   "Resignation of Editorial Team," May 6, 2016, *Enthemata*, https://enthemata.wordpress.com.

28.   Jan Hildebrand and Thomas Sigmund, "Study: Bailouts for Banks, Not Greeks," *Handelsblatt* 423, May 4, 2016, https://global.handelsblatt.com/edition/423/ressort/politics/article/study-finds-greek-bailouts-saved-banks -not-people.

29.   Leonid Bershidsky, "New Deal Aims to Forget Greece, Not Forgive It," *Bloomberg*, May 25, 2016, http://www.bloomberg.com/view/articles /2016-05-25/ new-deal-aims-to-forget-greece-not-forgive-it.

30.   Editorial, "New Syriza," April 6, 2016, *Red Notebook,* http://rednotebook.gr/2016/05/new-syriza-editorial-ton-theseon-tefchos-135/.

Index

6 6